ISNM 78:
International Series of Numerical Mathematics
Internationale Schriftenreihe zur Numerischen Mathematik
Série internationale d'Analyse numérique
Vol. 78

Birkhäuser Verlag
Basel · Boston · Stuttgart

Optimal Control of Partial Differential Equations II: Theory and Applications

Conference held at the Mathematisches Forschungsinstitut, Oberwolfach, May 18–24, 1986

Edited by

K.-H. Hoffmann
W. Krabs

1987

Birkhäuser Verlag
Basel · Boston · Stuttgart

Editors

K.-H. Hoffmann
Institut für Mathematik
Universität Augsburg
Memminger Str. 6
D–8900 Augsburg

Werner Krabs
Fachbereich Mathematik
Techn. Hochschule Darmstadt
Schlossgartenstr. 7
D–6100 Darmstadt

CIP-Kurztitelaufnahme der Deutschen Bibliothek

Optimal control of partial differential equations . . . : theory and applications ; conference . . . – Basel ; Boston ; Stuttgart : Birkhäuser
2. Held at the Mathematisches Forschungsinstitut, Oberwolfach, Mai 18–24, 1986. – 1987.
(International series of numerical mathematics ; Vol. 78)
ISBN 3-7643-1846-5 (Basel . . .)
ISBN 0-8176-1846-5 (Boston . . .)
NE: Mathematisches Forschungsinstitut <Oberwolfach>; GT

Printed in Germany
ISBN 3-7643-1846-5
ISBN 0-8176-1846-5

PREFACE

This volume contains the contributions of participants of the conference "Optimal Control of Partial Differential Equations" which, under the chairmanship of the editors, took place at the Mathematisches Forschungsinstitut Oberwolfach from May 18 to May 24, 1986.

The great variety of topics covered by the contributions strongly indicates that also in the future it will be impossible to develop a unifying control theory of partial differential equations. On the other hand, there is a strong tendency to treat problems which are directly connected to practical applications. So this volume contains real-world applications like optimal cooling laws for the production of rolled steel or concrete solutions for the problem of optimal shape design in mechanics and hydrodynamics. Another main topic is the construction of numerical methods. This includes applications of the finite element method as well as of Quasi-Newton-methods to constrained and unconstrained control problems. Also, very complex problems arising in the theory of free boundary value problems are treated. Finally, some contributions show how practical problems stimulate the further development of the theory; in particular, this is the case for fields like suboptimal control, necessary optimality conditions and sensitivity analysis.

As usual, the lectures and stimulating discussions took place in the pleasant atmosphere of the Mathematisches Forschungsinstitut Oberwolfach. Special thanks of the participants are returned to the Director as well as to the staff of the institute.

Karl-Heinz Hoffmann
Augsburg

Werner Krabs
Darmstadt

TABLE OF CONTENTS

ANGELL, T. S., KLEINMAN, R. E.: On a Domain Optimization Problem in Hydromechanics 9

BROKATE, M.: On a Certain Optimal Harvesting Problem with Continuous Age Structure 29

BUTKOVSKIY, A., LEPE, N., BABICHEV, A.: A Continuous Media: Interpretation Terms of Phase-Portrait Method for Dynamic Systems . . . 43

COLONIUS, F.: Optimal Periodic Control of Quasilinear Systems in Hilbert Spaces 57

ENGL, H. W., LANGTHALER, T., MANSELLIO, P.: An Inverse Problem for a Nonlinear Heat Equation Connected with Continuous Casting of Steel . . 67

FATTORINI, H. O.: Convergence of Suboptimal Controls for Point Targets 91

HASLINGER, J., NEITTAANMÄKI, P., TIBA, D.: On State Constrained Optimal Shape Design Problems 109

KELLEY, C. T., SACHS, E. W.: An Application of Quasi Newton Methods to Pseudoparabolic Optimal Control Problems 123

KENMOCHI, N.: Asymptotic Stability of Solutions to a Two-Phase Stefan Problem with Nonlinear Boundary Condition of Signorini Type . . . 139

NEITTAANMÄKI, P.: On the Control of the Secondary Cooling in the Continuous Casting Process 161

PAWLOW, I.: Optimal Control of Two-Phase Stefan Problems – Numerical Solutions 179

SEIDMAN, T. I.: Justification of Necessary Optimal Conditions for Certain Integral Functionals 207

TRÖLTZSCH, F.: Semidiscrete Finite Element Approximation of Parabolic Boundary Control Problems – Convergence of Switching Points . 219

International Series of
Numerical Mathematics, Vol. 78

ON A DOMAIN OPTIMIZATION PROBLEM IN HYDROMECHANICS

T.S. Angell and R.E. Kleinman

Abstract. Certain hydromechanical quantities associated with a floating or a totally immersed body depend explicitly on the body's geometry. We discuss some aspects of the mathematical description of such a physical system and consider the problem of choosing the shape of the body so that one such quantity is optimized. Certain families of solutions of the original boundary value problem are shown to be complete and a penalization method for treating the optimization problem is proposed.

1. INTRODUCTION

When a body, floating on the surface of an infinite, ideal, inviscid, irrotational fluid is subjected to a periodic vertical displacement, a wave pattern is created in the fluid. The problem of determining this pattern from a knowledge of the body geometry and applied forces is well known in fluid mechanics.

In problems with both partially and fully submerged objects quantities of physical interest are not only the wave patterns which may be derived from the velocity potential, but also functionals of the potential such as added mass and damping factors which measure the distribution of energy in the fluid, e.g. Weyhausen and Laitone [24 , p.567]. These factors are, of course, dependent on the body geometry and the natural question arises as to whether such quantities may be optimized over restricted classes of body geometry.

The question of optimizing the added mass (and similar) functionals was addressed by Angell, Hsiao, and Kleinman [2] who studied the problem for a body which is totally submerged in a fluid of finite depth. In the terminology of optimal control the problem is one of optimization of geometrical elements (see e.g. J.L. Lions [17]). Other optimization problems of this general class have been studied previously by, for example, Cea and his coworkers [7], [8], Chenais [9], and Pironneau [21], [22]. However, in contrast to much of the earlier work, the natural setting of our problem is in an unbounded rather than in a bounded domain.

It will come as no surprise to those familiar with the peculiar difficulties associated with exterior boundary value problems that it is particularly useful to reformulate the original boundary value problem (which here includes not only boundary conditions given on the bounded surface of the body, but also on the free surface and on the bottom both of which are of infinite extent) as a uniquely solvable integral equation defined on the boundary of the body.

Before summarizing the contents of the remaining sections of this paper, it is perhaps worthwhile to pause and make some comment on the boundary value problem itself and on its reformulation in terms of boundary integral equations. Unlike some other areas of mathematical physics as, for example the linearized theories of acoustics or electromagnetics, there are here certain basic questions to which we have only partial answers.

In his classic paper [13], F. John formulated the problem of a partially immersed heaving body as a boundary value problem for the velocity potential which satisfies Laplace's equation with given Neumann data on the submerged portion of the boundary, a linearized free surface condition on the mean free surface (the fluid-air boundary), a homogeneous Neumann condition on the bottom of the fluid, and a radiation condition. Successful application of the boundary integral equation method usually depends on knowing that the boundary value problem can have at most one solution, and it is just at this point that interesting problems appear. He established uniqueness only with restrictions on the body shape, in particular that it be convex, smooth and have normal intersection with the free surface and, moreover, that vertical rays from the free surface intersect the body at most once. Certainly, these restrictions are required by the technique of proof. To quote John: "There appears to be no physical reason why in [the contrary] cases the primary wave motion together with the motion of the obstacle should not determine the motion of the liquid uniquely." [13, p.49].

Since the appearance of John's paper in 1950 others have

returned to these and other questions raised by John's analysis. Thus, for example, Kleinman has shown in [15] that the geometrical conditions may be somewhat relaxed: corners are allowable as are non-normal intersections with the free surface, and convexity is not necessary. Concerning the requirement that vertical rays intersect the body only once, the condition has recently been relaxed in the two dimensional case by Simon and Ursell [23] although even their work does not constitute a general proof of uniqueness for all configurations. We will not give a complete review here of the work on the uniqueness question since the first part of this latter paper reviews the current knowledge on that topic.

When the body is completely submerged, John's uniqueness proof no longer applies. However Maz'ja [19] has provided a proof for a class of bodies delimited, once again, by certain geometric restrictions. The recent and interesting paper of A. Hulme [12] discusses the result of Maz'ja and most effectively describes the geometric meaning of the result. We will give a precise statement of this result in the next section. At this point, suffice it to say that the condition of Maz'ja provides a reasonable class of bodies for which, in the case that the body is totally submerged, we can assert the uniqueness of solutions of the boundary value problem.

In the reformulation of the exterior boundary value problem using boundary integral equations, John employed the Green's function for the entire fluid domain with no body present that satisfied the boundary condition at the bottom of the fluid (assumed flat) and the linearized free-surface condition, on the entire fluid-air boundary. Moreover, he demonstrated the existence of "irregular frequencies" i.e. values of the coupling parameter which appears in the free-surface condition, for which the integral equation is not uniquely solvable. We emphasize that this unique solvability question does not concern the original boundary value problem but rather the integral equation: we assume unique solvability of the former, and our object is to discover how to avoid irregular frequencies in the latter.

Recently, Kleinman [15] provided two methods of modifying the integral equation so that there were no irregular frequencies. In one case, the domain of the integral operator was enlarged and in the other the operator itself changed but both methods employed John's Green's function which is rather complicated. L. Wienert [25] has addressed the question of solvability of a boundary integral equation derived for the same class of bodies with this Green's function.

Another way to treat this problem is to employ a much simpler Green's function, one that satisfies only the boundary condition at the bottom of the fluid. Since this function does not satisfy the free surface condition one obtains an integral equation defined over both the surface of the body and the free surface. Such an integral equation was derived and even solved numerically for certain cases, e.g. Yeung [26] and Bai and Yeung [6]. Angell, Hsiao and Kleinman [1] showed that this integral equation, in the three dimensional case, has no irregular frequencies. More recently Liu [18] has studied the two dimensional case, both theoretically and numerically.

In the case of the totally submerged body we were able to show in our earlier paper [2] that the integral equation arising from the use of John's Green's function is uniquely solvable for all frequencies. It is the formulation of the boundary value problem, the statement of Maz'ja's theorem and the derivation of this boundary integral equation which form the content of the next section, while Section 3 contains a description of the optimization problem and a statement of the results obtained in [2] concerning the existence of an optimal body shape.

In the final section, Section 4, we turn to the question of a constructive method for finding approximate optimal surfaces. We prove there that certain families of functions form complete families of solutions and propose a penalization-type method for the constructive solution. The idea of using complete families to find approximate solutions to elliptic equations goes back at least to the work of Picone and of Fichera (see Miranda [20] for references). Angell and Kleinman [3], [4] have used such families in treating some optimization problems which arise in acoustic and in electromagnetic radiation problems. An approximation method similar to that proposed here is discussed in the context of an inverse transmission problem by Angell, Kleinman and Roach [5]. A related method in the inverse acoustic problem has been reported by Kirsch and Kress [14].

2. THE EXTERIOR BOUNDARY VALUE PROBLEM

We are concerned with solutions of Laplace's equation in an unbounded domain D^+ in $\mathbb{R}^3$ exterior to a bounded boundary, Γ, which is assumed to be a Lyapunov surface of index 1. A Cartesian coordinate system is fixed with origin in the unbounded region determined by Γ in terms of which the domain $D^+ = \mathbb{R}^2 \times [-h,0]$ as indicated in the accompanying figure:

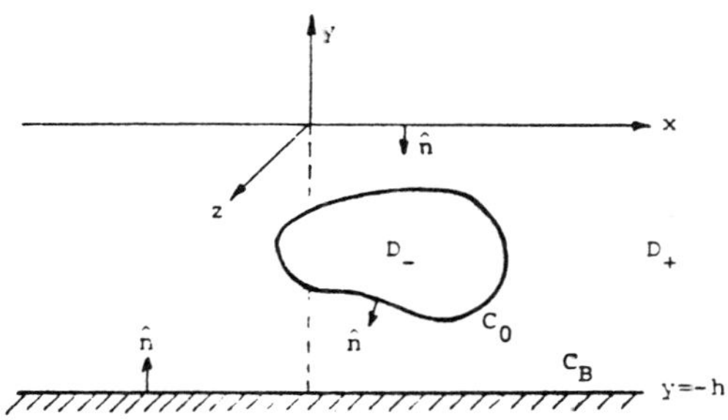

Fig.1

Indeed, the submerged body, whose interior we denote by D_-, will be assumed to be simply connected and lie in a strip $\mathbb{R}^2 \times [-h+\epsilon_o, \epsilon_o]$, $\epsilon_o > 0$. The condition that the surface be Lyapunov of index 1 guarantees, among other things, that there exists an Lipschitz continuous normal $\hat{n}$ at all points of Γ. We emphasize that $\hat{n}$ is oriented so that it points into D_+. Points will be denoted by $p = (x_p, y_p, z_p)$ with cylindrical coordinates $p = (\rho_r, \theta_r, y_p)$ and the subscripts will be omitted if there is no danger of confusion.

With these conventions in mind, we will concern ourselves with the following boundary value problem:

$$
\begin{array}{lll}
\text{(a)} & \Delta\phi = 0 & \text{in } D_+ , \\
\text{(b)} & \dfrac{\partial\phi}{\partial n} + k\phi = 0 & \text{on } y = 0 , \\
\text{(c)} & \dfrac{\partial\phi}{\partial n} = 0 & \text{on } y = -h , \\
\text{(d)} & \dfrac{\partial\phi}{\partial n} = g & \text{on } \Gamma ,
\end{array}
\tag{2.1}
$$

together with a radiation condition

$$\text{(e)} \quad \frac{\partial\phi}{\partial\rho} - ik_o\phi = 0(\rho^{-\frac{1}{2}}) .$$

In this formulation, $g \in C(\Gamma)$ and k_o is the root with the largest real part of the transcendental equation

$$k_n \sinh \; k_n h = k \cosh \; k_n h . \tag{2.2}$$

In [19] Maz'ja introduced a restricted class of boundaries for which this boundary value problem has at most one solution. We formulate that theorem as follows.

<u>Theorem 2.1</u>. Let V be the vector field in $\mathbb{R}^3$ defined by

$$V = \left[\frac{\rho(y^2 - \rho^2)}{\rho^2 + y^2}\right] \tilde{\rho} - \left[\frac{2\rho^2 y}{\rho^2 + y^2}\right] \tilde{y} .$$

Then the homogeneous boundary value problem (1) with $g = 0$ has only the trivial solution provided

$$V \cdot \hat{n} \geq 0 \quad \text{on} \quad \Gamma . \tag{2.3}$$

A discussion of this result and its geometric significance may be found in A. Hulme [12]. We will refer to the class of all such surfaces as the Maz'ja class.

Following John [13] we introduce the Green's function for this problem which is normalized to have the form

$$\gamma(p,q) = -\frac{1}{2\pi}\frac{1}{|p-q|} + R(p,q) \tag{2.4}$$

where the function R has bounded derivatives with respect to q for points $p \in \Gamma$ (see[13,p.96] and γ satisfies conditions 2.1b,c and e. Using this Green's function to define single and double layer potentials, the usual jump conditions can be established as in the potential-theoretic case since the singular behavior of γ and $\frac{\partial}{\partial n_q}\gamma$ is determined by the first term in (2.4). For convenience, we record these results here:

$$\lim_{p\to\Gamma^\pm} \frac{\partial}{\partial n_p} \int_\Gamma u(q)\,\gamma(p,q)\,d\Gamma_q = \pm u(p) + \int_\Gamma u(p) \frac{\partial\gamma(p,q)}{\partial n_p}\,d\Gamma_q , \tag{2.5}$$

$$\lim_{p\to\Gamma^\pm} \int_\Gamma u(q) \frac{\partial}{\partial n_q}\gamma(p,q)\,d\Gamma_q = + u(p) \mp \int_\Gamma u(q) \frac{\partial\gamma(p,q)}{\partial n_q}\,d\Gamma_q \tag{2.6}$$

where $p \to \Gamma^\pm$ means p approaches Γ from $D^\pm$, $u \in L_2(\Gamma)$ and the relations (2.5) and (2.6) hold in the L_2 sense [20].

Moreover, if ϕ is a solution of the boundary value problem (2.1) then one may use Green's Theorem to establish the familiar relation

$$\int_\Gamma \left[\gamma(p,q)\frac{\partial\phi(q)}{\partial n_q} - \phi(q)\frac{\partial}{\partial n_q}\gamma(p,q)\right] d\Gamma_q = \begin{cases} 2\phi(p), & p\in D^+ \\ \phi(p), & p \in \Gamma \\ 0, & p\in D^- \end{cases} . \tag{2.7}$$

If one then uses the boundary condition (2.1d) we have, for $p \in \Gamma$,

$$\int_\Gamma \gamma(p,q)\,g(q)\,d\Gamma_q - \int_\Gamma \phi(q)\frac{\partial}{\partial n_q}[\gamma(p,q)]\,d\Gamma_q = \phi(p) \tag{2.8}$$

or, in operator notation

$$(I + \bar{K}^*)\,\phi = \int_\Gamma \gamma(p,q)\,g(q)\,d\Gamma_q \tag{2.9}$$

where $\bar{K}^*$ is the boundary integral operator with kernel $\partial\gamma/\partial n_q$. We pause to remark that, given a solution, u, of this integral equation we may represent the solution of the boundary value problem according to the relation (2.7) by

$$\phi(p) = \frac{1}{2}\int_\Gamma \gamma(p,q)\,g(q)\,d\Gamma_q - \frac{1}{2}\int_\Gamma u(q)\frac{\partial\gamma(p,q)}{\partial n}\,d\Gamma_q , \quad p\in D^+ \tag{2.10}$$

and, again using the jump relations, one sees easily that

$$\phi\big|_\Gamma = u , \tag{2.11}$$

which is a direct relationship between the solution of the boundary integral equation and the boundary values taken on by the solution. Such a direct relation does not obtain when one uses a layer approach in which one assumes that the solution ϕ had a representation as a single layer,

$$\phi(p) = \int_\Gamma u(q)\,\gamma(p,q)\,d\Gamma_q ,$$

and then uses the boundary condition and jump relations to obtain an integral equation for u.

As we will see below when we consider the optimization problem, it is particularly convenient to have this formulation as the cost functional involves just the trace of the solution ϕ of (2.1) on Γ.

With the aid of these jump conditions, we have proved the unique solvability of the boundary integral equation (2.9). Specifically, we may state the following theorem referring to [2] for the proof:

Theorem 2.2: Let Γ be Lyapunov of index 1 and belong to the Maz'ja class. Let $g \in C(\Gamma)$. Then the integral equation (2.9) has a unique solution in $L^2(\Gamma)$.

Remark: In fact, the solution whose existence is guaranteed by this last theorem can be shown, by a standard argument to be continuous since $g \in C(\Gamma)$. However, we will not require this result in what follows.

3. THE OPTIMIZATION PROBLEM

Let $\Gamma_0 = \{p \in \mathbb{R}^3 \,|\, |p|=1\}$ denote the surface of the unit ball in $\mathbb{R}^3$ and let $C^{1,1}(\Gamma_0)$ denote the space of continuously differentiable functions whose first derivatives satisfy a Lipschitz condition and which is equipped with the usual Hölder norm $||\cdot||_{1,1}$ (see e.g. [10]). We will assume that we are given a family of surfaces which can be described by $C^{1,1}$ parameterizations:

$$\Gamma(f) = \left\{ p \in \mathbb{R}^3 \,|\, p = f(\tilde{p})\tilde{p} + p_0 \,,\ \tilde{p} = \frac{p - p_0}{|p - p_0|} \right\}$$

where $f:\Gamma_0 \to \mathbb{R}^3$ is an element of $C^{1,1}(\Gamma_0)$ and $p_0 \in \mathbb{R}^2 \times (-h+\epsilon_0, -\epsilon_0)$. Let a and b be two positive constants and define the subset $F_{a,b} \subset C^{1,1}(\Gamma_0)$ by

$$F_{a,b} = \{ f \in C^{1,1}(\Gamma_0) |\ ||f||_{1,1} \le b, f(\tilde{p})\tilde{p} + p_0 \in \mathbb{R}^2 \times (-h+\epsilon_0, -\epsilon_0) \quad (3.2)$$

$$\text{and} \qquad f(\tilde{p}) \ge a,\ \tilde{p} \in \Gamma_0 \} .$$

Definition 3.1. A surface S in $\mathbb{R}^3$ will be called admissible provided S can be described by a parametization $f \in F_{a,b}$ and S is contained in the Maz'ja class (c.f. Theorem 1.1).

Note that since each admissible surface is completely determined by the function f, we will henceforth simply refer to "the surface f" although, when convenient, we will use the notation $\Gamma(f)$. Clearly, each admissible surface describes a surface bounding a bounded region which contains a ball of radius a/2 and center p_0 in its interior.

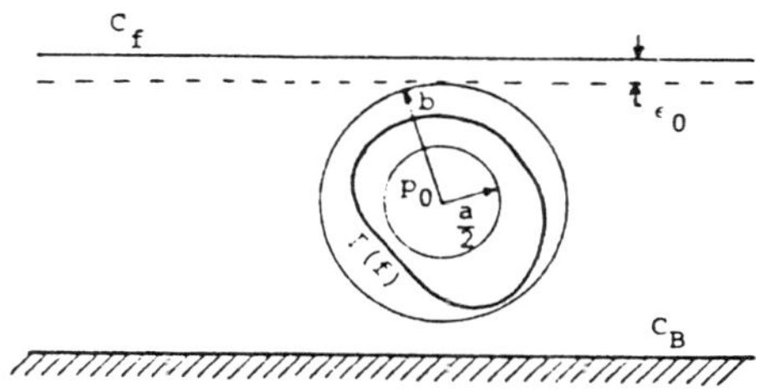

Fig. 2

We will, when necessary, denote the region in $\mathbb{R}^2 \times (-h, 0)$ exterior to an admissible surface f by D_f^+ and the interior of the surface by D_f^-.

Let U_{ad} be a compact subset of admissible surfaces. For example, since the imbedding $C^2(\Gamma_0) \to C^{1,1}(\Gamma_0)$ is compact, we may choose U_{ad} to be the subset of admissible functions in $C^2(\Gamma_0)$. This particular choice leads to a non-linear optimization problem over a closed convex set. The convexity will be advantageous for subsequent numerical considerations.

We now wish to consider a *family* of boundary value problems of the type discussed in Section 2 which may be considered as indexed by U_{ad}:

$$\begin{aligned}
&(a) \quad \Delta\phi(p) = 0, && p \in D_f^+ , \\
&(b) \quad \frac{\partial\phi}{\partial n} + k\phi = 0 && \text{on } y = 0 , \\
&(c) \quad \frac{\partial\phi}{\partial n} = 0 && \text{on } y = -h , \\
&(d) \quad \frac{\partial\phi}{\partial n} = g && \text{on } \Gamma(f) , \\
&(e) \quad \frac{\partial\phi}{\partial\rho} - ik_0\phi = o(\rho^{-\frac{1}{2}}) .
\end{aligned} \tag{3.3}$$

Note that, because we are considering a family of boundary value problems, the data g in (3.3d) must be defined throughout the domain formed by the union of all admissible surfaces. This is indeed the case for heaving motion where $g = -\hat{n} \cdot \hat{y}$.

With this understanding, each choice of surface $f \in U_{ad}$ gives rise, according to Theorem 2.1, to a potential $\phi = \phi(p;f)$, $p \in D_f^+$. The class of optimization problems that we discuss below then have the form: Let $J: C(\Gamma_0) \to \mathbb{R}$ be continuous and define a map $J[\cdot]: U_{ad} \to \mathbb{R}$ by

$$J[f] := J(\tilde{\phi}(\cdot;f)), \quad f \in U_{ad} \tag{3.4}$$

where

$$\tilde{\phi}(\tilde{p};f) := \phi(f(\tilde{p})\tilde{p} + p_0;f), \quad \tilde{p} \in \Gamma_0 . \tag{3.5}$$

The optimization problem is to find $f_0 \in U_{ad}$ such that

$$J[f_0] \le J[f] , \quad \text{for all } f \in U_{ad} \tag{3.6}$$

or

$$J[f_0] \ge J[f] , \quad \text{for all } f \in U_{ad} . \tag{3.7}$$

We will confine our discussion to the problem of minimization. This is sufficiently general since the problem of maximizing a functional J may always be replaced by that of minimizing $-J$.

Specific forms of the functional J of (3.4) may be chosen to reflect desirable design criteria. For example, as mentioned in the introduction one may choose J to represent the added mass of the hull. In this case, the problem of interest is that of minimizing the functional J in order to reduce the hydrodynamic force on the ship hull, a goal which is obviously of great importance to ship design. Indeed, it is well known (see [24,pp.563-567]) that the added mass of a particular hull may be represented by

$$M_a = \mathrm{Re} \int_{\Gamma(f)} \phi(p) \frac{\partial \phi}{\partial n} d\Gamma .$$

This form, in light of the boundary condition (3.3d), leads to the functional

$$J[f] = \mathrm{Re} \int_{\Gamma_0} \tilde{\phi}(\tilde{p};f) g(f(\tilde{p})\tilde{p} + p_0) J_f(\tilde{p}) d\Gamma_0 , \tag{3.8}$$

where J_f is the Jacobian of the transformation $p = f(\tilde{p})\tilde{p} + p_0$.

In [2] we proved the continuity of the mapping $f \to \tilde{\phi}(\cdot;f)$ from U_{ad} to $C(\Gamma_0)$. By introducing the functions

$$\tilde{\phi}(\tilde{p}) := \phi(f(\tilde{p})\tilde{p} + p_0) , \tag{3.9}$$

$$g_f(\tilde{p}) := g(f(\tilde{p})\tilde{p} + p_0) \tag{3.10}$$

and kernels

$$a_f(\tilde{p},\tilde{q}) := [\partial/\partial n_q \gamma(f(\tilde{p})\tilde{p} + p_0 , f(\tilde{q})\tilde{q} + p_0)]J_f(\tilde{q}) \tag{3.11}$$

and

$$b_f(\tilde{p},\tilde{q}) := [\gamma(f(\tilde{p})\tilde{p} + p_0) , f(\tilde{q})\tilde{q} + p_0)]J_f(\tilde{q}) \tag{3.12}$$

the integral equation (2.9) may be rewritten as

$$\tilde{\phi}(\tilde{p}) + \int_{\Gamma_0} a_f(\tilde{p},\tilde{q})\tilde{\phi}(\tilde{q})d\Gamma_{\tilde{q}} = \int_{\Gamma_0} b_f(\tilde{p},\tilde{q})g_f(\tilde{q})d\Gamma_{\tilde{q}} . \tag{3.13}$$

The integral operators A_f and B_f defined by the kernels a_f and b_f are in fact compact operators on $C(\Gamma_0)$, a fact which is established in [2] with the help of the following lemma.

Lemma 3.1. For any δ, $0<\delta<1/2$, the kernels a_f and b_f are weakly singular and satisfy the inequalities:

$$|a_f(\tilde{p},\tilde{q}) - a_g(\tilde{p},\tilde{q})| \le ||f - g||^{\delta}_{1,1} \frac{c_1}{|\tilde{p} - \tilde{q}|^{1+2\delta}} \tag{3.14}$$

and

$$|b_f(\tilde{p},\tilde{q}) - b_g(\tilde{p},\tilde{q})| \le ||f - g||^{\delta}_{1,1} \frac{c_2}{|\tilde{p} - \tilde{q}|^{1+\delta}} \tag{3.15}$$

where c_1 and c_2 are positive constants.

The basic results are the following theorem and its corollary which we will use in the following section.

Theorem 3.1. Let $\mathcal{B}(C(\Gamma_0))$ denote the space of bounded linear operators on $C(\Gamma_0)$ equipped with the uniform operator topology and assume that the map $f \to g_f$ from $C^{1,1}(\Gamma_0)$ into $C(\Gamma_0)$ is Hölder continuous. Then the mappings $f \to A_f$ and $f \to B_f$ of $C^{1,1}(\Gamma_0)$ into $\mathcal{B}(C(\Gamma_0))$ are Hölder continuous. Moreover, since the set U_{ad} is compact, the map $f \to \tilde{\phi}(\cdot;f)$ of U_{ad} into $C(\Gamma_0)$, where $\tilde{\phi}(\cdot;f)$ is the unique solution of the boundary integral equation (3.14), is Hölder continuous.

The continuity of the mappings $f \to \tilde{\phi}(\cdot;f)$ and $f \to G_f$ lead immediately to the following corollary which establishes the existence of solutions of our optimization problem.

Corollary 3.1. Under the hypotheses of Theorem 3.1, the functional $J[\cdot]$ defined by the equation (3.8) is continuous as a map from U_{ad} into $\mathbb{R}$ and consequently takes on its absolute minimum on the set U_{ad}.

4. COMPLETE FAMILIES AND APPROXIMATE OPTIMIZATION PROBLEMS

In this final section we turn to the question of developing a constructive procedure for the minimization problem. Our approach is based on the use of a complete family of solutions. We begin with a discussion of this family.

Recall that the class of admissible surfaces is defined in such a way that all contain a ball of radius $a/2$, centered at the point p_o, for some preassigned constant $a>0$. Certainly we may consider a surface Γ_{a_o} strictly interior to the surface of the ball $\Gamma_{a/2}$. We may thus prove the following result.

Theorem 4.1: Let $\{\phi_n\}_{n=1}^{\infty}$ be a linearly independent family of functions which is complete in $L^2(\Gamma_{a_o})$. For each n, define the function u_n by

$$u_n(p) = \int_{\Gamma_{a_o}} \gamma(p,q)\phi_n(q)d\Gamma_q \; , \; p \in \mathbb{R}^3 \backslash D^-_{a_o} \tag{4.6}$$

Then the functions

$$v_n(p) = (\partial u_n/\partial n)(p) \quad , \; p \in \Gamma(f) \quad , \; n = 1,2,\ldots$$

form a complete linearly independent family in

$L^2(\Gamma(f))$, for all $f \in U_{ad}$.

Remark: By linear independence of these countable families we mean that any finite subset is linearly independent.

Proof:

Consider the family $\{v_n\} \subset L^2(\Gamma(f))$ and suppose that there is some $\psi \in L^2(\Gamma(f)$ such that

$$0 = \langle \psi, v_n \rangle_{L_2(\Gamma(f))} \quad \text{for all} \quad n = 1,2,\ldots \quad .$$

Then, recognizing that $\Gamma(f) \cap \Gamma_{a_o} = \emptyset$,

$$\langle \psi, \nu_n \rangle_{L^2(\Gamma(f))} := \int_{\Gamma(f)} \psi(p) \left[\frac{\partial}{\partial n_p} \int_{\Gamma_{a_0}} \overline{\gamma}(p,q) \overline{\phi_n}(q) d\Gamma_q \right] d\Gamma_p$$

$$= \int_{\Gamma_{a_0}} \left[\int_{\Gamma(f)} \psi(p) \frac{\partial}{\partial n_p} \overline{\gamma}(p,q) d\Gamma_p \right] \overline{\phi}_n(q) d\Gamma_q$$

$$= \int_{\Gamma_{a_0}} \left[\overline{D}_{\Gamma(f)} \psi \right] (q) \overline{\phi_n}(q) d\Gamma_q$$

$$= \langle \overline{D}_{\Gamma(f)} \psi , \phi_n \rangle_{L^2(\Gamma_{a_0})}$$

Note that $\overline{D}_{\Gamma(f)} : L^2(\Gamma(f)) \to L^2(\Gamma_{a_0})$ and that the set $\{\phi_n\}$ is complete set $L^2(\Gamma_{a_0})$. Hence $\overline{D}_{\Gamma(f)} \psi = 0$ and hence $D_{\Gamma(f)} \psi = 0$ on Γ_{a_0}.

Now consider the function u, defined in D_f^- by

$$u_\psi(q) := \int_{\Gamma(f)} \frac{\partial}{\partial n_p} \gamma(p,q) \overline{\psi}(p) d\Gamma_p .$$

Then u_ψ is harmonic in D_f^-. Moreover, in the region $D_{a_0}^-$ i.e. in the region interior to Γ_{a_0}, u_ψ is harmonic and

$$u_\psi \Big|_{\Gamma_{a_0}} = 0 .$$

Hence u_ψ vanishes everywhere in $D_{a_0}^-$ and hence, by analytic continuation, everywhere in D_f^-. But, since $u_\psi = D_\Gamma \overline{\psi}$, we have, using the jump conditions

$$0 = \lim_{q \to \Gamma(f)^-} D_\Gamma \overline{\psi}(q) = (I + \overline{K}^*)\overline{\upsilon} .$$

The results of Section 2 guarantee that the only solution of

$$(I + \overline{K}^*) u = 0$$

is the trivial solution so we have $\psi = 0$. This establishes completeness.

To establish that any finite subset of the v_n is linearly independent, suppose, without loss of generality, that there exist constants $\alpha_1, \ldots, \alpha_N$ such that

$$\sum_{i=1}^{N} \alpha_i v_i = 0 \quad \text{on} \quad \Gamma(f) .$$

Then, by definition,

$$0 = \sum_{i=1}^{N} \alpha_i v_i = \frac{\partial}{\partial n} \sum_{i=1}^{N} \alpha_i \int_{\Gamma_{a_o}} \gamma(p,q)\phi_i(q)d\Gamma_q$$

$$= \frac{\partial}{\partial n}\left[\int_{\Gamma_{a_o}} \gamma(p,q) \sum_{i=1}^{N} \alpha_i\phi_i(q)\, d\Gamma_q\right]$$

$$= \frac{\partial}{\partial n} \int_{\Gamma_{a_o}} \gamma(p,q)w(q)d\Gamma_q$$

where $w(q) := \sum_{i=1}^{N} \alpha_i\phi_i(q)$.

Now, for $p \in D^+_{a_o}$, i.e. in the exterior of Γ_{a_o}, define the function $v = v(p)$ by

$$v(p) := \int_{\Gamma_{a_o}} \bar{\gamma}(p,q)w(q)d\Gamma_q .$$

Thus certainly v is harmonic in $D^+_{a_o}$ and, in particular, is harmonic in D^+_f. Moreover

$$\left.\frac{\partial}{\partial n} v\right|_{\Gamma(f)} = 0$$

and so v is a solution of the exterior homogeneous Neumann problem. By the uniqueness theorem, v vanishes identically in D^+_f and so, by analytic continuation, also vanishes in the region exterior to Γ_{a_o}. Hence, again using the jump conditions,

$$0 = \lim_{p\to\Gamma^+_{a_o}} \frac{\partial}{\partial n} Sw = (I + K_{a_o})w = 0 \qquad \text{where}$$

$$(K_{a_o}w)(p) := \int_{\Gamma_{a_o}} \frac{\partial\gamma}{\partial n_p}(p,q)w(q)d\Gamma_q .$$

Hence $(I + \overline{K}_{a_o})\overline{w} = 0$ and so $\overline{w}$ vanishes on Γ_{a_o} and therefore, so does w itself. From the linear independence of the $\{\phi_i\}_{i=1}^{N}$, we conclude that all the coefficients $c_i = 0$, $i=1,\ldots,N$ and this shows that the corresponding functions $v_i, i=1,\ldots,N$, are likewise linearly independent.

The completeness of the family (4.6) allows us to approximate any function in $L^2(\Gamma(f))$ as closely as desired with a finite linear combination of the normal derivatives $\partial u_n/\partial n$. Even more is true as a consequence of this choice of the functions u_n as harmonic functions. This additional approximation result is described in the next statement, in which Γ is a fixed surface.

Lemma 4.1: Let $g \in L^2(\Gamma)$ and let u be a solution of the system (4.4) with $\partial u/\partial n = g$. Suppose that, for each integer $N \geq 1$, the coefficients $\{c_\ell^{(N)} : \ell = 1, 2, \ldots, N\}$ are chosen so as to minimize $\left\| \sum_{\ell=1}^{N} c_\ell^{(N)} v_\ell - g \right\|_{L^2(\Gamma)}$. Then

$$\lim_{N\to\infty} \left\| \sum_{\ell=1}^{N} c_\ell^{(N)} u_\ell - \phi \right\|_{L^2(\Gamma)} = 0 . \tag{4.8}$$

when ϕ is the solution of the integral equation (2.9).

Proof: Since u and u_ℓ, $\ell=1,2,\ldots$, are harmonic and satisfy the radiation condition, Green's theorem yields the relations

$$(I + \overline{K}_\Gamma^*)u_\ell = \int_\Gamma \gamma(p,q) v_\ell(q)\, d\Gamma_q \tag{4.9}$$

and

$$(I + \overline{K}^*)u = \int_\Gamma \gamma(p,q) g(q)\, d\Gamma_q \tag{4.10}$$

where $\overline{K}_\Gamma^*$ is the double layer operator associated with the surface Γ (see (2.7)-(2.9)). We may conclude immediately that, since the integral equation (2.9) has a unique solution,

$$\sum_{\ell=1}^{N} c_\ell^{(N)} u_\ell - \phi = (I + \overline{K}^*)^{-1} \int_\Gamma \gamma(p,q) \left[\sum_{\ell=1}^{N} c_\ell^{(N)} N_\ell(q) - g(q) \right] d\Gamma_q \tag{4.11}$$

$$\left\| \sum_{\ell=1}^{N} c_\ell^{(N)} u_\ell - \phi \right\|_{L^2(\Gamma)} \leq \left\| (I+\overline{K}^*)^{-1} \right\|_{L^2(\Gamma)} \left\| S_\Gamma \right\| \left\| \sum_{\ell=1} c_\ell^{(N)} v_\ell - g \right\|_{L^2(\Gamma)} \tag{4.12}$$

where S_Γ is the single layer operator associated with Γ. The result follows from the boundedness of the two operators and the completeness of the v_ℓ.

Remark: The only restrictions on Γ_{a_o} are that $\Gamma_{a_o} \subset D_f^-$ for every $f \in U_{ad}$ and Γ_{a_o} be sufficiently smooth so that the jump conditions for single and double layers on Γ_{a_o} remain valid. For example Γ_{a_o} may be chosen to be a sphere of radius $a_o \leq \frac{a}{2}$ and $\{\phi_n\}$ may be taken as the spherical harmonics.

The family of harmonic functions $\{u_n\}$ defined in Theorem 4.1 individually satisfy the free surface condition, radiation condition and boundary condition on the sea floor and their normal derivatives are complete and linearly independent on $L^2(\Gamma(f))$ for all $f \in U_{ad}$. This makes them useful not only in approximating solutions of the submerged body problem (3.3) but also in formulating a sequence of approximate optimization problems.

Recall that the functional (3.8) may be written

$$J[f] = \text{Re} \int_{\Gamma(f)} \phi(p) g(p) d\Gamma \tag{4.13}$$

where ϕ is the trace on $\Gamma(f)$ of the solution of the boundary value problem (3.3). The functional has a miminum J_o on U_{ad}, as was established in the previous section. While the sign of J_o is not known a priori there exists a positive number M such that

$$J[f] + M > 0 \quad , \quad f \in U_{ad} , \tag{4.14}$$

and it is clear that $|J[f] + M|$ and $J[f]$ have the same minimizers though of course not the same minimum values. It is this form however that lends itself to the formulation of a sequence of functionals and related optimization problems which approximate the optimization problem we wish to solve. To this end we define

$$J^N[f;c_1,c_2,\ldots c_N] := \left| M + \mathrm{Re} \int_{\Gamma(f)} \sum_{n=1}^{N} c_n u_n(p) g(p) d\Gamma_f \right| + \nu \left\| \sum_{n=1}^{N} c_n \frac{\partial u_n}{n} - g \right\|_{L^2(\Gamma(f))}$$

and the associated sequence of optimization problems: determine $f^N \in U_{ad}$ and $c_n^N \in \mathbb{C}$, $n=1, \ldots N$ to minimize $J^N[f;c_1,\ldots c_N]$.

The second term on the right in (4.15) measures the defect in satisfying the boundary conditions and the factor ν may be chosen to adjust the penalty for failing to satisfy the boundary condition. The minimum J_o of $J[f]$ will in general be unknown therefore unless a lower bound of $J[f]$ can be found. A suitable M in (4.15) will have to be determined through numerical experimentation as will suitable values of ν. This awaits numerical implementation of an algorithm to solve the approximate optimization problems. These points as well as questions of existence of minimizers of J^N and their convergence to minimizers of J will be discussed elsewhere.

Acknowledgement: This work was supported under National Science Foundation Grant DMS-8507063 and Office of Naval Research Grant N00014-85-K-0532.

References

[1] T.S. Angell, G.C. Hsiao and R.E. Kleinman, An Integral Equation for the Floating-Body Problem, J. Fluid Mech. 166 (1986), 161-177.

[2] T.S. Angell, G.C. Hsiao and R.E. Kleinman, An Optimal Design Problem for Submerged Bodies, Math. Meth. in the Appl. Sci. 8 (1986), 50-76.

[3] T.S. Angell and R.E. Kleinman, A Galerkin Procedure for Optimization in Radiation Problems, SIAM J. Appl. Math. 44 (1984), 1246-1257.

[4] T.S. Angell and R.E. Kleinman, A New Optimization Method for Antenna Design, Ann. Télécommun. 40 (1985), 341-349.

[5] T.S. Angell, R.E. Kleinman and G.F. Roach, An Inverse Transmission Problem for the Helmholtz Equation, Inverse Problems, to appear.

[6] K.J. Bai and R.W. Yeung, Numerical Solutions to Free Surface Flow Problems, 10th Symposium on Naval Hydrodynamics, MIT, (1974), 609-647.

[7] J. Cea, Identification de Domaines. Lecture Notes in Computer Science 3 (1975), Springer-Verlag, 92-102.

[8] J. Cea, A. Gioan, J. Michel, Adaptation de la Méthode du Gradient à un Probléme d'Identification de Domame Lecture Notes in Computer Science 11 (1974) Springer-Verlag.

[9] D. Chenais, On the Existence of a Solution in a Domain Identification Problem, J. Math. Anal. Appl. 52 (1975), 189-209.

[10] D. Colton and R. Kress, Integral Equation Methods in Scattering Theory, John Wiley, New York 1983.

[11] S. DeJulio, Numerical Solution of Dynamical Optimization Problems, SIAM J. Control 8 (1970), 135-147.

[12] A. Hulme, Some Application of Maz'ja's Uniqueness Theorem to a Class of Linear Water Wave Problems, Math. Proc. Comb. Phil. Soc. 95 (1984), 165-174.

[13] F. John, On the Motion of Floating Bodies II, Comm. Proc. Appl. Math. 3 (1950), 45-101.

[14] A. Kirsch and R. Kress, On An Integral Equation of the First Kind in Inverse Acoustic Scattering, to appear.

[15] R.E. Kleinman, On the Mathematical Theory of the Motion of Floating Bodies - an Update, David W. Taylor Naval Ship Research and Development Center Report DTNSRDC-82/074 Bathesda, MD.

[16] J.L. Lions, Optimal Control of Systems Governed by Partial Differential Equations, S.K. Mitter, tr. Springer-Verlag 1971.

[17] J.L. Lions, Some Aspects of the Optimal Control of Distributed Parameter Systems, Regional Conference Series in Appl. Math., SIAM, 1972.

[18] Y. Liu, A Boundary Integral Method for the Two-Dimensional Floating Body Problem. Ph.D. Dissertation, Department of Mathematical Sciences, University of Delaware, 1987.

[19] V.G. Maz'ja, Solvability of the Problem on the Oscillations of a Fluid Containing a Submerged Body, J. Soviet Math. 10 (1978), 86-89.

[20] C. Miranda, Partial Differential Equations of Elliptic Type, Second Revised Edition, Springer-Verlag, 1970.

[21] O. Pironneau, On Optimum Profiles in Stokes Flow, J. Fluid Mech. 59 (1973), 117-128.

[22] O. Pironneau, On Optimal Design in Fluid Mechanics, J. Fluid Mech. 64 (1974), 97-110.

[23] N.J. Simon and F. Ursell, Uniqueness in Linearized Two-Dimensional Water-Wave Problems, J.Fluid Mech. 148 (1984), 137-154.

[24] J.V. Wehausen and E.V. Laitone, Surface Waves. In: Handbuch der Physik, Bd.IX: Strömungsmechanik III, S. Flügge ed. Springer Verlag (1960), 446-778.

[25] L. Wienert, Ein Existenzbeweis für ein Randwertproblem aus der Theorie der Wasserwellen, Diplomarbeit, Institut für Numerische und Angewante Mathematik, Universität Göttingen

[26] R.W. Yeung, A Hybrid Integral Equation Method for Time Harmonic Free Surface Flows. Proc. First Inst. Conf. on Numerical Ship Hydrodynamics, Gaithersburg, MD, 581-607.

International Series of
Numerical Mathematics, Vol. 78

ON A CERTAIN OPTIMAL HARVESTING PROBLEM WITH CONTINUOUS AGE STRUCTURE

Martin Brokate
Institut für Mathematik
Universität Augsburg
8900 Augsburg, F . R. G.

Abstract: We consider an optimal harvesting problem for a population with continuous age and time structure. On the basis of a version of Pontryagin's principle, we investigate the form of an optimal solution in a special situation.

1. Problem formulation and preliminary results.

We consider the following optimal harvesting problem, whose dynamics are described by the Gurtin-MacCamy equations [1] and which is a special case of an optimal harvesting problem presented in [2] and discussed further in [3] , [4]:

For $0 < T < \infty$ fixed,

$$\text{maximize} \int_0^T\int_0^\infty u(a,t)\rho(a,t)\,da\,dt \tag{1}$$

where for $(a,t) \in \mathbb{R}_+\times[0,T]$ (resp. in the interior)

$$\left(\frac{\partial}{\partial a} + \frac{\partial}{\partial t}\right) \rho(a,t) + (\mu(p(t)) + u(a,t))\,\rho(a,t) = 0 \tag{2}$$

$$\rho(a,0) = \rho_o(a) \tag{3}$$

$$\rho(0,t) = b(t) \tag{4}$$

$$b(t) = \int_0^\infty \beta(a)\,\rho(a,t)\,da \tag{5}$$

$$p(t) = \int_0^\infty \rho(a,t)\,da \tag{6}$$

$$0 \leq u(a,t) \leq u_{max} \tag{7}$$

The death rate μ, the fertility function β, and the initial age distribution ρ_o are given functions; the harvesting effort u is the control function (bounded by a given $u_{max} > 0$); the population density ρ, the birth rate b and the total population p are the state variables.
Our basic assumptions are:

Assumption (A1)

(i) $\mu, \beta, \rho_o : \mathbb{R}_+ \to \mathbb{R}_+$, i.e. they are nonnegative.

(ii) $\rho_o \in L^1(0,\infty) \cap L^\infty(0,\infty)$, not identically zero.

(iii) β is bounded.

(iv) μ and β are twice continuously differentiable.

□

For mathematical convenience, we transform (1) - (7) into characteristic (x,t) - coordinates by

$$x = a - t \quad , \quad a = x + t$$

and rewrite (2) - (4) as an integral equation. We set

$$y(x,t) = \rho(x+t,t) \ , \ 0 \leqq t \leqq T \ , \ -t \leqq x < \infty \ ,$$

and obtain the following problem:

$$\text{Maximize} \int_0^T \int_{-t}^\infty u(x,t)y(x,t) \, dx \, dt \tag{8}$$

subject to

$$y(x,t) = y_o(x) - \int_0^t \chi(s+x) \left[\mu(p(s)) + u(x,s) \right] y(x,s) \, ds \tag{9}$$

$$y_o(x) = \begin{cases} \rho_o(x) & , \ x \geqq 0 \\ b(-x) & , \ -T \leqq x < 0 \end{cases} \tag{10}$$

$$b(t) = \int_{-t}^\infty \beta(x+t) y(x,t) \, dx \tag{11}$$

$$p(t) = \int_{-t}^{\infty} y(x,t)\,dx \tag{12}$$

$$0 \leqq u(x,t) \leqq u_{max} \tag{13}$$

Here χ denotes the Heaviside function ($\chi(t) = 0$ for $t < 0$, $\chi(t) = 1$ for $t \geqq 0$) .

Given $u \in L^{\infty}$, the system equations (9) - (12) have a unique and nonnegative solution (y,b,p) . This has been basically proved in [2]; see [3], [5], [6], [7], [8] for various weakenings of the assumptions in [2]. It has been proved in [4] by weak convergence arguments, that the optimal harvesting problem (8) - (13) has a solution:

THEOREM 1

If (A1) holds, then (8) - (13) has a solution $L^{\infty}([-T,\infty)\times[0,T])$ with corresponding state (y,b,p) , also termed solution, in the spaces

$$y \in C(0,T;L^{\infty}(-T,\infty)) \cap C(0,T;L^{1}(-T,\infty))$$
$$b \in L^{\infty}(0,T)\ ,\ p \in C[0,T]\ .$$

□

In [3], the Pontryagin principle for a more general optimal harvesting problem has been proved. Specialized to the problem (8) - (13) above, we obtain:

THEOREM 2

If (A1) holds and (y,b,p,u) is a solution of (8) - (13), then there exist adjoint functions

$$\eta \in C(0,T;L^{\infty}(-T,\infty))\ ,\zeta,\theta \in L^{\infty}(0,T)$$

such that the adjoint equations

$$\eta(x,t) = -\int_t^T \chi(s+x)\Big[(u(x,s) + \mu(p(s)))(1+\eta(x,s)) - \qquad (14)$$
$$- (\mu(p(s)) + \beta(x+s)\zeta(s) + \theta(s))\Big]\,ds$$

$$\zeta(t) = \eta(-t,t) \qquad (= \eta\ (-t,0)) \qquad (15)$$

$$\theta(t) = -\mu'(p(t))\int_{-t}^{\infty} y(x,t)\eta(x,t)\,dx \qquad (16)$$

hold. The optimal control satisfies

$$u(x,t) = \begin{cases} u_{max}, & \text{if } \eta(x,t) > -1 \\ 0, & \text{if } \eta(x,t) < -1 \end{cases} \qquad (17)$$

Proof: This is a special case of Theorem 4 in [3].

□

2. Properties of an optimal solution.

We henceforth assume, that (A1) holds, and denote by (y,b,p,u) a solution of (8) - (13) and by (η,ζ,θ) the adjoints satisfying (14) - (17). At first we note that we have more regularity.

Lemma 1

(i) For the distributional time derivatives we have

$$y_t \in L^\infty((-T,\infty)\times(0,T)) \cap L^\infty(0,T;L^1(-\infty,T))$$
$$b',p',\theta' \in L^\infty(0,T) \quad .$$

(ii) Furthermore η and η_t are Lipschitz-continuous on
$$H = \{(x,t) : 0 \leq t \leq T\ ,\ -t \leq x < \infty\}\quad ,$$
and $\zeta' \in L^\infty(0,T)$.

Proof: Assertion (i) follows directly from formulas (9), (11), (12) and (16), if one applies basic lemmas for distributional derivatives. To prove (ii), we combine (14) - (17) to obtain in H the integral equation

$$\eta(x,t) = -\int_t^T u_{max}(1+\eta(x,s))_+ + \mu(p(s))\eta(x,s) -$$

$$- \beta(x+s)\ \eta(-s,s) - \theta(s)\ ds \quad ,$$

which has the form

$$\eta(x,t) = \int_t^T f(x,s,\eta(x,s)) + g(x,s,\eta(-s,s))\ ds \quad , \tag{18}$$

where f and g are Lipschitz-continuous on $[-T,M]\times[0,T]\times\mathbb{R}$ for every $M > 0$. By standard contraction arguments, (18) has a unique continuous solution in $[-T,\infty) \times [0,T]$ which coincides on H with the solution of (14). For $z \in C\,[0,T]$, $x \in [-T,M]$, we consider the equation

$$z = F(z,x) + G(x) \tag{19}$$

with

$$F(z,x)(t) = \int_t^T f(x,s,z(s))\ ds$$

$$G(x)(t) = \int_t^T g(x,s,\eta(-s,s))\ ds$$

From the parameter-dependent version of the Banach contraction principle [9,p.18f], applied to $C[0,T]$ with norm

$$\|z\| = \sup_{t\in[0,T]} e^{-C(T-t)}\,|z(t)|$$

for C sufficiently large, we obtain a unique solution

$z = z(x)$ of (19) which depends Lipschitz-continuously upon x Since by uniqueness $z(x)(t) = \eta(x,t)$, η is Lipschitz-continuous, therefore also η_t and ζ .

□

The optimal distributed control $u(\cdot,t)$ at any given time must be some balance between maximizing the cost function and not depleting the population too much for future use. In the model (8) - (13) with fixed finite T it is clear that for t near T the conservation of the population is ignored.

Lemma 2

There exists a $\delta_o > 0$ such that for all t with $T-\delta_o \leq t < T$ we have

$$u(x,t) = u_{max} \quad \text{for all } x$$

$$\eta_t(x,t) > 0 \quad \text{a.e. in } x$$

$$\eta(x,t) < \eta(x,T) = 0 \quad \text{a.e. in } x$$

Proof: By (14), there exists a $\delta_o > 0$ such that $\eta(x,t) > -1$ a.e. for $t \geq T - \delta_o$, therefore $u = u_{max}$ for $t \geq T - \delta_o$. Making δ_o smaller if necessary we see from (14) - (16) and Lemma 1 that $|\eta_t(x,t) - u_{max}|$ can be made small uniformly in (x,t) .

□

The next question is: What happens if $\eta > -1$ no longer holds?

Definition 1

$$G_t := [-T,\infty) \times [t,T]$$

$$t^* := \inf \{t \in [0,T] : \eta(x,s) > -1 \text{ a.e. in } G_t\}$$

$$G^* := G_{t^*}$$

We first derive some properties of θ which depend only on assumptions for μ .

Assumption (A2)

(i) $\mu(p) > 0$, $\mu'(p) > 0$ for all $p > 0$

(ii) $\mu'' \equiv 0$, i.e. $\mu(p) = \alpha_o + \alpha_1 p$.

□

Lemma 3

For θ we have $\theta(T) = 0$ and

$$\theta'(t) = \gamma(t)\theta(t) - \mu'(p(t)) \int_{-t}^{\infty} y(x,t)u(x,t)\, dx \tag{20}$$

where

$$\gamma(t) = \mu'(p(t))p(t) + \frac{\mu''(p(t))p'(t)}{\mu'(p(t))} \tag{21}$$

If (A2 i) holds, we have

$$\epsilon(t) > 0 \quad \text{for all} \quad t < T \quad . \tag{22}$$

If furthermore (A2 ii) holds, we have

$$\epsilon(t) < u_{max} \quad \text{for all} \quad t < T \tag{23}$$

Proof: Formulas (20), (21) follow by differentiation using (14) - (16). The integral in (20) is greater than 0 for t near T because of (A1 ii) and Lemma 2. If one applies the variation of constants formula to (20), then one obtains (22). For (23), set

$$z(t) = u_{max} - \theta(t) .$$

Then

$$z'(t) = \mu'(p(t))p(t)z(t) + f(t)$$

with $f \geq 0$, and because of $z(T) < 0$ we again conclude $z(t) < 0$ for all $t < T$.

□

We further need one assumption concerning β.

Assumption (A3)

We have

$$\beta'(a) < 0 \quad \text{for all} \quad a \geq 0 .$$

□

This assumption is sufficient for the nonexistence of singular optimal controls:

Lemma 4

If (A2 i) holds and if $\{a : \beta'(a) \neq 0\}$ is dense in $\{a : \beta(a) \neq 0\}$, which is implied by (A3), then there is no open set S such that $\eta(x,t) = -1$ for all $(x,t) \in S$.

Proof: If there where such an S, then we would have

$$0 = \mu(p(t)) + \beta(x+t)\zeta(t) + \theta(t) , \quad (x,t) \in S ,$$

by (14). Differentiating with respect to x yields

$$0 = \beta'(x+t)\zeta(t) \qquad , \qquad (x,t) \in S \quad .$$

Both equations together imply $\beta(x+t)\zeta(t) = 0$ in S , therefore

$$\theta(t) = -\mu(p(t))$$

which contradicts (22).

□

To proceed further we write down the variation of constants formula for η and ζ .

Lemma 5

If $t < \tau \leqq T$

$$\eta(x,t) = k(x,t,\tau)\eta(x,\tau) + \int_t^\tau k(x,t,s)\Big[-u(x,s) + \beta(x+s)\zeta(s) + \theta(s)\Big]\,ds \tag{24}$$

$$\zeta(t) = \int_t^T k(-t,t,s)\Big[-u(-t,s) + \beta(s-t)\zeta(s) + \theta(s)\Big]\,ds \tag{25}$$

where

$$k(x,t,s) = \exp\Big(\int_t^s -u(x,r) - \mu(p(r))\,dr\Big) \tag{26}$$

Proof. The proof follows immediately from (14) and (15).

□

We now return to Definition 1.

Lemma 6

(i) The functions η,ζ,k are C^1 in G^*, and for $t^* \leqq t < \tau \leqq T$ we have

$$\eta_x(x,t) = k(x,t,\tau)\eta_x(x,\tau) + \int_t^\tau k(x,t,s)\beta'(x+s)\zeta(s)\,ds \tag{27}$$

(ii) If (A2) holds, then $\zeta(t) < 0$ for $t \in [t^*,T)$.

(iii) If (A2) and (A3) hold, then

$$\eta_x(x,t) > 0 \quad \text{for} \quad (x,t) \in G^* \quad .$$

Proof. Since $u = u_{max}$ in G^*, $k_x = 0 = u_x$. Now (i) follows from Lemma 5, since $\eta(\cdot,T) = 0$ is C^1 in x . Because of Lemma 2, $\zeta(t) < 0$ for $t \geqq T - \delta_o$, and (ii) is then implied by (23). At last, (iii) follows from (ii) and (i) if we set $\tau = T$ in (27).

□

This yields the next structural assertion concerning the optimal control.

Lemma 7

If (A2) and (A3) hold and if $t^* > 0$, then

$$\zeta(t^*) = \eta(-t^*,t^*) = -1 \quad ,$$
$$\eta(x,t^*) > -1 \qquad \text{for all} \quad x > -t^*$$
$$\zeta(t) > -1 \qquad \text{for all} \quad t > t^*$$

This means, that the first switching curve must start at the left boundary (in the sense of reverse t-direction).

Proof: See Lemma 6.

□

In a neighborhood of t^*, we obtain regularity for the switching curve.

Lemma 8

If the assumptions of Lemma 7 hold, then there exists a $t_* < t^*$ and a C^1- curve $\tilde{\sigma} : [t_*,t^*] \to \mathbb{R}$ with C^1-inverse σ

(i) $\tilde{\sigma}' < 0$, $\sigma' < 0$

(ii) η is C^1 in $G_* := G_{t_*}$,

$\eta_x > 0$ in G_*

$\eta(x,\sigma(x)) = -1$.

This implies that $u = 0$ below σ and $u = u_{max}$ above and to the right of σ .

Proof: Because of Lemma 6 and 7, from above we have

$$\eta_t(-t^*,t^*) = \zeta'(t^*) + \eta_x(-t^*,t^*) > 0 .$$

Since η_t is continuous by Lemma 1,

$$\eta_t(x,t) > 0 \qquad \text{for} \quad (x,t) \in N$$

in some neighbourhood N of $(-t^*,t^*)$. We now denote by $\tilde{\eta},\tilde{k}$ the solution of (24), (26) with ζ and θ as before, but u replaced by the constant u_{max} . Then $\tilde{\eta}$ is C^1 in (x,t) , $\tilde{\eta}_t > 0$ in N and we may also assume $\tilde{\eta}_x > 0$ in N.

By the implicit function theorem there exists a C^1-curve $\tilde{\sigma} : [t_*,t^*] \to \mathbb{R}$ for some t_* with a C^1-inverse σ and

$$\tilde{\eta}(\tilde{\sigma}(t),t) = -1 \ , \ \tilde{\sigma}(t^*) = -t^* \ .$$

In the region above $\tilde{\sigma}$ we have $\eta = \tilde{\eta}$ since the defining equations are identical. In the region below $\tilde{\sigma}$ we have $\eta < -1$ because of $\eta_t > 0$. It remains to prove that η_x exists below σ and is continuous across σ . For this one writes down (24) for some $t < \sigma(x) < \tau$ in the form

$$\eta(x,t) = k(x,t,\tau)\eta(x,\tau) - \int_{\sigma(x)}^{\tau} u_{max} \cdot k(x,t,s)\, ds + $$

$$+ \int_{t}^{\tau} k(x,t,s)\Big[\beta(x+s)\zeta(s) + \theta(s)\Big]\, ds$$

and a similar equation for k . This implies differentiability with respect to x . One carries out the differentiation and passes to the limit $t\uparrow\sigma(x), \tau\downarrow\sigma(x)$ to obtain continuity of η_x across σ .

□

One notices that the critical point in the proof above is that η_t stays positive and $-\infty < \sigma' < 0$. The author could not find a sufficient condition for this. On the other hand, we have

<u>Lemma 9</u>

If the assumptions of Lemma 7 hold, and if the switching curve σ from Lemma 8 can be continued to a C^1-curve $\sigma:[-t^*,A]$ with $\sigma(A) = 0$, $\sigma' < 0$ and

$$\eta(x,\sigma(x)) = -1 \quad , \quad x \in [-t^*,A] \quad ,$$

then

$$u(x,t) = \begin{cases} 0 \quad , & x \in (-t^*,A),\ t < \sigma(x) \\ u_{max} & , \text{ otherwise} \end{cases}$$

Proof: Starting from some G_t , the assertions of Lemma 8 can be obtained for G_s with some $s < t$ by the same arguments as in the proof of Lemma 8, because

$$\eta_t(\tilde{\sigma}(t),t) = - \eta_x(\tilde{\sigma}(t),t)\tilde{\sigma}'(t) > 0 \quad .$$

On the other hand, if they hold for a sequence G_{t_n} with $t_n \downarrow t$, they also hold for t , because $\zeta < -1$ in $(t,T]$ and by (27)

$$\lim_{n\to\infty} \eta_x(x,t_n) > 0$$

and therefore $\eta_t(\tilde{\sigma}(t),t) > 0$.

□

This means, that if the first switching curve is regular in the sense of Lemma 9, then under assumptions (A2) and (A3) there can be no more switching curves.

REFERENCES

[1] Gurtin, M., MacCamy, R.: Non-linear age-dependent population dynamics. Arch. Rat. Mech. Anal. 54 (1974), 281-300.

[2] Gurtin, M., Murphy, L.: On the optimal harvesting of age-structured populations. In: Busenberg, S., Cooke, K. (eds.), Differential equations and applications in ecolgy,

epidemics, and population problems, 115-129.
Academic Press, New York 1981.

[3] Brokate, M.: Pontryagin's principle for control problems in age-dependent population dynamics. J. Math. Biology 23 (1985), 75-101.

[4] Brokate, M.: Optimal control of age-structured populations. To appear in: LN Control and Information Sciences, Proc. IFIP Conference at Budapest 1985.

[5] Webb, G.F.: Theory of nonlinear age-dependent population dynamics. Dekker, New York-Basel 1985.

[6] Chipot, M.: On the equations of age-dependent population dynamics. Arch. Rat. Mech. Anal. 82 (1983), 13-25.

[7] Marcus, M.: Global existence theory for models of population dynamics. Arch. Rat. Mech. Anal. 82 (1983), 191-201.

[8] Elderkin, R.: Nonlinear, globally age-dependent population models: Some basic theory. J. Math. Anal. Appl. 108 (1985), 546-562.

[9] Zeidler, E.: Nonlinear Functional Analysis and its Applications I. Springer, New York 1986.

International Series of
Numerical Mathematics, Vol. 78

CONTINUOUS MEDIA: INTERPRETATION IN TERMS OF PHASE-PORTRAIT METHOD FOR DYNAMIC SYSTEMS WITH CONTROL

Anatoliy Butkovskiy, Nikolai Lepe, Alexandr Babichev

Abstract. The paper concerns an investigation of a substance propagation process in a continuous medium by representing it as a finite-dimensional dynamic system with control (DSC). A correspondence is established between the Laplacian of this process and the Hamiltonian of the DSC. To analyse DSC in a differential inclusion form an original phase-portrait method is proposed. Some general results on DSC qualitative behavior obtained with the phase-portrait method are also presented in the paper.

1. INTRODUCTION

Throughout most part of the paper we shall study DSC in the form of

(1.1) $\dot{q} = f(q,u) \ , \ q \in R^n \ , \ u \in U(q) \subset R^m$

where q is a vector in DSC phase-space R^n and u is a control, with constraint $U(q)$ being an arbitrary previously given set. Let q be fixed and u take the values throughout $U(q)$. Then $\dot{q}$ produces a set $\phi(q) = f(q,U(q))$ of admissible DSC speeds. This permits differential inclusion

(1.2) $\dot{q} \in \phi(q) \ , \ \phi(q) \subset R^n$

to be substituted for the DSC description (1.1).

DSC may be considered as a representation of a substance propagation process subjected to the partial differential equation by interpreting $\phi(q)$ as a set of admissible substance flow vectors. It leads to a generalization of Laplace differential operator for such a process.

For the DSC may be studied independently, the basic concept of appropriate phase-portrait method is worth to be introduced. Let $\phi(q) \subset R^n$ be a complete bounded convex set. Define the DSC Hamiltonian by

(1.3) $$H(p,q) = \max_{\dot{q}\in\phi(q)} p\dot{q} = \max_{u\in U(q)} pf(q,u) \quad , \quad p \in R^n \quad .$$

Hamiltonian $H(p,q)$ is obviously seen to be a support function of the set $\phi(q)$ [2]. In accordance with Hamilton system theory the problem

(1.4) $$\begin{cases} \dot{q} = \dfrac{\partial H}{\partial p} \\ \dot{p} = -\dfrac{\partial H}{\partial q} \end{cases}$$

under initial conditions

(1.5) $$q(0) = q^o \ , \ p(0) = p_o \ , \ H(p_o,q_o) = 0$$

generates a set of trajectories $q(t) \in R^n$ starting at the point q_o . Geometrically speaking the trajectories $q(t)$ constitute a funnel surface in R^n with the vertex at q_o .

In accordance with the Hamilton system theory the relation $H(p(t) \ , \ q(t)) = H(p_o,q_o) = 0$ holds. The corresponding vector $p(t)$ may be interpreted as being a gradient vector $\frac{\partial z}{\partial q}$ for a function $z(q)$ that permits the trajectory funnel surface to be defined by equation $z(q) = 0$. Therefore, formula (1.3) combined with relation mentioned above make the vectors $\dot{q} \in \phi\ (q)$ to be directed either tangently or inside the funnel surface whenever it is defined. As a consequence, all admissible DSC trajectories starting at q_o can be located only inside or at the surface of the funnel. Moreover, some other DSC trajectories can cross the funnel surface only from outside into the funnel. To see this funnel property, the trajectory funnel surface will be shaded outside. There is a family of shaded trajectory funnel surfaces filling the DSC phase-space, which will be called DSC phase-portrait. An approach to analyse the DSC phase-portrait is proposed in sections 3-6.

2. INTERRELATION BETWEEN FINITE-DIMENSIONAL DSC AND CONTINUOUS MEDIUM

In this section we establish a correspondence between a DSC and a substance propagation process in continuous medium.

The reason is that the dynamic equations for both phenomena tend to be derived from the same maximum principle.

Suppose that propagation process of a substance, say heat, is caused by gradient grad $z = \frac{\partial z}{\partial q}$ of a corresponding potential $z = z(q)$. Let the substance flow vector $\kappa(q)$ be identified with DSC speed vector $\dot{q}$ and gradient grad $z(q)$ with p-vector of this DSC. Then, if $H(p,q)$ is Hamiltonian of this DSC, the substance flow vector $\kappa(q)$, depending on the potential gradient, will be defined by relation

$$\kappa(q) = \dot{q} = \frac{\partial H(p,q)}{\partial q}, \quad p(q) = \frac{\partial z}{\partial q}(q) \tag{2.1}$$

which is called continuous medium material relation.
It can be easily seen from (2.1) that Laplacian $\Delta_H z(q)$ for the substance propagation process is of the form

$$\Delta_H z(q) = \operatorname{div} \kappa(q) = \operatorname{div} \frac{\partial H}{\partial p}(p(q),q) = \operatorname{div} \frac{\partial H}{\partial p}\left(\frac{\partial z}{\partial q}, q\right),$$

which results in the expression

$$\Delta_H z(q) = \operatorname{tr}\left(\frac{\partial^2 H}{\partial p^2}, \frac{\partial^2 z}{\partial q^2} + \frac{\partial^2 H}{\partial p \partial q}\right) \tag{2.2}$$

where tr is a trace of matrix in brackets.

Formula (2.2) states a correspondence between DSC and Laplacian for a substance propagation process in continuous medium. For instance, Hamiltonian $H(p,q) = \frac{1}{2}p^2$ leads to the traditional Laplacian

$$\Delta_H z(q) = \frac{\partial^2 z(q)}{\partial q^2}$$

Physical sense of the correlation discussed above is that the extending of DSC extreme time attainable surface proves to be analogous to the substance propagation in a continuous medium.

This permits one to draw an interesting analogy between DSC and complex nonlinear nonisotropic continuous media.

3. CLASSIFICATION OF ADMISSIBLE DIRECTION CONES AT

One may describe DSC by differential inclusion

(3.1) $\dot{q} \in K(q)$, $K(q) = \{\alpha\dot{q} : \alpha > 0 , \dot{q} \in \phi(q)\}$, $q \in R^n$,

where $K(q)$ is a cone of DSC admissible speed directions, just as an ordinary differential equation is determined with speed direction field. Thus a classification problem for $K(q)$ arises.

$K(q)$ is obviously a convex cone with the vertex at 0 in tangent space R^n . There exist m which is the dimension of minimal linear subspace $L^m (L^m \subset R^n)$ containing $K(q)$ and τ which is the maximum number of linearly independent support planes for $K(q)$ vertex in L^m . Thus, for each $K(q)$ its type can be denoted by a_τ^m . We shall distinguish the two cases, $0 \in K(q)$ and $0 \notin K(q)$. It can be easily seen that $\tau < m$ leads to the inclusion $0 \in K(q)$, for $K(q)$ is convex. If $\tau < m$ and $m \neq 0$, the two mentioned above cases may exist. We shall use the symbol a_m^m for the former and $\bar{a}_m^m$ for the latter. All possible types of cones $K(q)$ are presented in Fig. 1. The number of $K(q)$ types is $1+2+..+(n+1)+n= = 1+(n^2+5n)/2$.

One of the fundamental problems of phase-portrait method is to divide DSC phase-space into domains of a fixed cone type. This problem has been solved for two-dimensional DSC defined by differential inclusion

(3.2) $\dot{q} \in \phi(q)$, $q \in R^2$, $\phi(q) = \omega(f_1(q)\ldots f_\ell(q))$

where $f_1(q),\ldots f_\ell(q)$ are analytic vector fields and ω is convex spanning of $f_1,\ldots,f_\ell$ at point q . It should be noted that the DSC form (3.2) is equivalent in the aspect discussed above to the form

(3.3) $\dot{q} = f(q) + \sum_{i=1}^{p} u_i g_i$, $g \in R^2$, $u \in U(q)$

for some analytic fields $f(q)$, $g_i(q)$ and some set $U(q)$.

Denote the determinant of matrix formed with vectors $f_i(q)$ and $f_j(q)$ at point q by $d_{ij} = |f_i, f_j|$ and the scalar production of these vectors by (f_i, f_j). The following theorem is valid.

THEOREM 3.1. The cone $K(q)$ at point q is of type

1) a_o^o if and only if $\forall i\ f_i=0$.

2) a_o^1 $\qquad \forall i,j\ d_{ij} = 0\ ;\ \exists\ m,n:\ (f_m, f_n) < 0$.

3) a_1^1 $\qquad \forall i,j\ d_{ij} = 0\ ,\ (f_i, f_j) > 0$.

4) $\bar{a}_1^1$ $\qquad \forall i,j\ d_{ij} = 0\ ,\ (f_i, f_j) \geqq 0 ; \exists m,n: (f_m, f_n) = 0$.

5) a_o^2 $\qquad \exists i \neq j \neq k: d_{ij} \neq 0, d_{ik} \neq 0, d_{jk} \neq 0, \text{sign } d_{ij} = \text{sign } d_{ik} = \text{sign } d_{jk}$.

6) a_1^2 $\qquad \exists i \neq j: d_{ij} \neq 0; \exists x \in R^2, x \neq 0: \forall i\ (x, f_i) \geqq 0$.

7) a_2^2 $\qquad \exists i \neq j: d_{ij} \neq 0; \exists x \in R^2: \forall m (x, f_m) > 0$.

8) $\bar{a}_2^2$ $\qquad \exists i \neq j: d_{ij} \neq 0; \exists m: f_m = 0; \exists x \in R^2:$

$$(\forall n: f_n \neq 0) \rightarrow (x, f_n) > 0 \ .$$

Related with the admissible direction cone classification is the definition below.

DEFINITION 3.1. Point $q_o \in R^n$ is called a singular point of DSC if the dimension m of a minimal linear subspace L^m containing $K(q_o)$ is smaller than the dimension n of R^n .

It proves to be crucial for DSC controllability investigation to analyse the sets of singular points (or singular sets) in R^n .

A detailed DSC controllability investigation based on such analysis for the plane R^2 is presented at [4,5]. In those articles there are also presented relations between singular sets, domains of full controllability and points of local controllability.

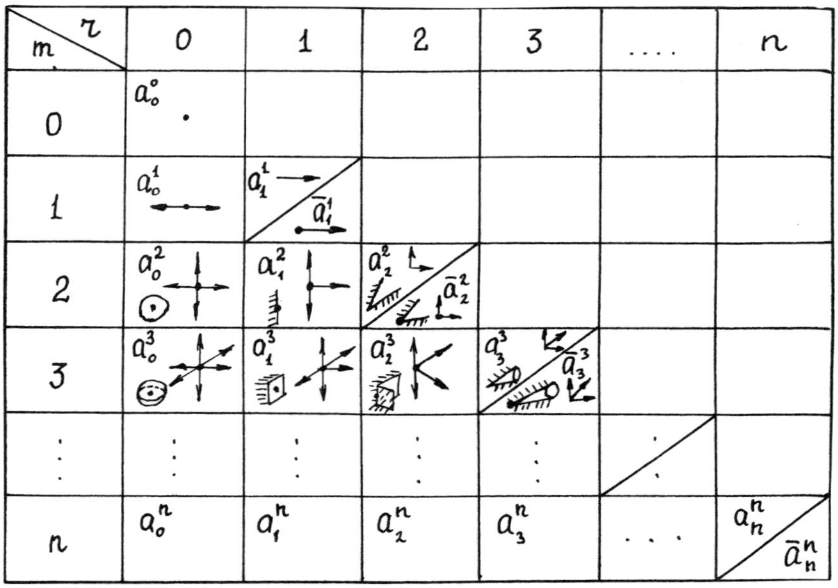

Fig. 1. The types a_τ^m of DSC admissible direction cones $K(q)$.

4. SINGULAR SETS AT THE PLANE

Let DSC be defined by differential inclusion

$$\dot{q} \in \phi(q) \; , \; q \in R^2 \; , \; \phi(q) = \mathrm{co}(f(q), g(q)) \; . \tag{4.1}$$

It follows that the condition $\rho(q) \equiv |f(q), g(q)| = 0$ is a criterium for q to be singular. Suppose $f(q_o) \neq 0$ and $g(g_o) \neq 0$ at some point g_o . Then there are two main cases where q_o is singular.

Let exist the trajectories of differential equations $\dot{q} = f(q)$ and $\dot{q} = g(q)$, which will be denoted $q = \varphi(t), \varphi(0) = q_o$ and $q = \gamma(t)$, $\gamma(0) = q_o$ respectively.

DEFINITION 4.1. Singular point $q_o, f(q_o) \neq 0, g(q_o) \neq 0$ is said to be point of DSC (4.1) invariant manifold if there exists $\varepsilon > 0$ such, that

$$(4.2) \qquad \rho(\varphi(t)) \equiv 0 \ , \ |t| \leq \varepsilon \ .$$

In this formula trajectory $\gamma(t)$ may be substituted for $\varphi(t)$, since the singularity of corresponding Couchi problem solution is assumed.

DEFINITION 4.2. Singular point $q_o, f(q_o) \neq 0, g(q_o) \neq 0$ is said to be the shading change point for DSC (4.1) if there exists $\varepsilon > 0$ such, that the two inequalities hold:

$$(4.3) \qquad \rho(\varphi(t)) \cdot \rho(\varphi(-t)) < 0 \ ,$$

$$(4.4) \qquad \rho(\gamma(t)) \cdot \rho(\gamma(-t)) < 0 \ , \ 0 < t \leq \varepsilon \ .$$

Definition 4.2. means that the cone $K(q)$ is directed into opposite side of curve $\varphi(t)(\gamma(t))$ on parts of $\varphi(t)(\gamma(t))$ divided by q_o. Observe, that the trajectories $\varphi(t)$ and $\gamma(t)$ produce the boundaries (surface) of trajectory funnel for DSC (4.1). Thus, on two different parts of $\varphi(t)(\gamma(t))$ divided by q_o the shadings of $\varphi(t)(\gamma(t))$ is opposite. In terms of qualitative differential equation theory it means that the trajectory $\varphi(t)$ is an arc of generalized contact with trajectory $\gamma(t)$ at point q_o [3]. The contact point q_o proves to be singular DSC point isolated along the trajectories $\varphi(t)$ and $\gamma(t)$. It's worth to be stated that there exist other points of generalized contracts in each small neighbourhood of q_o, as it follows from continuous solution dependency on initial data for equations $\dot{q} = f(q)$ and $\dot{q} = g(q)$. However, these points may be non-isolated along the trajectories $\varphi(t)$ and $\gamma(t)$.

Define, by the analogy, the shading change point for DSC

$$(4.5) \qquad \dot{q} \in \omega(f(q), g(q), -g(q)) \ , \ q \in R^2$$

being of equivalent representation in differential equation form

$$(4.6) \qquad \dot{q} = f(q) + ug(q) \ , \ q \in R^2 \ , \ u \in [-\infty, \infty] \ .$$

DEFINITION 4.3. Singular point $q_o, f(q_o) \neq 0, g(q_o) \neq 0$, $\rho(q_o) = 0$ is the shading change point for DSC (4.5) (or (4.6)) if there exists $\varepsilon > 0$ such, that

$$\rho(\gamma(t)) \cdot \rho(\gamma(-t)) < 0 \ , \ 0 < t \leqq \varepsilon \ .$$

Some differential criteria for defined above sorts of DSC singular points can be derived. These permit one to determine the sort of singular point without integrating equations $\dot{q} = f(q)$ and $\dot{q} = g(q)$. See for reference [4].

5. LOCAL CONTROLLABILITY

In this section the local controllability (LC), depending on singular points locations, is studied for DSC:

(5.1) $$\dot{q} = \tilde{f}(q) + u\tilde{g}(q) \ , \ q \in R^2 \ , \ u \in [-1,1] \ .$$

The functions $\tilde{f}(q)$ and $\tilde{g}(q)$ are supposed to be of C^1 - - class.

DEFINITION 5.1. It is said that $q_o \in R^2$ is a point of local controllability for DSC (1.1) if for any $\varepsilon > 0$ there exists $\delta : 0 < \delta < \varepsilon$ such, that for two any points $q_1, q_2 \in S_\delta$ (S_r is an r - ball with centre at q_o) there exists an admissible DSC trajectory which starts at q_1 and terminates at q_2 in finite time T, without leaving S_ε at any moment $t \leqq T$.

We shall first consider LC in a domain $D \subset R^2$ inside which differential equations $\dot{q} = f(q)$ and $\dot{q} = g(q)$ have no singular point. We denote here $\tilde{f}(q) + \tilde{g}(q)$ by $f(q)$ and $\tilde{f}(q) - \tilde{g}(q)$ by $g(q)$. The following theorem formulates necessary LC condition for $q_o \in D$.

THEOREM 5.1. Suppose that $q_o \in D$ is a point of LC for DSC (5.1). Then the two relations hold:

(5.2) $$\rho(q_o) = |f(q_o), g(q_o)| = 0 \ ,$$

(5.3) $$(f(q_o), g(q_o)) < 0 \ .$$

An additional assumption about relative location of the trajectories $\varphi(t), \varphi(0) = q_o$ and $\gamma(t), \gamma(0) = q_o$ for the equations

$\dot{q} = f(q)$ and $\dot{q} = g(q)$ respectively results in the next theorem.

THEOREM 5.2. Suppose that $q_o \in D$ is a DSC singular point isolated along the trajectories $\varphi(t)$ and $\gamma(t)$. Then for q_o to be LC point it is necessary and sufficient that the condition (5.3) be satisfied and q_o be a shading change point.

COROLLARY 5.1. Let vector fields $f(q)$ and $g(q)$ be analytical. Then for q_o to be LC point it is necessary and sufficient that the condition (5.3) be satisfied and q_o be a shading change point.

Now we consider LC for DSC (5.1), where $q_o \notin D$. If $f(q_o) = g(q_o) = 0$ is satisfied, the q_o is a DSC invariant point rather than a point of LC. Thus we consider only the case $f(q_o) \neq 0$, $g(q_o) = 0$ without loosing generality. Suppose that q_o is a simple equilibrium point for differential equation $\dot{q} = g(q)$. As it is stated in [3] $g(q)$ can be presented in the form of

$$g(q) = A(q-q^o) + G(q)$$

where A - is an 2x2 matrix, det $A \neq 0$, and vector-function $G(q)$ being of class C^1 vanishes at q_o together with its first derivatives. Note, that the case of two equal eigenvalues will not be considered here, because the condition $g(q) \in C^1$ is not sufficient for determining the differential equation trajectory behavior in a neighbourhood of q_o in this case.

THEOREM 5.4. If the eigenvalues of matrix A are real and unequal, the point q_o is not a LC point for DSC (5.1).

THEOREM 5.5. If the eigenvalues of matrix A are complex, the q_o is a LC point for DSC (5.1).

Analogous results can be obtained for the DSC

$$(5.4) \qquad \dot{q} = f(q) + ug(q), \quad u \in [-\infty,\infty] .$$

THEOREM 5.6. For point $q_o, f(q_o) \neq 0$, $g(q_o) \neq 0$ to be LC point for DSC (5.4), it is necessary and sufficient that q_o be a shading change point.

THEOREM 5.7. Suppose that $f(q_o) \neq 0, g(q_o) = 0$ and eigenvalues of matrix A are real and unequal. Then q_o is not a LC point for DSC (5.4).

THEOREM 5.8. Suppose that $f(q_o) \neq 0$, $g(q_o) \neq 0$ and eigenvalues of matrix A are complex. Then q_o is a LC point for DSC (5.4).

Let $(\mathrm{ad}\, g)^n f(q) = [g,\ldots,[g,f]\ldots](q)$, where $(\mathrm{ad}\, g) f(q) = [g,f] = g \frac{\partial q}{\partial q} - f \frac{\partial g}{\partial q}$ - is commutator of fields $g(q)$ and $f(q)$, and $(\mathrm{ad}\, g)^o f(q) \equiv f(q)$ is assumed.

THEOREM 5.9. Suppose that $f(q_o) \neq 0$, $g(q_o) \neq 0$; $f(q)$, $g(q) \in C^{N+1}$ and there exists $n \leqq N$ such, that the two conditions hold:

$$|(\mathrm{ad}\, g)^k f(q_o), g(q_o)| = 0, \quad 0 \leqq k < n,$$
$$|(\mathrm{ad}\, g)^n f(q_o), g(q_o)| \neq 0 .$$

Then q_o is LC point for DSC (5.4) if and only if n is odd. It's worth be mentioned for reference that there are articles [4,5] concerned with relations between local and global controllability in terms of phase-portrait method. In addition, we present the following theorem.

THEOREM 5.10. Suppose that fields $f(q)$ $g(q)$ have no singular points (i.e. $f(q) \neq 0$ and $g(q) \neq 0$). Then DSC (5.4) is globally controllable if and only if each trajectory of differential equation $\dot{q} = g(q)$ contains an LC point.

Remark. The sufficient condition for global controllability remains correct for a field $f(q)$ of an arbitrary sort and for DSC of an arbitrary dimension.

6. GRAPH OF DYNAMIC SYSTEM WITH CONTROL

It is usefull to consider the structure of DSC phase-portrait in terms of attainability problem. Suppose that the DSC phase-space is divided into open unintersecting domains. Let's take the domains to be the DSC graph vertices of one of the two following conditions is satisfied.

Denote by A and B two arbitrary adjacent domains and by ∂A and ∂B its boundaries respectively:

1. For each point $q_o \in A$ there exists an admissible DSC trajectory starting at q_o and terminating at some point $q_1 \in B$ without leaving the set $A \cup \partial A \cup B \cup \partial B$; and for each point $q_1 \in B$ there exists an admissible DSC trajectory terminating at q_1 and starting at some point $q_o \in A$.
2. There is no admissible DSC trajectory connecting two arbitrary points one of which belongs to A and the other to B inside the set $A \cup \partial A \cup B \cup \partial B$.

With the first condition satisfied, the vertex A will be connected with the vertex B by an arc directed from A to B.

Consider as an example following system:

$$\begin{aligned} \dot{q}_1 &= q_1 + u \\ \dot{q}_2 &= -q_2 + u , \qquad |u| \leq \text{´} \; . \end{aligned} \tag{6.1}$$

DSC (6.1) phase-portrait presented at Fig. 2 is obtained by putting on R^2 of two saddles with equilibrium points (1,-1) and (-1,1) respectively. The DSC (6.1) singular set $q_2 = -q_1$ is constituted by shadding change points (except the points (1,-1) and (-1,1)), the points defined by $q_2 = -q_1$, $|q_1| < 1$, $|q_2| < 1$ to be LC points.

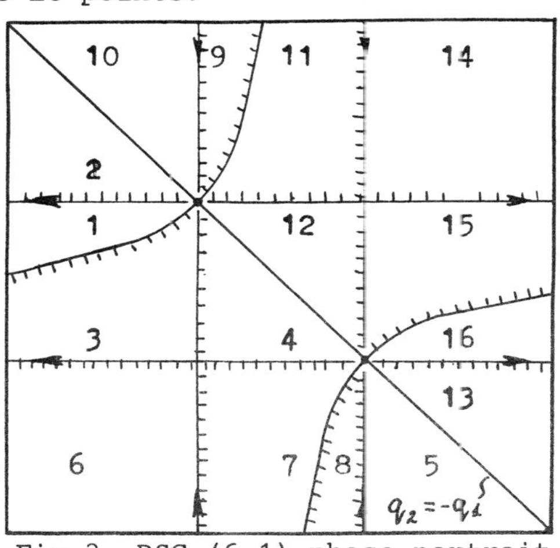

Fig.2. DSC (6.1) phase portrait

Corresponding DSC graph is presented at Fig.3, which demonstrates following DSC (6.1) graph properties:

1) There exists the full controllability domain denoted by FC.

2) There exist the domains 1,16 into which the admissible DSC trajectories can only enter, and which can not be leaved. There exist the domains 8,9, which can be leaved and into which no admissible DSC trajectory can enter.

3) In DSC graph there exist the path connected the domains 8 and 1, which passes through the full controllability domain. Thus, for each points $q_o \in 8$ and $q_1 \in 1$ there exist an admissible DSC trajectory starting at q_o and terminating at q_1 .

If for any points $q_o \in A$ and $q_1 \in B$ of the adjacent domains A and B there exist an admissible DSC trajectory from q_o to q_1 , the vertices A and B will be connected by dotted arc.

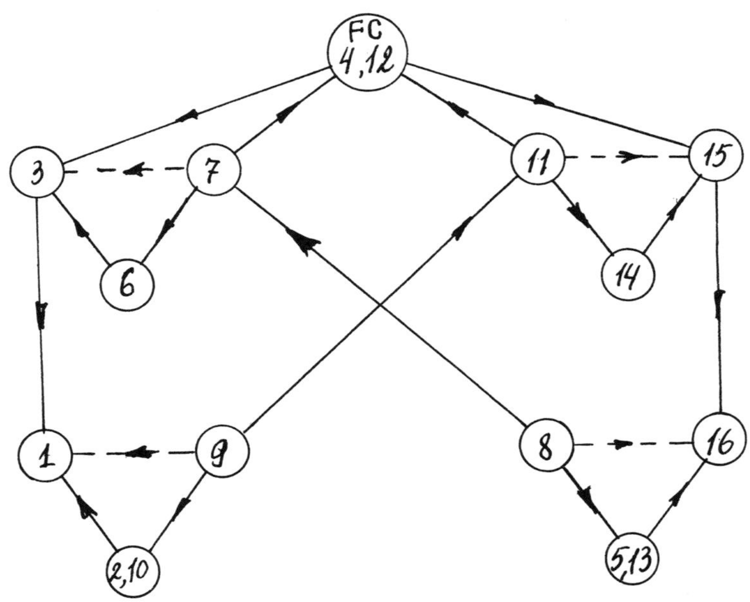

Fig. 3. DSC (6.1) graph

Remark. It can be easily seen that the base for the DSC phase-space division into such domains is produced by the boundaries of dynamic cells of the equations $\dot{q} = f(q)$ and $\dot{q} = g(q)$ [3] together with DSC singular sets which are topological invariants. Furthermore it seems to be true that among all singular sets for DSC (4.1) with fields $f(q)$ and $g(q)$: $f(q) \neq 0, g(q) \neq 0$ only LC points are topological invariants.

REFERENCES

1. Butkovskiy A.G.,Phase-portraits of controlled dynamic systems. Nauka, Moscow (1985).

2. Rund H.,The differential geometry of Finsler spaces. Springer-Verlag, Berlin-Göttingen-Heidelberg (1959).

3. Andronov A.A., Leontovich E.A., Gordon I.I., Mayer A.G.,Qualitative theory of the second order dynamic systems. Nauka, Moscow (1966).

4. Babichev A.V., Butkovskiy A.G., Lepe N.L.,Singular sets at phase-portraits of dynamic systems with control. Avtomatika i telemekhanika 5 (1986), 24-31.

5. Butkovskiy A.G., Babichev A.V., Lepe N.L.,Phase-portraits of dynamic systems with control at the plane. Preprint, Institute of Control Sciences (1985).

Butkovskiy A.G.
Lepe N.L.
Babichev A.V.
Institute of Control Sciences,
Moscow, Profsoyuznaya, 65.

Acknowledgement. The authors are grateful to professor Filippov for his important discussion.

International Series of
Numerical Mathematics, Vol. 78

OPTIMAL PERIODIC CONTROL OF QUASILINEAR SYSTEMS IN HILBERT SPACES

Fritz Colonius

Abstract. This paper discusses optimal periodic control problems for quasilinear systems in Hilbert spaces. Using Ekeland's variational principle, a global maximum principle is proven.
Then the question of local properness is discussed, i.e. if an optimal steady state can be improved by allowing proper periodic controls and trajectories. This discussion is based on second order necessary optimality conditions obtained from general optimization theory in Banach spaces.

1. INTRODUCTION

This paper deals with optimal periodic control problems for quasilinear systems of the following form

Minimize

$$(1.1) \qquad 1/\tau \int_0^\tau g(y(t),u(t))dt \qquad \text{s.t.}$$

$$(1.2) \qquad y'(t) = Ay(t) + f(y(t),u(t)), \quad t \in T := [0,\tau]$$

$$(1.3) \qquad y(0) = y(\tau)$$

$$(1.4) \qquad u \in \mathcal{U}_{ad} := \{u: T \to \Omega, \text{ strongly measurable}\}$$

where A is the infinitesimal generator of a strongly continuous semigroup $\{T(t), t \geq 0\}$ in a Hilbert space Y, Ω is a bounded subset of a Banach space U, $g: Y \times U \to \mathbb{R}$ and $f: Y \times U \to Y$ have continuous Fréchet derivatives $\partial_y g(y,u)$, $\partial_y f(y,u)$, with respect to y and f,g(resp. $\partial_y f$, $\partial_y g$) are continuous (resp. strongly continuous) and bounded on bounded subsets of $Y \times U$.

By definition, a solution of (1.2) is a continuous solution of the integrated version

$$y(t) = T(t)y(0) + \int_0^t T(t-s)f(y(s),u(s)ds, \quad t \in T$$

We assume that $T(t)$ is compact for $t > 0$.

For ordinary differential systems and for functional differential systems, optimal periodic control problems have been studied for quite a while (cp. [3] for recent results and references). This paper aims at developing a similar theory for the quasilinear system described above (with parabolic partial differential equations in mind).

In section 2, a global maximum principle is given. The proof relies on Ekeland's Variational Principle and is only sketched; it uses similar arguments as [4,5,3]. Section 3 discusses the problem of local properness, i.e., the problem how one can decide if near an optimal steady state the average system behaviour can be improved by introducing oscillations. In particular, second order necessary optimality conditions for weak optima are derived and applied.

2. A GLOBAL MAXIMUM PRINCIPLE

This section gives necessary optimality conditions for a strong minimum.

The first proposition assures existence and uniqueness of solutions of (1.2).

<u>Proposition 2.1</u> Assume

(2.1) $A - \omega I$ is dissipative for some $\omega \in \mathbb{R}$, that is

$$\langle y^*, Ay \rangle \le \omega \|y\|^2$$

for $y \in \mathcal{D}(A)$, $y^* \in \theta(y) := \{y^* \in Y^*: \|y^*\|^2 = \|y\|^2 = \langle y^*, y \rangle\}$.

(2.2) There is $C > 0$ such that

$$\langle y^*, f(y,u) \rangle \le C(1 + \|y\|^2)$$

for $y \in Y$, $y^* \in \theta(y)$, $u \in \Omega$.

Then for every initial condition $y(0) = y_0 \in Y$, and every $u \in \mathcal{U}_{ad}$, equation (1.2) has a unique solution $y(\cdot) = y(\cdot, u, y_0)$.

<u>Proof</u>: cp. [6, Section 5].

The linearized system corresponding to (1.2) is

$$(2.3)\qquad \begin{aligned} z'(t) &= Az(t) + \partial_y f(y(t),u(t))z(t), \quad t \in [s,\tau]. \\ z(s) &= z_0 \end{aligned}$$

The solutions of (2.3) are, by definition, solutions of the integrated version

$$z(t) = T(t-s)z_0 + \int_s^t T(t-\sigma)\partial_y f(y(\sigma),u(\sigma))z(\sigma)d\sigma, \quad 0 \le s \le t \le \tau.$$

The corresponding solution operator is denoted by $\Phi(t,s,y,u)$.

Lemma 2.2 Let $0 \le s \le t \le \tau$, $u \in \mathcal{U}_{ad}$. Then the operator $\Phi(t,s,y,u) : Y \to Y$ is compact.

Proof: Follows as [6, Theorem 6.4].

The next theorem presents a global maximum principle for Problem (1.1) - (1.4).

Theorem 2.3 Let conditions (2.1) and (2.2) be satisfied and assume that (y^o,u^o) is a strong minimum for Problem (1.1) - (1.4), i.e.

$$(2.4)\qquad 1/\tau \int_0^\tau g(y^o(t),u^o(t)dt \le 1/\tau \int_0^\tau g(y(t),u(t))dt$$

for all (y,u) satisfying (1.2) - (1.4).

Then there are $\lambda \ge 0$ and a solution y^* of the adjoint equation

$$(2.5)\qquad y^{*\prime}(s) = A^*y^*(s) + \partial_y f(y^o(s),u^o(s))^* y^*(s) + \lambda\partial_y g(y^o(s),u^o(s)), \quad s \in T$$

$$(2.6)\qquad y^*(0) = y^*(\tau)$$

such that (λ,y) is not identically zero and

$$(2.7)\qquad \lambda\, g(y^o(t),u^o(t)) + \langle y^*(t),f(y^o(t),u^o(t))\rangle$$

$$= \min_{u\in\Omega} \{ \lambda\, g(y^o(t),u) + \langle y^*(t),f(y^o(t),u)\rangle \quad \text{for a.a. } t \in T.$$

Proof: The proof is a slight variant of the one given in [5] and will only be sketched.

The space $\mathcal{U}_{ad}$ becomes a complete metric space under the Ekeland distance defined by

$$d(u,v) = \text{meas } \{t: u(t) \neq v(t)\}.$$

Consider a sequence $\delta_n \to 0$, $\delta_n > 0$, and define functionals F_n on $\mathcal{U}_{ad} \times Y$ by

$$(2.8) \quad F_n(u,y_o) := [|y(\tau,u,y_o)-y_o|^2 + |J(u,y_o) - (m-\delta_n)|^2]^{1/2}$$

where

$$J(u,y_o) := 1/\tau \int_0^\tau g(y(t,u,y_o),u(t))dt$$

and

$$m := \inf \{J(u,y_o): u \in \mathcal{U}_{ad}, y_o \in Y\} .$$

Then $F_n(u,y_o) > 0$ for all (u,y_o). Using Ekeland's variational principle one finds (u^n,y_o^n) approximating $(u^o,y^o(0))$ and $\lambda^n \geq 0$, $z^n \in Y^*$ such that $|(\lambda^n,z^n)| = 1$ and

$$[\Phi(\tau,0,y^n,u^n) - Id]x = -\lambda^n/\tau \int_0^\tau \partial_y g(y^n(\sigma),u^n(\sigma))\Phi(\sigma,0,y^n,u^n)x d\sigma \quad \text{for}$$

all $x \in Y$ and

$$\begin{aligned} -\varepsilon_n^{1/2} \leq\ & z^n\, \Phi(\tau,s,y^n,u^n)\ [f(y^n(s),u) - f(y^n(s),u^n(s))] \\ & + \lambda^n \int_0^\tau \partial_y(y^n(\sigma),u^n(\sigma))\, \Phi(\sigma,s,y^n,u^n)[f(y^n(s),u)-f(y^n(s),u^n(s))]d\sigma \\ & + \lambda^n[g(y^n(s),u) - g(y^n(s),u^n(s))] \end{aligned}$$

for all $u \in \Omega$ and almost all $s \in T$.

Now compactness of $\Phi(\tau,0,y^n,u^n)$ and convergence of $u^n \to u^o$, $y^n \to y^o$ can be used to establish the assertion.

For details cp. [5] and also [3] for similar arguments applied to functional differential equations.

Remark

Observe that no constraint qualification (comparable to Fattorini's "fat cone condition") is required in the proof of the maximum principle above. This is due to the consideration of periodic boundary conditions.

3. LOCAL PROPERNESS AND SECOND ORDER CONDITIONS

Associated with the periodic problem (1.1) - (1.4) is the following steady state problem:

(3.1) Minimize $g(y,u)$ over $(y,u) \in \mathcal{D}(A) \times U$ s.t.

(3.2) $0 = Ay + f(y,u)$

(3.3) $u \in \Omega$

Let (y^o,u^o) be an optimal solution of this problem. Then a natural question is to ask whether the constant functions $y^o(\cdot) \equiv y^o$, $u^o(\cdot) \equiv u^o$, which obviously satisfy the constraints (1.2) - (1.4) of the periodic problem, are an optimal solution of the latter problem. If this is not the case, (y^o,u^o) are called locally proper. In order to decide whether an optimal solution of (3.1) - (3.3) is locally proper, it is convenient to check if it satisfies necessary optimality conditions for (1.1) - (1.4).

Such "tests" for local properness in ordinary differential systems based on the Pontryagin maximum principle are given in [7].

However, frequently, the maximum principle is equivalent to the first order necessary optimality conditions obtained by weak variations, and it is well-known that these conditions do not give a test for local properness since they are always satisfied by solutions of the steady state problem. A similar result is true for the infinite dimensional problem considered here:

<u>Proposition 3.1</u> Suppose that f and g are continuously Frèchet differentiable and let (y^o,u^o) be optimal for (3.1) - (3.3).

(3.4) Suppose that the cone $\{Ay+\partial_y f(y^o,u^o)y + \partial_u f(y^o,u^o)u : y \in \mathcal{D}(A) u \in \mathbb{R}_+(\Omega-u^o)\}$ contains a subspace of finite codimension in Y, Ω is closed and convex.

Then there are $(0,0) \neq (\lambda,y^*) \in \mathbb{R}_+ \times Y^*$ with

(3.5) $0 = \lambda\, \partial_y g(y^o,u^o) + y^*A + y^*\partial_y f(y^o,u^o)$

(3.6) $[\lambda\, \partial_u g(y^o,u^o) + y^*\, \partial_u f(y^o,u^o)]\,[u-u^o] \geq 0$ for all $u \in \Omega$.

This follows as standard Lagrange multiplier theorems. This result

shows in particular, that if (3.4) holds and f and g are affine in u, an optimal solution of the steady state problem satisfies the maximum principle, Theorem 2.3, for the periodic problem. Hence in order to decide the question of local properness, we have to recur to second order optimality conditions for the periodic problem.
The following result shows that only Lagrange multipliers of the steady state problem have to be considered.

Proposition 3.2 Suppose that f and g are continuously Fréchet differentiable in a neighbourhood of an optimal solution (y^o,u^o) of Problem (1.1) - (1.4).
Assume

(3.7) the homogeneous linearized equation

$$z'(t) = [A + \partial_y f(y^o,u^o)]z(t), \quad t \geq 0$$

has only the trivial τ-periodic solution.

Then (2.5) - (2.7) can only hold with $\lambda \neq 0$ and there exists a unique τ-periodic solution y^* of (2.5) with $\lambda = 1$.
In particular, if (y^o,u^o) is constant, y^* is constant and given by (3.5).

Proof: A Standard Lagrange multiplier theorem implies $\lambda \neq 0$. Uniqueness of the solution of (2.5) follows from compactness of the solution operator of the linearized system equation, Lemma 2.2, and hence of its adjoint. Furthermore, the constant solution y^* of (3.5) is the unique solution of (2.5). □

We turn to the second order necessary optimality conditions and consider for simplicity an optimal steady state solution (y^o,u^o).
Our analysis is based on the following general 2nd order conditions in Banach spaces.

Theorem 3.3 Let x^o be a local optimum of the problem.

Minimize $G(x)$ s.t.
$F(x) = 0, \ x \in C,$

where $G: X \to \mathbb{R}$, $F: X \to Z$, X,Z Banach spaces, are twice continuously Fréchet differentiable and $C \subset X$ is closed and convex. Assume

(3.8) $F'(x^o)(\mathbb{R}_+(C-x^o))$ contains a subspace of finite codimension in Z.

Then for every $h \in X$ with $G'(x^o)h \le 0$, $F'(x^o)h = 0$, $x^o + h \in \text{int } C$ there exists $(0,0) \neq (\lambda,z^*) \in \mathbb{R}_+ \times Z^*$ with

(3.9) $\lambda_o\, G'(x^o) - z^*\, F'(x^o) = 0;$

(3.10) $[\lambda_o\, G''(x^o) - z^*\, F''(x^o)](h,h) \ge 0.$

If $F'(x^o)\,(\mathbb{R}_+(C-x^o)) = Z$ and there exists $\tilde{x} \in \mathbb{R}_+(C-x^o) \cap \text{Ker } F'(x^o)$, then $\lambda \neq 0$.

<u>Proof</u>: [3, Corollary II. 2.15].

In the following we assume

(3.11) The maps f and g are twice continuously Fréchet differentiable and together with their derivatives bounded in a neighbourhood of (y^o,u^o), the set Ω is closed and convex.

Before we can apply the theorem above, the solution operator of equation (1.2) has to be analysed:

Define

$$S: L^\infty(0,\tau;U) \times Y \to C(0,\tau;Y)$$

$$S(u,y_o) := y(\cdot,u,y_o).$$

<u>Lemma 3.4</u> The map S is twice continuously Fréchet differentiable; the first derivative $z := \mathcal{D}S(u^o,y^o)(u,y)$ is the solution of

(3.12) $z(t) = \Phi(t,0)y + \int_0^t \Phi(t,s)\partial_u f(y^o(s),u^o(s))u(s)ds,\ t \in T;$

the second derivative $\xi := \mathcal{D}\mathcal{D}S(u^o,y^o)((u,y),(u,y))$ is the solution of

$$(3.13)\quad \xi(t) = \int_0^t \Phi(t,s)[\partial_y\partial_y f(y^o(s),u^o(s))(z(s),z(s)) + 2\partial_y\partial_u f(y^o(s),u^o(s))(z(s),u(s)) + \partial_u\partial_u f(y^o(s),u^o(s))(u(s),u(s))]ds,\ t \in T.$$

Proof: This follows by implicitly differentiating equation (1.2); use the second order chain rule (cp. e.g. [3, Lemma II.2.5]).

For an application of Theorem 3.3 let

$$X := L^\infty(0,\tau,U)\times Y,\quad Z := Y,\quad C := \mathcal{U}_{ad} \times Y$$

$$F(u,y_0) := y(\tau,u,y_0) - y_0$$

$$G(u,y_0) := 1/\tau \int_0^\tau g(y(t,u,y_0),u(t))dt.$$

Using Lemma 3.4 and the chain rule one can show that F and G are twice continuously Frêchet differentiable.

Introduce a function

$$\mathcal{H} : Y \times U \times Y^* \to \mathbb{R}$$

$$\mathcal{H}(y,u,y^*) := g(y,u) + y^* f(y,u)$$

Definition 3.5 An optimal solution $(y^0,u^0) \in Y \times U$ of problem (3.1)-(3.3) is locally proper, if for every $\varepsilon > 0$ there are (y,u) satisfying (1.2) - (1.4) with

$$\text{(3.14)}\quad \begin{aligned} &\sup_{t\in T}|y(t)-y^0| \le \varepsilon,\ \operatorname*{ess\,sup}_{t\in T}|u(t) - u^0| \le \varepsilon \\ &1/\tau \int_0^\tau g(y(t),u(t))dt < g(y^0,u^0). \end{aligned}$$

Theorem 3.6 Let $(y^0,u^0) \in Y \times U$ be an optimal solution of Problem (3.1) - (3.3) and assume that conditions (3.7) and (3.11) hold. Then (y^0,u^0) is locally proper if there exists (y,u) with

$$\text{(3.15)}\quad \int_0^\tau [\partial_y g(y^0,u^0)y(t) + \partial_u g(y^0,u^0)u(t)]dt \le 0$$

$$\text{(3.16)}\quad y(0) = y(\tau),\ y'(t) = Ay(t) + \partial_y f(y^0,u^0)y(t) + \partial_u f(y^0,u^0)u(t),\quad t \in T$$

$$\text{(3.17)}\quad u^0 + u \in \operatorname{int} \mathcal{U}_{ad}$$

$$\text{(3.18)}\quad \int_0^\tau [\mathcal{D}_1\mathcal{D}_1\mathcal{H}(y^0,u^0,y^*)(y(t),y(t)) + 2\mathcal{D}_1\mathcal{D}_2\mathcal{H}(y^0,u^0,y^*)(y(t),u(t)) + \mathcal{D}_2\mathcal{D}_2\mathcal{H}(y^0,u^0,y^*)(u(t),u(t))]dt < 0$$

where $y^* \in Y^*$ is given by

$$0 = \partial_y g(y^o,u^o) + y^* \partial_y f(y^o,u^o) + y^*A \tag{3.19}$$
$$0 = \partial_u g(y^o,u^o) + y^* \partial_u f(y^o,u^o)$$

Proof: Using Lemma 3.4 one shows that the assumptions of Theorem 3.3 are satisfied. Now suppose that (y^o,u^o) is an optimal solution of Problem (1.1) - (1.4). Then Theorem 3.3 yields necessary optimality conditions. Using assumption (3.7) and Proposition 3.2 one sees that the corresponding Lagrange multiplier coincides with the Lagrange multiplier of the steady state problem (3.1) - (3.3). Thus it satisfies (3.5), (3.6).

Using Lemma 3.4, one computes the concrete form of the necessary optimality conditions. These must be violated if (y^o,u^o) is locally proper.
This yields the assertion.

Remark: This result may be applied to parabolic partial differential systems along the lines of [6].

Remark: For ordinary differential systems this criterion for local properness was developed in [1], [2].

References

[1] S. Bittanti, G. Fronza, G. Guarbadassi, Periodic control: a frequency domain approach, IEEE Trans.Aut. Control, AC-18 (1973), 33-38.

[2] D.S. Bernstein, E.G. Gilbert, Optimal periodic control: the Π-Test revisited, IEEE Trans.Aut. Control, AC-25 (1980), 673-684.

[3] F. Colonius, Optimal Periodic Control, Habilitationsschrift, Universität Bremen, Bremen 1986.

[4] I. Ekeland, Nonconvex minimization problems, Bull.Amer.Math. Soc. 1(NS) (1979), 443-474.

[5] H.O. Fattorini, The maximum principle for nonlinear nonconvex systems in infinite dimensional spaces, Distributed Parameter Systems, F.Kappel, K. Kunisch, W. Schappacher, eds., Springer-Verlag, Berlin 1986, 162-178.

[6] H.O. Fattorini, Optimal control of nonlinear systems: convergence of suboptimal controls I, University of California, Department of Mathematics, Los Angeles, 1986.

[7] E.G. Gilbert, Optimal Periodic control: a general theory of necessary conditions, SIAM J. Control Optim. 15 (1977), 717-746.

[8] A. Pazy, Semigroups of Linear Operators and Applications to Partial Differential Equations, Springer-Verlag, Berlin 1983.

Present address:
Fritz Colonius
Institut für Dynamische Systeme
Universität Bremen
Postfach 330 440
D-2800 Bremen 33
West Germany

International Series of
Numerical Mathematics, Vol. 78

ON AN INVERSE PROBLEM FOR A NONLINEAR HEAT EQUATION CONNECTED WITH CONTINUOUS CASTING OF STEEL

Heinz W. Engl, Thomas Langthaler *
Johannes-Kepler-Universität Linz
Austria

and

Paolo Manselli **
Università degli Studi Firenze
Italy

ABSTRACT:

After describing the technical background that led to the inverse problem for a nonlinear heat equation considered in this paper, we prove existence, uniqueness and continuous-dependence results for the direct problem, uniqueness for the inverse problem and show how the stability can be restored in the inverse problem by a suitable a-priori bound.

---

* Supported by the Austrian Fonds zur Förderung der wissenschaftlichen Forschung (project S32/o3)

** Supported in part by a grant within the Cultural Exchange Treaty between Austria and Italy (project no. 55)

I. Continuous casting

Continuous casting is the linking process between steel making and hot rolling and has become the dominant process route in modern steel production. Liquid steel is cast into the mould, which must be capable of extracting sufficient heat from the incoming metal to solidify a shell which can support the liquid pool at the mould exit. The heat extraction process is continued by spraying water onto the surface of the strand ("secondary cooling"). In this so-called "spray cooling zone" sufficient heat must be removed from the steel to virtually complete solidification. There are many thermal requirements if steel is to be cast efficiently with a minimum of defects. It is of major importance for the quality of the resulting product how the surface temperature and the front of solidification (i.e., the boundary between liquid and solid phase) behave as functions of time. As a logical consequence one tries to control the solidification process in such a way that the outcome is "optimal" in a certain sense. From metallurgical considerations, the engineer can provide information about the optimal behaviour of the front of solidification. Thus, it is important that one is able to compute cooling rates in the spray cooling zones that lead to a solidification front which is as close to the optimal one as possible. In [3], the first two authors report about the implementation of an algorithm for computing these cooling rates in an industrial environment (VOEST-ALPINE AG, Linz).

The mathematical formulation of this problem can be reduced (see [3] for details) to an inverse problem for a heat-equation in one space variable with coefficients that depend on the temperature in a nonlinear way and nonlinear mixed boundary conditions. Since only secondary cooling can be influenced to a reasonable extent, we fix time $t = 0$ to be that moment when the strand leaves the mould. The movement of the strand is modeled in such a way as if it were kept fixed and the cooling zones were moved upward. Thus, the boundary conditions which describe the cooling depend on time and on the casting speed. Some physical and technical considerations (see [3]) justify further simplifications, which finally lead to the following mathematical model:

$$(1.1)\qquad \frac{\partial}{\partial x}\,[k(u(x,t)).\frac{\partial u}{\partial x}\,(x,t)] = \rho.c(u(x,t))\,\frac{\partial u}{\partial t}\,(x,t)$$

$$\text{for } (x,t) \in\,]0, \tfrac{d}{2}[\times]0,T_s[$$

$$(1.2)\qquad k(u(0,t))\,\frac{\partial u}{\partial x}\,(0,t) = g_v(t).[u(0,t)-U_w] \quad \text{for } t \in [0,T]$$

$$(1.3)\qquad k(u(0,t))\,\frac{\partial u}{\partial x}\,(0,t) = \sigma.\varepsilon.[u(0,t)^4-U_a{}^4] \quad \text{for } t \in\,]T_c,T_s]$$

$$(1.4)\qquad \frac{\partial u}{\partial x}\,(\tfrac{d}{2}, t) = 0 \quad \text{for } t \in [0,T_s]$$

$$(1.5)\qquad u(x,0) = f(x) \quad \text{for } x \in [0, \tfrac{d}{2}]$$

$$(1.6)\qquad u(s(t),t) = U_s \quad \text{for } t \in [0,T_s].$$

Here, the variables and constants have the following meaning:

u .... temperature, depending on space x and time t
k .... thermal conductivity, see Fig. 1.1
ρ .... density
c .... specific heat, see Fig. 1.1
g_v .... heat transfer function; v: casting speed
U_w .... temperature of the water used in the spray cooling zones
T_c, T_s .... times when the strand leaves the spray cooling zones and is completely solid, respectively
T .... $\min\{T_c, T_s\}$
U_a .... temperature of the surrounding air
σ .... Stefan-Boltzmann-constant
ε .... emission factor (depends on the material)
U_s .... temperature at which the material is completely solidified
s .... distance of the boundary between solid phase and liquid phase from the left boundary of the strand
f .... temperature distribution at time 0; for technological reasons (see above) f is given in such a way that $s(0) > 0$, i.e., the strand is already supported by a thin solid layer.

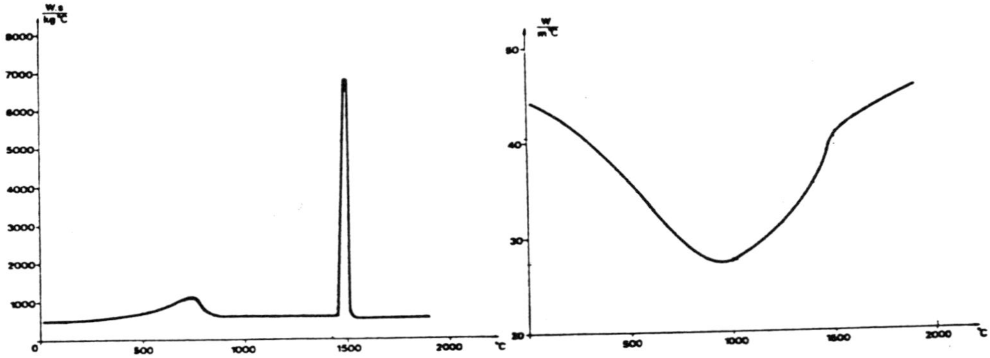

Heat capacity c

Thermal conductivity k

Fig. 1.1: Thermal properties of steel

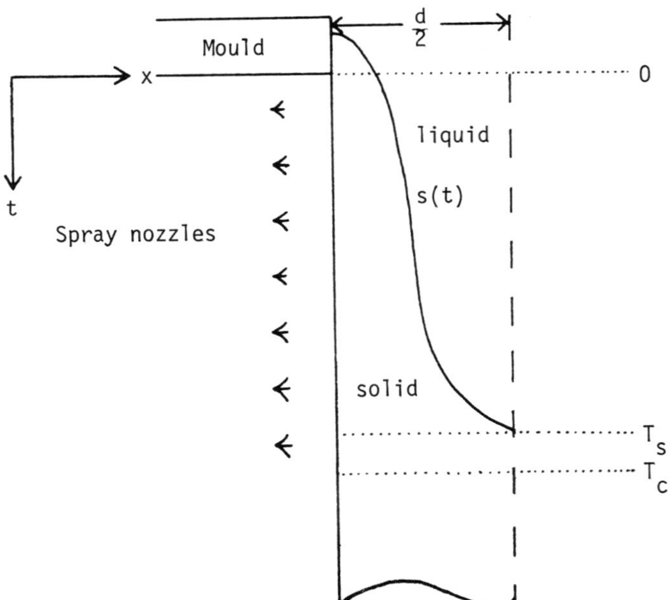

Fig. 1.2

Note that T_c, T_s and hence also T depend on the casting speed v; by definition of T_s, $s(T_s) = \frac{d}{2}$. See Fig. 1.2 for a one-dimensional sketch illustrating the model. A sketch of an actual casting machine can be found in [3]. In connection with equations (1.1) through (1.6), we will use the term "direct problem" for the problem of computing the temperature u and the solidification front s, where all the other quantities are given. This looks like a free-boundary value problem of Stefan type (cf. e.g. [4]). More precisely, because of (1.5), (1.1) - (1.5) is a boundary value problem on a fixed domain that determines u; the solidification front is then determined by (1.6). Nevertheless, we will call s the "free boundary".

Actually, we are interested in the "inverse problem": From s (given as a function of time), we want to compute g_v and u, fulfilling (1.1) - (1.6), where all the other quantities are given. This is an inverse problem similar to an inverse Stefan problem. Even for a linear heat equation, this problem is ill-posed in the sense that a solution g_v does not depend continuously on the "data" s. For a comprehensive treatment of inverse Stefan problems governed by the linear heat equation see e.g. [6]. Numerical aspects are treated e.g. in [2], [5] and [1o].

The ill-posedness of the problem leads to the need of some kind of regularization. In the environment described in [3], this regularization was "built into" the casting machine, since there, spray cooling could be controlled only in such a way that in six different regions, g_v could assume different values (which were constant in each region). Thus, the control variable g_v could be treated as a finite-dimensional variable. However, [3] contains no theoretical investigation about the well-posedness of that problem. For the following theoretical investigations about the problem we treat the control variable g_v as a function which we do not assume to be piecewise constant any longer; instead, we assume that g_v is continuously differentiable and that a-priori bounds for this function and for its first derivative are available.

In the next section we slightly simplify the system (1.1) - (1.6) to make it suitable for our analysis.

II. Transformation of the problem

In the sequel we treat the following equations, which are a slight variation of (1.1) - (1.6):

(2.1) $[k(u(x,t))u_x(x,t)]_x = c(u(x,t))u_t(x,t) \quad (x,t) \in D: =]-1,1[\times]0,T[$

(2.2) $k(u(1,t))u_x(1,t) = g(t)u(1,t) \quad t \in [0,T]$

(2.3) $-k(u(-1,t))u_x(-1,t) = g(t)u(-1,t) \quad t \in [0,T]$

(2.4) $u(x,0) = f(x) \geq 0 \quad x \in [-1,1]$

$(f(x) = f(-x) \text{ for } x \in [-1,1])$

(2.5) $u(s(t),t) = U_s \quad t \in [0,T_s]$

(2.6) $u(-s(t),t) = U_s \quad t \in [0,T_s]$

Comparing equations (2.1) - (2.6) with (1.1) - (1.6) one can see easily that the domains are slightly different. We take 2 as value for d and set $T_c = T$, i.e., we omit the effects of radiation contained in (1.3) and assume a constant casting speed, which implies that the cooling function g is always defined on the same interval [0,T]. Besides, we use a constant density $\rho = 1$ and a temperature of the cooling water of $U_w = 0$. In (2.1) - (2.6) we consider the complete strand (i.e., $x \in [-1,1]$) whereas in (1.1) - (1.6) we considered only one half of the strand and used symmetry. Since the cooling is done in a symmetric way, both approaches are equivalent.

If not mentioned otherwise we assume from now on that there exists a constant K such that for all $(x,t) \in D$, $0 \leq u(x,t) \leq K$. Besides we assume that the functions k and c are strictly positive on the interval [0,K]. We remark that both assumptions are realistic.

REMARK 2.1: If the functions k and c were constant, equation (2.1) would be linear. For that problem one could get existence, uniqueness and continuous dependence on the data for the direct problem under less restrictive assumptions than in the nonlinear case (cf. e.g. [4], [6]).

Moreover, if one has an a-priori bound for the solution or assumes its positivity, one can even get continuous dependence on the data for the inverse problem, in special cases convergence rates can be proven (cf. [2]).

Now we make a further transformation:
Let h be an antiderivative for c with $h(0) = 0$, which exists under the assumptions to be made about c later. Since c is assumed to be strictly positive, h is strictly monotonically increasing, hence the inverse function h^{-1} exists and is also strictly monotonically increasing. For any function u with values in $[0,K]$, we define $\tilde{u}(x,t) := h(u(x,t))$. By definition of h, we have that $\tilde{u}_t = c(u)u_t$ and $\tilde{u}_x = c(u)u_x$. Since k,c are strictly positive, we can define (for any function u with values in $h([0,K])$)

$$\tilde{k}(\tilde{u}) := \frac{k(h^{-1}(\tilde{u}))}{c(h^{-1}(\tilde{u}))} ;$$

$\tilde{k}$ is strictly positive. Under the assumptions about $\tilde{k}$ to be made later, we can perform the differentiations needed in the following transformations; we obtain for any solution u of (2.1) - (2.6) on the same domains as there:

$$\tilde{u}_t = c(u)u_t = (k(u)u_x)_x = \left(\frac{k(u)}{c(u)} \quad \tilde{u}_x \right)_x =$$

$$= \left(\frac{k(h^{-1}(\tilde{u}))}{c(h^{-1}(\tilde{u}))} \tilde{u}_x \right)_x = (\tilde{k}(\tilde{u})\tilde{u}_x)_x,$$

$$g(t)h^{-1}(\tilde{u}) = g(t)u = k(u)u_x = \frac{k(u)}{c(u)} \tilde{u}_x = \tilde{k}(\tilde{u})\tilde{u}_x,$$

$$\tilde{u}(x,0) = h(u(x,0)) = h(f(x)) =: \tilde{f}(x),$$

$$\tilde{u}(s(t),t) = h(u(s(t),t)) = h(U_s) =: \tilde{U}_s .$$

Since h is strictly monotonically increasing and $h(0) = 0$, the correspondence between u and $\tilde{u}$ is one-to-one. In this sense, the system (2.1) - (2.6) is equivalent to the transformed system

$$(2.7)\qquad [\tilde{k}(\tilde{u}(x,t))\tilde{u}_x(x,t)]_x = \tilde{u}_t(x,t) \qquad (x,t) \in D$$

$$(2.8)\qquad \tilde{k}(\tilde{u}(1,t))\tilde{u}_x(1,t) = g(t)h^{-1}(\tilde{u}(1,t)) \qquad t \in [0,T]$$

$$(2.9)\qquad -\tilde{k}(\tilde{u}(-1,t))\tilde{u}_x(-1,t) = g(t)h^{-1}(\tilde{u}(-1,t)) \qquad t \in [0,T]$$

$$(2.1o)\qquad \tilde{u}(x,0) = \tilde{f}(x) \qquad x \in [-1,1]$$

$$(2.11)\qquad \tilde{u}(s(t),t) = \tilde{U}_s \qquad t \in [0,T_s]$$

$$(2.12)\qquad \tilde{u}(-s(t),t) = \tilde{U}_s \qquad t \in [0,T_s].$$

If we refer to the "transformed problem" below, we mean (2.7) - (2.12), which we will abbreviate by "TP". The aim of this transformation was to remove the nonlinearity from the derivative with respect to t, as a comparison between (2.1) and (2.7) shows. In referring to TP we will now omit the superscripts "~". To reinterpret the results of Section III for (2.1) - (2.6), one has to translate the assumptions to be made in terms of the quantities appearing in (2.1) - (2.6).

III. Results for the transformed problem

In this chapter, we solve most of the basic problems for TP concerning existence, uniqueness and continuous dependence for the direct and the inverse problem. The plan of this chapter is as follows:

Under some assumptions about the behaviour of the functions appearing in TP and the main assumption that a solution for the inverse problem connected with TP always exists, we can show the uniqueness of that solution. Under certain assumptions we will show existence and uniqueness of the solution of the direct problem (2.7) - (2.1o). Under further assumptions concerning the existence of a classical solution with certain additional properties we will show the uniqueness of the resulting free boundary s.

Further restrictions guarantee the continuous dependence on the data (i.e.,on g) for the solution of the direct problem connected with TP. All assumptions together with the assumption of a-priori bounds for the cooling function and its first derivative lead to continuous dependence on the data (i.e., on s) for the solution of the inverse problem (i.e., u and g) connected with TP up to time T_s. Unfortunately, this result is only a qualitative stability result for the inverse problem. So far we did not succeed in obtaining a quantitative result, i.e., a modulus of continuity, which would be useful for designing a regularization algorithm for the inverse problem in the spirit of [8]. However, we did succeed in proving Lipschitz continuous dependence on the data for a linear functional (namely the mean value) of g (for a slightly simplified problem).

Now we carry out this plan in detail. From now on we assume (unless stated otherwise) the existence of a constant $\tilde{K} > 0$ (where we again omit the superscript ~) such that for all $(x,t) \in \bar{D}$, $u(x,t) \in [0,K]$ for all solutions of TP we consider. Furthermore, we assume the function k to be strictly positive on the interval $[0,K]$. Our continuous initial temperature distribution f is assumed to satisfy

(i) $f(x) = f(-x) > 0$ for $x \in [-1,1]$

and

(ii) $f(0) > U_s > f(1)$.

(i) is merely a symmetry property; (ii) assures the existence of $x \in]0,1[$ with $f(x) = U_s$, which means that at time $t = 0$ the strand has already a solidified shell. Both assumptions are fulfilled for the practical problem as discussed in the first two chapters.

All assumptions are to be understood in the sense that the results are valid only for those functions for which the assumptions hold.

ASSUMPTION 3.1:

(i) Given s, there exists a classical solution u of the inverse problem for TP, i.e., of the problem of finding u and g solving TP for a given s.

(ii) u is analytic, k is twice continuously differentiable, s is continuously differentiable on $[0,T_s[$.

(iii) u is strictly positive on the domain $\bar{D}$.

(iv) For all $\bar{t} < T_s$, s is strictly positive on the interval $[0,\bar{t}]$.

Note that Assumption 3.1 (i) is a restriction on the free boundaries that we consider. For Assumption 3.1 (ii) see Remark 3.3.

PROPOSITION 3.2 (Uniqueness for the inverse problem):

Under Assumption 3.1, the (classical) solution of the inverse problem for TP is unique up to time T.

Proof: Let u_1, u_2 be two arbitrary solutions of TP (fulfilling Assumption 3.1), i.e.,

$$(3.1)\qquad u_{it} = k(u_i)u_{ixx} + k'(u_i)u_{ix}^2 \qquad i = 1,2.$$

From (3.1) we obtain by subtraction the following equation for $v: = u_1-u_2$:

$$(3.2)\qquad \begin{aligned} v_t &= \frac{k(u_1)+k(u_2)}{2}\, v_{xx} + \frac{k'(u_1)+k'(u_2)}{2}\,(u_{1x}+u_{2x})v_x + \\ &+ \Big[\frac{u_{1xx}+u_{2xx}}{2}\int_0^1 k'(\theta u_1+(1-\theta)u_2)d\theta + \frac{u_{1x}^2+u_{2x}^2}{2}\int_0^1 k''(\theta u_1+(1-\theta)u_2)d\theta\Big]v. \end{aligned}$$

With $\tilde{A}_1: = \frac{1}{2}[k(u_1)+k(u_2)]$, $\tilde{A}_2: = \frac{1}{2}[k'(u_1)+k'(u_2)](u_{1x}+u_{2x})$ and

$$\tilde{A}_3: = \frac{1}{2}\Big[(u_{1xx}+u_{2xx})\int_0^1 k'(\theta u_1+(1-\theta)u_2)d\theta + (u_{1x}^2+u_{2x}^2)\int_0^1 k''(\theta u_1+(1-\theta)u_2)d\theta\Big],$$

v satisfies the linear parabolic equation

$$(3.3)\qquad v_t = \tilde{A}_1(x,t)v_{xx} + \tilde{A}_2(x,t)v_x + \tilde{A}_3(x,t)v \qquad (x,t) \in D.$$

Since u_1 und u_2 are solutions of TP, the function v fulfills the following boundary conditions:

$$(3.4)\qquad \begin{aligned} v(x,0) &= 0 \qquad x \in [-1,1] \\ v(s(t),t) &= 0 \qquad t \in [0,T_s] \\ v(-s(t),t) &= 0 \qquad t \in [0,T_s]. \end{aligned}$$

From now on we restrict the domain to $[-1,1] \times [0,\bar{t}]$ for some $\bar{t} < T_s$ arbitrarily close to T_s. Now we transform the domain as follows:
For $0 \leq t \leq \bar{t}$ and $x \in [-s(t),s(t)]$ we define $\xi(x,t): = \frac{1}{2}\left(\frac{x}{s(t)} + 1\right)$ and $w(\xi,t): = v(x,t)$, where $\xi = \xi(x,t) \in [0,1]$. Then we have the following correspondence:

$$(3.5)\qquad w_\xi \cdot \frac{1}{2s(t)} = v_x$$

$$(3.6)\qquad w_{\xi\xi}\cdot\left(\frac{1}{2s(t)}\right)^2 = v_{xx} \qquad 0 \leq t \leq \bar{t},\ x \in [-s(t),s(t)]$$
$$\xi = \xi(x,t) \in [0,1]$$

$$(3.7)\qquad w_t + w_\xi\left(\frac{-xs'(t)}{2s^2(t)}\right) = v_t.$$

Note that for $t \in [0,\bar{t}]$, $s(t) \neq 0$ because of Assumption 3.1. From (3.3) and (3.5) - (3.7), it follows that w satisfies a parabolic equation

$$(3.8)\qquad w_t = \bar{A}_1(\xi,t)w_{\xi\xi} + \bar{A}_2(\xi,t)w_\xi + \bar{A}_3(\xi,t)w,\ (\xi,t) \in]0,1[\times]0,\bar{t}[.$$

The boundary conditions (3.4) are transformed into

$$(3.9)\qquad \begin{aligned} w(\xi,0) &= 0 \quad 0 \leq \xi \leq 1\\ w(1,t) &= 0 \quad 0 \leq t \leq \bar{t}\\ w(0,t) &= 0 \quad 0 \leq t \leq \bar{t}. \end{aligned}$$

Problem (3.8), (3.9) fulfills the requirements of Theorem 8 in [9, p.176], from which we can conclude that $w = 0$. Hence also $v(x,t)$ vanishes for $t \in [0,\bar{t}]$, $x \in [-s(t),s(t)]$. Thus $u_1 = u_2$ on this domain.
Since v is analytic, this implies that v varishes everywhere, i.e., $u_1 = u_2$ and thus $g_1 = g_2$ (by (2.8), (2.9) and Assumption 3.1 (iii)). □

REMARK 3.3: Assumption 3.1 is not as restrictive as it seems to be. Assumption 3.1 (iii) is of course always true; Assumption 3.1 (iv) is always fulfilled for our model of the continuous casting process, since T_s is by definition the moment when solidification is completed. If one does not want to assume analyticity of u, the result of Proposition 3.2 could also be obtained by referring to Theorem 4 of "M.H.Protter, Properties of solutions of parabolic equations and inequalities, Canad.J.Math. 13 (1961), pp.331-345" instead of to the analyticity of u at the end of the proof. This argument removes the analyticity of u from Assumption 3.1 (ii).

ASSUMPTION 3.4:

(i) k is twice continuously differentiable on the interval [0,K].
(ii) g is continuously differentiable on the interval [0,T].

To prove an existence result, we drop (only for Proposition 3.5) the assumption that $u \leq K$; we can continue c and k in such a way that the assumed smoothness requirements are fulfilled and h^{-1} is still defined in order to get a relationship between the solutions of (2.1) - (2.6) and (2.7) - (2.12) as in Section II without the bound K.

We cannot prove existence of a solution with values in [0,K]; thus, the existence of such a solution (which is of course physically reasonable) is a general assumption for everything except the next proposition:

PROPOSITION 3.5 (Existence and uniqueness in the direct problem): Under Assumption 3.4, there exists a unique classical solution of the direct problem (2.7) - (2.1o) (for given g).

Proof: With

$$a(x,t,u) \triangleq k(u)$$

$$b(x,t,u,u_x) \triangleq k'(u)u_x^2$$

$$\psi(x,t,u) \triangleq -g(t)h^{-1}(u)$$

$$\psi_0(x) \triangleq f(x),$$

one can easily show that Theorem 7.4 of [7, p.491] can be applied; from this Theorem and the remark concerning the inhomogenous initial condition in [7, p.49o], the result follows.

□

REMARK 3.6: Assumption 3.4 (i) is no real restriction for the technical situation (see Fig. 1.1). Assumption 3.4 (ii) is the point where these theoretical considerations differ from the situation treated in [3], where g was a step function.

ASSUMPTION 3.7: Given g as in Assumption 3.4, there exists a classical solution u of the problem (2.7) - (2.1o) which is for all $t \in [0,T]$ strictly monotonically increasing for $x \in [-1,0[$ and strictly monotonically decreasing for $x \in [0,1]$ as a function of x.

PROPOSITION 3.8 (Uniqueness of the direct problem including the free boundary):

Under Assumptions 3.4 and 3.7, the solution (u,s) of the direct problem (2.7) - (2.12) is unique.

Proof: Assumption 3.7 guarantees the existence of a solution u to problem (2.7) - (2.1o), which is unique by Proposition 3.5. Assumption 3.7 also assures that the level curves s(t),-s(t), defined by $u(\pm s(t),t) = U_S$ $(t \in [0,T_S])$ are unique. □

REMARK 3.9: Because of the permanent "super-cooling" on each side of the strand, in the continuous casting process it is reasonable to assume that for any fixed moment t, the temperature of the strand is strictly monotonically increasing as a function of the location between strand-surface and the center of the strand. From this point of view, Assumption 3.7 and other similar assumptions are not very restrictive, if one thinks of the continuous casting process as motivation for the governing equation of our problem.

From Assumption 3.7, one can also conclude the continuity of s. The argument goes as follows: If s were discontinuous at time t, there would exist two sequences of points where the temperature has the value U_s converging to different points (x_1,t), (x_2,t). By continuity of u, this would imply $u(x_1,t) = u(x_2,t) = U_s$ in contradiction to Assumption 3.7. Whenever $u_x \neq 0$ holds, there it follows from the Implicit Function Theorem that s is as smooth as u.

ASSUMPTION 3.1o:

(i) k is twice continuously differentiable in $[0,K]$

All considered solutions of the direct problem (2.7)-(2.12) fulfill:

(ii) There exists a (uniform) constant $L > 0$ such that $u \geq L$ in D.

(iii) For all $t \in [0,T]$, u is strictly monotonically increasing for $x \in [-1,0[$ and strictly monotonically decreasing for $x \in [0,1]$ as a function of x.

(iv) There exists a (uniform) constant $M > 0$ such that $|u_{xx}| \leq M$ and $|u_x| \leq M$ holds in D.

(v) For all $x \in [-1,1]$, $u(x,t)$ is strictly monotonically decreasing (as a function of t) in $[0,T]$.

(vi) There exists $T_s \leq T$ with $u(0,T_s) = U_s$.

PROPOSITION 3.11 (Continuous dependence on the data for the direct problem):

Under Assumptions 3.4, 3.7 and 3.1o, the solution (u,s) of the direct problem depends continuously on the data g in the following sense: There is a $c_1 > 0$ such that

$$\|u_1-u_2\|_\infty \leq c_1\|g_1-g_2\|_\infty$$

holds. Furthermore, if $\|g_n-g_o\|_\infty \to 0$, then $(T_{s_n}) \to T_{s_o}$ and (s_n) converges pointwise to s_o on $[0,T_{s_o}[$. Here, (u_n,s_n) stands for the solution of the direct problem determined by the cooling function g_n.

Proof: $v: = u_1-u_2$ satisfies the following conditions:

$$(3.1o)\quad \begin{aligned} &v_t = \tilde{A}_1(x,t)v_{xx} + \tilde{A}_2(x,t)v_x + \tilde{A}_3(x,t)v \qquad (x,t) \in D \\ &v(x,0) = 0 \qquad x \in [-1,1], \end{aligned}$$

where the $\tilde{A}_i$ are as in the proof of Proposition 3.2. Now we develop the boundary conditions satisfied by v.

u_1 and u_2 fulfill $k(u_i)u_{ix} = \pm g_i h^{-1}(u_i)$ (see (2.8), (2.9)).

We treat only the boundary condition at $x = 1$ explicitely; for $x = -1$, the only difference is that g_1-g_2 has to be replaced by g_2-g_1.

We define (for $u \in [L,K]$) $H(u): = \frac{k(u)}{h^{-1}(u)}$; because of our assumptions about k (and c in Section II), h^{-1} is strictly positive and continuously differentiable and hence H is well-defined and continuously differentiable (for any $t \in [0,T]$ and $x = 1$).

By subtracting the boundary conditions we obtain

$$\frac{H(u_1)+H(u_2)}{2} v_x + \frac{u_{1x}+u_{2x}}{2} (H(u_1)-H(u_2)) = g_1-g_2,$$

which can be formulated as

$$(3.11)\qquad B_1(t)v_x + B(t)v = g_1-g_2 \qquad t \in [0,T]$$

with $B_1(t): = \frac{H(u_1)+H(u_2)}{2} > 0$ and $B(t): = \int_0^1 H'(\theta u_1+(1-\theta)u_2)d\theta$.

Because of our assumptions, B_1 and B are continuous functions in $[0,T]$. Notice that, because of Assumption 3.1o (iv), $\tilde{A}_1$, $\tilde{A}_2$ and $\tilde{A}_3$ as well as B_1 and B can be bounded by constants depending on L and M only.

This guarantees that (3.1o) - (3.11) meets the requirements of Theorem 2.3 in [7,p.16]. Since all bounds are independent of u_1 and u_2 (and g_1 and g_2), it follows from that Theorem that with a constant c_o independent of u_1, u_2, g_1, and g_2,

$$\|u_1-u_2\|_\infty \leq c_o\|g_1-g_2\|_\infty$$

holds. The only thing left to do is to show that the resulting boundary s depends also continuously on the data g (in the sense of pointwise convergence). Let (g_n) be such that $\|g_n-g_o\|_\infty \to 0$.

For $n \in \mathbb{N}_o$, $s_n(t)$ is that value of x for which $u_n(x,t)$ equals U_s. Our assumptions guarantee that s_n is a continuous curve (cf. Remark 3.9). By T_{s_n} we denote that time at which complete solidification occurs (i.e., $u_n(0,T_{s_n}) = U_s$, or equivalently, $s_n(T_{s_n}) = 0$).

The estimates to be obtained may depend on g_o, u_o, s_o, but not on g_n, u_n, s_n.

There are two different situations possible:

(i) $T_{s_n} < T_{s_o}$, i.e., g_n causes faster solidification than g_o.

(ii) $T_{s_n} \geq T_{s_o}$.

We now show that

$$(3.12) \qquad (T_{s_n}) \to T_{s_o}.$$

Since all T_{s_n} are in $[0,T]$, every subsequence has a further subsequence that converges to some $\bar{T}$; it suffices to show that $\bar{T} = T_{s_o}$. Dropping the index for the subsequence, let $(T_{s_n}) \to \bar{T}$. Since $|u_n(0,T_{s_n})-u_o(0,\bar{T})| \leq$
$\leq |u_n(0,T_{s_n})-u_o(0,T_{s_n})| + |u_o(0,T_{s_n})-u_o(0,\bar{T})| \leq c_o\|g_n-g_o\|_\infty +$
$+ |u_o(0,T_{s_n})-u_o(0,\bar{T})| \to 0$ and $u_n(0,T_{s_n}) = U_s$, we have that $u_o(0,\bar{T}) = U_s$, which implies by Assumption 3.1o (v) that (3.12) holds.

Let $t < T_{s_o}$ be arbitrary, but fixed, and $n_o \in \mathbb{N}$ sufficiently large for $T_{s_n} \geq t$ to hold for $n \geq n_o$. For those n, we argue as above: Every subsequence of $(s_n(t))$ has a convergent subsequence converging to, say, $\bar{s}$. It suffices to show that $\bar{s}=s_0(t)$ to conclude that $(s_n(t))\to s_0(t)$. To this end, note that from $|u_n(s_n(t),t)-u_0(\bar{s},t)| \leq |u_n(s_n(t),t)-u_0(s_n(t),t)| + |u_0(s_n(t),t)-u_0(\bar{s},t)| \leq$ $\leq c_0\|g_n-g_0\|_\infty + |u_0(s_n(t),t)-u_0(\bar{s},t)| \to 0$ and $u_n(s_n(t),t) = U_s$ we obtain that $u_0(\bar{s},t) = U_s$. Since also $u_0(s_0(t),t) = U_s$, we conclude from Assumption 3.1o (iii) that $\bar{s} = s_0(t)$. $\square$

REMARK 3.12: As before, Assumption 3.1o seems to be realistic for the practical problem we have in mind; since positivity of all solutions is no restriction for steel close to the melting point. For (iii), see Remark 3.9. Assumption (v) means that due to the permanent cooling, no reheating takes place at any point in the strand, which is realistic. We remark that in practice, there is the possibility of reheating as soon as the strand leaves the spray cooling zone, i.e., in the zone where (1.3) is valid (which is not considered in problem TP, however). Assumption (vi) means that we consider only solutions that lead to solidification within [0,T]. Note that our proof would imply that $(s_n(t)) \to s_0(t)$ for $t \leq T_{s_0}$ also if $T_{s_n} \geq T \geq T_{s_0}$.

As to Proposition 3.11: The solution u_0 depends on the data g_0 even in a Lipschitz-continuous way (uniformly on D). For the free boundary s, we could only prove continuous dependence with respect to the topology of pointwise convergence. If one would strengthen Assumption 3.1o (iii) in such a way that $u_x(x,t) \neq 0$ for $x \neq 0$, then one could obtain an estimate $|s_n(t)-s_0(t)| \leq C\|g_n-g_0\|_\infty$, where C depends on t and on s_0, i.e., local pointwise Lipschitz-continuity.

ASSUMPTION 3.13: There is a constant $B > 0$ such that for all data s considered and for the resulting cooling functions g, $|g(t)| \leq B$ and $|g'(t)| \leq B$ hold for all $t \in [0,T]$.

THEOREM 3.14 (Continuous dependence on the data for the inverse problem):

Under Assumptions 3.1, 3.4, 3.7, 3.1o and 3.13, the solution g of the inverse problem depends continuously on the data s in $[0,T_s]$ in the following sense: If $(T_{s_n}) \to T_s$ and (s_n) converges pointwise to s on $[0,T_s[$, then the resulting cooling functions (g_n) converge to g uniformly on [0,T].

Proof: By the Arzela-Ascoli-Theorem and Assumption 3.13, the set of functions g we consider is relatively compact with respect to uniform convergence. By G we denote the operator that maps a given admissible boundary s onto the resulting cooling function g on [0,T]; we will call it the "inverse operator".
By S we denote the operator that maps a given cooling function g onto the resulting boundary s. We will call it the "direct operator". Because of our assumptions and results, S and G are well-defined. Due to the previous results we know that S is continuous (from the uniform to the pointwise topology, see Proposition 3.11).

Now, let $(T_{s_n}) \to T_s$ and $(s_n) \to s$ pointwise on $[0,T_s[$ and let g_n and g be the resulting cooling functions, i.e., $g_n = G(s_n)$, $g = G(s)$. Because of compactness, each subsequence of g_n, without loss of generality again denoted by g_n, has another subsequence, again denoted by g_n, that converges to some $\bar{g}$. Because of Poposition 3.11, $(S(g_n))$ converges to $S(\bar{g})$ pointwise on $[0,T_{S(\bar{g})}[$ and $(T_{S(g_n)}) \to T_{S(\bar{g})}$; since by Proposition 3.8, $S(g_n) = s_n$, and since $(T_{s_n}) \to T_s$ was assumed, $T_s = T_{S(\bar{g})}$, so that $(S(g_n))$ converges to $S(\bar{g})$ pointwise on $[0,T_s[$. Since $S(g_n) = s_n$ was assumed to converge to s there, we have $S(\bar{g}) = s$, i.e., $G(S(\bar{g})) = G(s) = g$.
Given $S(\bar{g})$, both $\bar{g}$ and $G(S(\bar{g}))$ are solutions of the inverse problem. Hence, by Proposition 3.2, $\bar{g}$ and $G(S(\bar{g}))$ agree on [0,T]. Combining the results, we obtain that $\bar{g} = g$ on [0,T]. Thus, all subsequences of (g_n) have subsequences converging uniformly on [0,T] to g.

□

REMARK 3.15: Theorem 3.14 is only a qualitative stability result. The proof of Theorem 3.14 is based on a compactness argument (namely that the inverse of an invertible continuous operator on a compact set is also continuous) and hence cannot be modified as to give some kind of quantitative stability result; other techniques are needed there. So far, we did not succeed in proving convergence rates of (g_n) in dependence of (s_n), but one might expect logarithmic dependence or Hölder-continuity under some assumptions (cf. [6], [8]).

REMARK 3.16: For the theoretical considerations of this section, we used continuously differentiable cooling functions, whereas in [3], piecewise constant step functions were used. However, we can approximate these step functions that were defined in such a way that they could assume different values on six fixed intervals by functions as needed in Assumption 3.13 by interpolating in a suitable way between $[t_i-\varepsilon, t_i+\varepsilon]$, where t_i is one of the points of discontinuity. The a-priori bound on the derivative depends on the a-priori bound for these step functions (which is known from technological considerations) and on a fixed lower bound on ε. Thus, our results are also relevant for the setting considered in [3]. As an alternative, one could try to use the fact that in [3] only these special step functions were used to prove results in the spirit of this Section.

For a slightly simplified problem (namely (3.13) - (3.17)) we can finally prove the following quantitative stability result for the mean-value of the cooling function. In this result, the general assumptions about k, g and u are not needed any more; k and g should be such that classical solutions of (3.13) - (3.17) exist for the prescribed free boundaries.

PROPOSITION 3.17:

Consider the problem

(3.13) $\quad [k(u(x,t))u_x(x,t)]_x = u_t(x,t) \qquad (x,t) \in]0,1[\times]0,T[$

(3.14) $\quad k(u(1,t))u_x(1,t) = g(t) \qquad t \in [0,T]$

(3.15) $\quad u_x(0,t) = 0 \qquad t \in [0,T]$

(3.16) $\quad u(x,0) = f(x) \qquad x \in [0,1]$

(3.17) $\quad u(s(t),t) = U_s \qquad t \in [0,T_s],$

where T_s has the same meaning as in TP. Let s_1, s_2 be continuously differentiable on $[0,T_{s_1}[$ and $[0,T_{s_2}[$, respectively, with $\max\{T_{s_1},T_{s_2}\} \leq T$, $t_o < \min\{T_{s_1},T_{s_2}\}$. Assume that on $[0,t_o]$, s_1' and s_2' are strictly negative. By (u_1,g_1), (u_2,g_2) we denote the solutions of (3.13) - (3.17) with given s_1,s_2, respectively. We assume that $(u_2)_{tx}$ exists and is bounded. Then the following estimate holds:

$$\left|\int_o^{t_o} (g_1(t)-g_2(t))dt\right| \leq c_1(u_2)\|s_1-s_2\|_{L^1[0,t_o]} +$$

$$\text{(3.18)} \qquad + \|(u_1-u_2)(.,t_o)\|_{L^1[s_1(t_o),1]} + c_2\|(u_1-u_2)(s_1(.),.)\|_{L^1[0,t_o]} +$$

$$+ c_3\|(u_1-u_2)_t(s_1(.),.)\|_{L^1[0,t_o]} + c_4(u_2)\|s_1'-s_2'\|_{L^1[0,t_o]}.$$

Here, c_2 and c_3 are constants independent of the solutions (but dependent on bounds for s_1' and s_2'), while c_1 and c_4 depend on quantities determined by u_2 (see the proof for details).

Proof: In the sequel, $i \in \{1,2\}$, $t \in [0,t_o]$. By (3.14) and (3.15),

$$g_i(t) = \int_o^1 (k_i(u_i(x,t))u_{ix}(x,t))_x \, dx \underset{(3.13)}{=}$$

$$= \int_{s_i(t)}^1 u_{it}(x,t)dx + k(u_i(s_i(t),t)u_{ix}(s_i(t),t) \underset{(3.17)}{=}$$

$$= \int_{s_i(t)}^1 u_{it}(x,t)dx + k(U_s).u_{ix}(s_i(t),t).$$

From (3.17), we obtain $u_{ix}(s_i(t),t) = -\dfrac{u_{it}(s_i(t),t)}{s_i'(t)}$.

Hence we get $g_i(t) = \int_{s_i(t)}^{1} u_{it}(x,t)dx - k(U_s)\dfrac{u_{it}(s_i(t),t)}{s_i'(t)}$. Now we begin to estimate the left-hand side of (3.18):

$$\left|\int_0^{t_o}(g_1(t)-g_2(t))dt\right| = \left|\int_0^{t_o}\left[\int_{s_1(t)}^{1} u_{1t}(x,t)dx - \int_{s_2(t)}^{1} u_{2t}(x,t)dx - \right.\right.$$

$$\left.\left.- k(U_s)\left(\frac{u_{1t}(s_1(t),t)}{s_1'(t)} - \frac{u_{2t}(s_2(t),t)}{s_2'(t)}\right)\right]dt\right| \leq$$

$$\leq \underbrace{\left|\int_0^{t_o}\left[\int_{s_1(t)}^{1} u_{1t}(x,t)dx - \int_{s_2(t)}^{1} u_{2t}(x,t)dx\right]dt\right|}_{=:\, I_1} +$$

$$+ |k(U_s)| \cdot \underbrace{\left|\int_0^{t_o}\frac{u_{1t}(s_1(t),t)}{s_1'(t)} - \frac{u_{2t}(s_2(t),t)}{s_2'(t)}\,dt\right|}_{=:\, I_2}.$$

We estimate I_1 and I_2 separately. Let $A_i := \{(x,t)/t \in [0,t_o], x \in [s_i(t),1]\}$. Let $A_1 \triangle A_2 := (A_1 \setminus A_2) \cup (A_2 \setminus A_1)$ be the symmetric difference of A_1 and A_2 and let $\bar{u}_2$ be u_2 on A_1 and $-u_2$ on A_2. By (3.16), $s_1(0) = s_2(0) =: b$.

$$I_1 = \int_0^{t_o}\left[\int_{s_1(t)}^{1} u_{1t}(x,t)dx - \int_{s_2(t)}^{1} u_{2t}(x,t)dx\right]dt = \int_{A_1}(u_1-u_2)_t(x,t)d(x,t) +$$

$$+ \int_{A_1} u_{2t}(x,t)d(x,t) - \int_{A_2} u_{2t}(x,t)d(x,t) = \int_b^1\int_0^{t_o}(u_1-u_2)_t(x,t)dt\,dx +$$

$$+ \int_{s_1(t_o)}^{b}\int_{s_1^{-1}(x)}^{t_o}(u_1-u_2)_t(x,t)dt\,dx + \int_{A_1\triangle A_2}\bar{u}_{2t}(x,t)d(x,t) \underset{(3.16)}{=}$$

$$= \int_b^1 (u_1-u_2)(x,t_o)dx + \int_{s_1(t_o)}^b (u_1-u_2)(x,t_o)dx - \int_{s_1(t_o)}^b (u_1-u_2)(x,s_1^{-1}(x))dx +$$

$$+ \int_{A_1\Delta A_2} \bar{u}_{2t}(x,t)d(x,t) = \int_{s_1(t_o)}^1 (u_1-u_2)(x,t_o)dx - \int_{s_1(t_o)}^b (u_1-u_2)(x,s_1^{-1}(x))dx +$$

$$+ \int_{A_1\Delta A_2} \bar{u}_{2t}(x,t)d(x,t).$$

Thus, $|I_1| \leq \|(u_1-u_2)(.,t_o)\|_{L^1[s_1(t_o),1]} + \|(u_1-u_2)(.,s_1^{-1}(.))\|_{L^1[s_1(t_o),b]} +$

$\int_{A_1\Delta A_2} |u_{2t}(x,t)|d(x,t)$. By assumption, there exist $e,E > 0$ with $e \leq |s_i'| \leq E$ on $[0,t_o]$. Since $\|(u_1-u_2)(.,s_1^{-1}(.))\|_{L^1[s_1(t_o),b]} \leq E.\|(u_1-u_2)(s_1(.),.)\|_{L^1[0,t_o]}$, we have: $|I_1| \leq \|(u_1-u_2)(.,t_o)\|_{L^1[s_1(t_o),1]} + E.\|(u_1-u_2)(s_1(.),.)\|_{L^1[0,t_o]} +$

$+ |A_1 \Delta A_2| \sup_{(x,t)\in A_1\Delta A_2} |u_{2t}(x,t)|$. Since $|A_1 \Delta A_2 = \|s_1-s_2\|_{L^1[0,t_o]}$ and $|u_{2t}|$ is bounded, there is a constant $\bar{c}_1 = \bar{c}_1(u_2)$ such that with $c_2 := E$,

$$|I_1| \leq \|(u_1-u_2)(.,t_o)\|_{L^1[s_1(t_o),1]} + c_2\|(u_1-u_2)(s_1(.),.)\|_{L^1[0,t_o]} +$$

$$+ \bar{c}_1(u_2)\|s_1-s_2\|_{L^1[0,t_o]}.$$

Now we turn to estimating I_2. For this, we use the Mean-Value-Theorem to obtain with suitable $\xi(t) \in A_1 \Delta A_2$:

$$s_1'(t)s_2'(t)\left[\frac{u_{1t}(s_1(t),t)}{s_1'(t)} - \frac{u_{2t}(s_2(t),t)}{s_2'(t)}\right] = [s_2'(t)u_{1t}(s_1(t),t) - s_2'u_{2t}(s_1(t),t)] +$$

$$+ [s_2'u_{2t}(s_1(t),t) - s_1'(t)u_{2t}(s_1(t),t)] + [s_1'(t)u_{2t}(s_1(t),t) - s_1'(t)u_{2t}(s_2(t),t)] =$$

$= s_2'(t)(u_{1t}(s_1(t),t)-u_{2t}(s_1(t),t)) + u_{2t}(s_1(t),t)(s_2'(t)-s_1'(t)) +$

$+ s_1'(t)u_{2tx}(\xi(t),t)(s_1(t)-s_2(t)) =: F(t)$. Thus,

$$|I_2| = \left|\int_0^{t_o} \frac{F(t)}{s_1'(t)s_2'(t)}\,dt\right| \leq \int_0^{t_o} \left|\frac{F(t)}{s_1'(t)s_2'(t)}\right| dt \leq$$

$$\leq \int_0^{t_o} \left|\frac{1}{s_1'(t)s_2'(t)}\right| . \left|(u_1-u_2)_t(s_1(t),t)\right| . \left|s_2'(t)\right| dt +$$

$$+ \int_0^{t_o} \left|\frac{1}{s_1'(t)s_2'(t)}\right| . \left|u_{2t}(s_1(t),t)\right| . \left|s_2'(t)-s_1'(t)\right| dt +$$

$$+ \int_0^{t_o} \left|\frac{1}{s_1'(t)s_2'(t)}\right| . \left|u_{2tx}(\xi(t),t)\right| . \left|s_1(t)-s_2(t)\right| dt \leq$$

$$\leq \frac{1}{e} \int_0^{t_o} \left|(u_1-u_2)_t(s_1(t),t)\right| dt +$$

$$+ \frac{1}{e^2} \sup_{t\in[0,t_o]} \left|u_{2t}(s_1(t),t)\right| . \int_0^{t_o} \left|s_2'(t)-s_1'(t)\right| dt +$$

$$+ \frac{1}{e^2} \sup_{\xi\in A_1\Delta A_2} \left|u_{2tx}(\xi,t)\right| . \int_0^{t_o} \left|s_1(t)-s_2(t)\right| dt =:$$

$$=: c_3\|(u_1-u_2)_t(s_1(.),.)\|_{L^1[0,t_o]} + c_4(u_2)\|s_2'-s_1'\|_{L^1[0,t_o]} +$$

$$+ \tilde{c}_3(u_2)\|s_1-s_2\|_{L^1[0,t_o]} .$$

With $c_1(u_2) := \bar{c}_1(u_2) + \tilde{c}_3(u_2)$ we obtain (3.18) by combining the estimates for $|I_1|$ and $|I_2|$. □

Note that the only simplification of problem (3.13)- (3.17) compared to the transformed problem TP is that we omitted the temperature u on the right-hand side of the heat-flux boundary-condition (3.14). Proposition 3.17 gives quantitative information (even local Lipschitz-continuity) for the inverse problem, but only for one linear functional, namely the mean value of the solution on those time intervals $[0,t_0]$ for which we have information on the temperature at t_0.

References:

[1] D.L.Colton, "Analytic Theory of Partial Differential Equations", Pitman, Boston 198o.

[2] D.L.Colton, R.Reemtsen, "The Numerical Solution of the Inverse Stefan Problem in Two Space Variables", SIAM J.Appl.Math., Vol. 44, Nr. 5 (1984), pp. 996 - 1o13.

[3] H.W.Engl, T.Langthaler, "Numerical Solution of an Inverse Problem Connected with Continuous Casting of Steel", ZOR - Zeitschrift für Operations Research, Volume 29 (1985), pp. B185 - B199.

[4] A.Fasano, M.Primicerio, "General free boundary problems for the heat equation", J.Math.Anal.Appl. 59 (1977), pp. 1-14.

[5] P.Jochum, "The numerical solution of the Inverse Stefan Problem", Numer.Math. 34(198o), pp. 411 - 429.

[6] P.Knabner, "Fragen der Rekonstruktion und der Steuerung bei Stefan-Problemen und ihre Behandlung über lineare Ersatzaufgaben", Inauguraldissertation, Universität Augsburg 1983.

[7] O.A.Ladyženskaja, V.A.Solonnikov, N.N.Ural'ceva, "Linear and Quasilinear Equations of Parabolic Type", Translations of Mathematical Monographs, Vol. 23, Amer.Math.Soc., Providence 1968.

[8] P.Manselli, K.Miller, "Calculation of the Surface Temperature and Heat Flux on One Side of a Wall from Measurements on the Opposite Side", Annali di Matematica pura ed applicata (IV), Vol CXXIII (198o), pp. 161 - 183.

[9] M.H.Protter, H.E.Weinberger, "Maximum Principles in Differential Equations", Prentice Hall, Inc., Englewood Cliffs, N.J. 1967.

[1o] R.Reemtsen, A.Kirsch, "A Method for the Numerical Solution of the One-dimensional Inverse Stefan Problem", Numer.Math. 45 (1984), pp.253-273.

Authors' adresses:

Prof.Dr.H.Engl, Dipl.-Ing.T.Langthaler, Institut für Mathematik, Johannes-Kepler-Universität Linz, Altenbergerstraße 69, A-4o4o Linz, Austria.

Prof.Dr.P.Manselli, Istituto Matematico "Ulisse Dini", Università degli Studi, Viale Morgagni 67/A, I-5o134 Firenze, Italy.

International Series of
Numerical Mathematics, Vol. 78

CONVERGENCE OF SUBOPTIMAL CONTROLS FOR POINT TARGETS

H. O. Fattorini

Abstract. We consider sequences of suboptimal (i.e. close to optimal) controls in the context of optimal control problems for general input-output systems involving a point target condition. A *sequence maximum principle* for these sequences is obtained using Ekeland's variational principle, and is then applied to show convergence of suboptimal controls for quasilinear distributed parameter systems, both of parabolic and hyperbolic type.

1. INTRODUCTION

Recent developments in nonlinear analysis, such as Ekeland's variational principle, make now possible the development of a theory of optimal control for general nonlinear input-output maps without explicit reference to a state equation. This has been done in [2], [3], [4]; the final result in these works is a form of Pontryagin's maximum principle that applies equally well to input-output maps generated by ordinary differential equations, partial differential equations (distributed and boundary control), functional differential equations, etc. The optimal control problems considered deal with point target ([2], [4]) or set target conditions ([3], [4]). One advantage of the input-output approach is the simplicity and generality of the treatment; other, no less important, is that it is in the nature of Ekeland's variational principle that approximate maximum principles can be obtained for *suboptimal* (that is, close to optimal) controls, a fact that was exploited for the first time in [8] in relation to optimal control problems for hyperbolic equations. These approximate maximum principles can then be translated in certain situations into convergence results for suboptimal controls in L^p topologies. This was done in [5] and [6] for target sets; the results in [5] apply to quasilinear parabolic distributed parameter systems and to target sets satisfying the *fat cone condition* introduced in [3], while those in [6] apply to quasilinear hyperbolic distributed parameter systems, but are restricted to the time optimal problem and to balls as target sets. We sketch in this paper several results on convergence of sequences of suboptimal controls for general systems, this time for the point target problem, (see §2), whose proofs will appear in full in [7]. The strategy is about the same as that in [5] and [6] and consists of three steps. In the first, we establish a *sequence maximum principle*, that is, a separate approximate maximum principle for each of the suboptimal controls in the sequence. In the second, we combine these separate maximum principles into a *convergence principle*. The third step consists in translating the convergence principle into actual convergence of optimal controls. At this point, it seems more productive to descend from the level of general systems and work with particular examples, which we did in [5], [6] and [7] and we do here as well. The main difference between the treatment of set targets and point targets can be summarized as follows. In the set target case, the passage from the sequence maximum principle to the convergence principle is automatic if we choose carefully the function to which Ekeland's principle is applied. No controllability properties are necessary (either for the sequence maximum principle or for the convergence principle), although approximate controllability plays a role in the final convergence results. In contrast, in the point target case treated in this paper, the maximum principle and the convergence principle can only be deduced from the sequence maximum principle via controllability properties of the linearized system (see §5 and §6) and, in fact, may not be true when controllability is absent. This makes the point target problem more demanding than the set target problem. This is of course not news in the linear case, where the point target problem requires separation of a point from a convex set by a hyperplane (not always possible) whereas in the set target case we only have to separate two convex sets, one of them having an interior point. However, things are somewhat less trivial in the nonlinear nonconvex case, even for target sets with nonempty interior.

2. SYSTEMS. OPTIMAL CONTROL PROBLEMS

We summarize the setup of [2], [3] and [4]. E and F are arbitrary Banach spaces; U is a subset of F called the *control set*. Given $k \geq 0, T > 0,$ the *control space* $W(-k,T; U)$ is the set of all strongly measurable F-valued functions $u = u(t)$ defined in $-k \leq t \leq T$ such that $u(t) \in U$ a.e. The space $W(-k,T; U)$ is a complete metric space equipped with the distance

$$d(u,v) = \text{meas}\ \{t; u(t) \neq v(t)\}\ . \tag{2.1}$$

The *trajectory* or *output* space $C(0,T; E)$ consists of all E-valued continuous functions $y(t)$ defined in $0 \leq t \leq T$. We define a *system* as a map

$$X : W(-k,T; U) \to C(0,T; E) \tag{2.2}$$

that satisfies the following postulates: (a) *Causality*. Let $0 \leq \bar{t} \leq T$. Then the *trajectory* $y(t,u) = (Xu)(t)$ in $0 \leq t \leq \bar{t}$ depends only on the values of u in $0 \leq t \leq \bar{t}$. (b) *Pointwise continuity*. For $\bar{t}$ as in (a), the map

$$u(t) \to y(\bar{t},u)$$

from $W(-k,\bar{t}; U)$ into E is continuous. (c) *Differentiability* (with respect to spike variations). For every $u(t) \in W(-k,\bar{t};U)$ there exists a set $e = e(u)$ of full measure in $0 \leq t \leq \bar{t}$ such that, if $s \in e$, the limit

$$\xi(\bar{t},s,u,v,u(s)) = \lim_{\rho \to 0+} \rho^{-1}(y(\bar{t},u_{s,\rho,v}) - y(\bar{t},u)) \tag{2.3}$$

exists; here $u_{s,\rho,v}(t)$ is the *spike variation* of the control $u(t)$ defined by $u_{s,\rho,v}(t) = v$ in $s - \rho < t \leq \rho$, $u_{s,\rho,v}(t) = u(t)$ elsewhere.

At this level of generality, systems can be used to describe input-output relationships generated by a wide variety of state equations (not necessarily differential), or even more general entities. The constant k in the control space $W(-k,T; U)$ is meant to account for possible time delays in the control action (see [4] for examples where $k > 0$). In this paper, $k = 0$.

Let $X : W(-k,T; U) \to C(0,T; E)$ be a system as defined above and consider a second system $X_0 : W(-k; T; U) \to C(0,T; \mathbf{R})$ ($\mathbf{R}$ the real numbers) called the *cost functional*. We denote by $\xi_0(t,s,u,v,w)$ the function in (2.3) corresponding to the system X_0. The *augmented system* $\tilde{X}$ is defined by

$$(\tilde{X}u)(t) = ((X_0,X)u)(t) = (y_0(t,u),y(t,u)) , \tag{2.4}$$

where $y_0(t,u) = (X_0u)(t)$. We also use the notation $\tilde{y}(t,u) = (\tilde{X}u)(t)$ for the trajectories of the augmented system in $\mathbf{R} \times E$; in the same fashion, we write $\tilde{\xi}(t,s,u,v,w) = (\xi_0(t,s,u,v,w), \xi(t,s,u,v,w))$.

Optimal control problems are the usual ones: the target condition is

$$y(\bar{t},\bar{u}) = \bar{y}$$

and optimality means

$$y(\bar{t},\bar{u}) = m = \inf \ y(t,u) ,$$

the infimum taken over all times $t > 0$ and all controls $u(t)$ in $W(-k; t; U)$ such that $y(t,u) = \bar{y}$. Obviously, we have $-\infty < m < \infty$ if y_0 is bounded below and if $\bar{y}$ can be hit at all.

A control u in $W(-k,\bar{t}; U)$ is called $(\bar{t},\epsilon)$-*suboptimal* if

$$\|y(\bar{t},u) - \bar{y}\| \le \epsilon, \qquad y_0(\bar{t},u) \le m + \epsilon . \tag{2.5}$$

3. THE SEQUENCE MAXIMUM PRINCIPLE

Under an additional condition (see [7]) that guarantees, among other things, that $(\bar{t},\delta)$-suboptimal controls will satisfy $y_0(\bar{t},u) \ge m - \epsilon$ for δ small enough, we have the following result.

THEOREM 3.1 (*The sequence maximum principle*). *Let* $\{u^n\}$ *be a sequence of* (t_n,u^n)*- suboptimal controls with* $\{t_n\}$ *bounded,* $\epsilon_n \to 0$. *Then there exists a subsequence of* $\{u^n\}$ *(which we denote by the same symbol) such that*

$$(3.1) \qquad t_n \to \bar{t}, \qquad y_0(t_n,u^n) \to m, \qquad y(t_n,u^n) \to \bar{y}\,,$$

a second sequence $\{\bar{u}^n\}$ of controls with $\bar{u}^n \in W(-k,t_n;\,U)$ such that

$$(3.2) \qquad d_n(u^n,\bar{u}^n) \to 0\,,$$

a sequence $\{\tilde{y}^n\} = \{(\mu_n,y^n)\}$ in $\mathbf{R} \times E$ *with* $\|\tilde{y}^n\| = 1$ *and a set* e_n *of full measure in* $0 \le s \le t_n$ *such that*

$$(3.3) \qquad \mu_n\xi_0(t_n,s,\bar{u}^n,v,\bar{u}^n(s)) + \langle y^n,\xi(t_n,s,\bar{u}^n,v,\bar{u}^n(s))\rangle =$$

$$\langle \tilde{y}^n,\tilde{\xi}(t_n,s,\bar{u}^n,v,\bar{u}^n(s))\rangle \ge -\,\delta_n \to 0 \quad (v \in U,\ s \in e_n)\,.$$

For the proof, we apply Ekeland's variational principle ([1]) *to the function*

$$(3.4) \qquad F_n(u) = \{(y_0(t_n,u) - (m - \epsilon_n))^2 + \|y(t_n,u) - \bar{y}\|^2\}^{1/2}$$

in the metric space $W(-k,t_n;\,U)$ (which is complete) deducing existence of a control $\bar{u}^n \in W(-k,t_n;\,U)$ such that

$$(3.5) \qquad F_n(\bar{u}^n) \le F(u^n) = 5^{1/2}\,\epsilon_n\,,$$

$$(3.6) \qquad d_n(u^n,\bar{u}^n) \le 5^{1/4}\,\epsilon_n^{\ 1/2}\,,$$

$$(3.7) \qquad F_n(w) \ge F_n(\bar{u}^n) - 5^{1/4}\,\epsilon_n^{\ 1/2} d_n(w,\bar{u}^n) \qquad (w \in W(-k,t_n,U))\,.$$

We exploit (3.7) for spike variations $w = (\bar{u}^n)_{s,\rho,v}$ of $\bar{u}^n$ using (c) (see [3], [4]). The result is (3.3) with $\tilde{y}^n = (\mu_n,y^n) = (\lambda_n,x^n)/\|(\lambda_n,x^n)\|$,

$$(\lambda_n,x^n) = \tilde{y}(t_n,\bar{u}^n) - \tilde{y}_n = (y_0(t_n,\bar{u}^n) - (m - \epsilon_n),\ y(t_n,\bar{u}^n) - y_n))\,.$$

Obviously, (3.2) is a consequence of (3.6).

As usual, a separate theorem is required for the time optimal problem, where, since $\xi_0 = 0$, (3.3) may be empty (in case $\mu_n = 0$).

THEOREM 3.2 (*The sequence maximum principle for the time optimal problem*). *Let* $\{u^n\}$ *be a sequence of* (t_n,u^n)*-suboptimal controls with* $t_n < \bar{t}$, $\epsilon_n \to 0$. *Then there exists a* *subsequence of* $\{u^n\}$ *(which we denote with the same symbol) such that*

(3.8) $$t_n \to \bar{t}, \quad y(t_n,u^n) \to \bar{y}\,,$$

($\bar{t}$ *the optimal time), a sequence* $\{\tilde{u}^n\}$ *of controls,* $\tilde{u}^n \in W(-k,t_n;U)$ *such that*

(3.9) $$d_n(u^n,\tilde{u}^n) \to 0\,,$$

a sequence $\{y^n\}$ *in* E *such that* $\|y^n\| = 1$ *and a set* e_n *of full measure in* $0 \le s \le t_n$ *such that*

(3.10) $$\langle y^n, \xi(\bar{t}_n,s,\tilde{u}^n,v,\tilde{u}^n(s))\rangle \ge -\,\delta_n \to 0 \qquad (v \in U,\ s \in e_n)\,.$$

The proof is entirely similar to that of Theorem 3.1: we consider this time the function

(3.11) $$F_n(u) = \|y(t_n,u) - \bar{y}\|\,.$$

The vector y^n in (3.10) is $y^n = x^n/\|x^n\|$, where

$$x^n = y(t_n,\tilde{u}^n) - \bar{y}\,.$$

The condition that $t_n < t$ can be dropped (see [7]).

4. SYSTEMS DEFINED BY ABSTRACT DIFFERENTIAL EQUATIONS

Roughly speaking, a sequence maximum principle becomes a *convergence principle* if we can show that the sequence $\{y^n\}$ in (3.3) or (3.10) has a subsequence (denoted with the same symbol) such that

(4.1) $$y^n \to y \ne 0 \ \text{ weakly}\,.$$

In some cases (as seen below), (4.1) implies convergence of sequences of suboptimal controls; in others (see §9), weak convergence is not enough and we need to prove *strong* convergence of the subsequence. Of course, in case E is *finite dimensional*, the passage from the sequence maximum principle to the convergence principle is automatic via the Bolzano-Weierstrass theorem.

We consider below the initial value problem

$$y'(t) = Ay(t) + f(t,y(t),u(t)) \qquad (0 \le t \le T)\,, \tag{4.2}$$

$$y(0) = y_0\,, \tag{4.3}$$

where A is the infinitesimal generator of a strongly continuous semigroup $\{S(t); t \ge 0\}$ in the Banach space E. By definition, a *solution* of (4.2)-(4.3) is a continuous solution of the integrated version

$$y(t) = S(t)y_0 + \int_0^t S(t-\sigma)f(\sigma,y(\sigma),u(\sigma))\,d\sigma \qquad (0 \le t \le T)\,. \tag{4.4}$$

We assume that U is bounded, that $f(t,y,u)$ has a Fréchet derivative $\partial_y f(t,y,u)$ with respect to y and that f (resp. $\partial_y f$) is continuous (resp. strongly continuous) and bounded on bounded subsets of $[0,T] \times E \times U$. These conditions being satisfied, (4.4) can be locally solved by succesive approximations. To insure the solution can be extended to the whole interval $[0,T]$, we assume the *a priori* bound

$$\|y(t)\| \le C \qquad (0 \le t \le T_0)$$

for any solution of (4.4) in an arbitrary interval $[0,T_0]$. The system X is defined by

$$(Xu)(t) = y(t,u) = y(t)\,, \tag{4.5}$$

where $y(t)$ is the only solution of (4.4). We show easily that X satisfies postulates (a), (b) and (c) in §2: the function $\xi(t,s,u,v,w)$ in (2.3) is

$$\xi(t,s,u,v,w) = S(t,s;u)\,\{f(s,y(s,u),v) - f(s,y(s,u),w)\}\,. \tag{4.6}$$

where $S(t,s;u)$ is the solution operator of the *linearized equation* $z'(t) = (A + B(t))z(t)$, $B(t) = \partial_y f(t,y(t,u),u(t))$, that is, the only strongly continuous solution of the operator equation

$$S(t,s;u)z = S(t-s)z + \int_s^t S(t-\sigma)B(\sigma)S(\sigma,s;u)z\,d\sigma \tag{4.7}$$

$$(0 \le s \le t \le T)\,.$$

The operator $S(t,s;u)$ defined by (4.6) is strongly continuous in $0 \le s \le t \le T$. For complete proofs, see [4].

5. THE WEAK CONVERGENCE PRINCIPLE

We consider in this section the systems defined in §4. We assume from now on that the control set U is *bounded, closed and convex* and that the nonlinearity $f(t,y,u)$ in (4.2) has the form

$$f(t,y,u) = f(t,y) + Bu , \tag{5.1}$$

where $B : F \to E$ is a bounded operator. For simplicity, we treat only the time optimal problem: general cost functionals are handled in the same way (see [7] for full details).

In view of (3.10) we have

$$\langle y^n, S(t_n,s;\bar{u}^n)\,(v - \bar{u}^n(s))\rangle \ge -\,\delta_n \to 0 . \tag{5.2}$$

We take $v = v(s)$ in (5.2) ($v(s)$ a function in $W(-k; t_n; U)$) and integrate in $0 \le s \le t_n$. We obtain

$$\langle y^n, \int_0^{t_n} S(t_n,s;\bar{u}^n)Bv(s)\,ds - \int_0^{t_n} S(t_n,s;\bar{u}^n)B\bar{u}^n(s)\,ds\rangle \ge -\,\delta_n \to 0 . \tag{5.3}$$

In order to take advantage of (5.3), convergence of the right hand side in the scalar product must be proved. Assuming that $S(t)$ is compact for all $t > 0$, the three results below follow:

LEMMA 5.1. *The map* $(t,s;u) \to S(t,s;u)$ *is continuous in the uniform topology of operators for* $0 < s < t < \bar{t}$, $u \in W(0,\bar{t};U)$ *(* u *moving in the weak topology of* $L^2(0,\bar{t};F)$*).*

LEMMA 5.2. *The operator* $S(t,s;u)$ *is compact for* $0 < s < t < T$.

LEMMA 5.3. *Let* $\Lambda : L^2(0,T;E) \to C(0,T;E)$ *be the nonlinear operator defined by*

$$(\Lambda u)(t) = \int_0^t S(t,s;u)Bu(s)\,ds .$$

Let $\{u^n\}$ *be a sequence in* $W(0,\bar{t}; U)$ *converging weakly to* $u \in W(0,\bar{t}; U)$ *in the weak topology of* $L^2(0,\bar{t}; E)$. *Then, if necessary passing to a subsequence, we have*

$$\Lambda u^n(t) \to \Lambda u(t) \text{ uniformly in } 0 \leq t \leq \bar{t}.$$

The proofs are in [5] and [7].

Making use of Lemma 5.3, of the definition of suboptimal control and of the integral equation defining $S(t,s; u)$ we prove:

LEMMA 5.4. *Let* $\{\bar{u}^n\}$ *be the sequence in Theorem* 3.2. *Then there exists a subsequence of* $\{\bar{u}^n\}$ *such that*

$$\{\Lambda \bar{u}^n(t_n)\}$$

is convergent.

Let $\{\Delta_n\}$ be a sequence of sets in a Hilbert space H. We say that $\{\Delta_n\}$ *has full dimension* if the set

$$\Delta = \cap_{n\geq 1} \overline{\text{conv}}(\Delta_n)$$

has nonempty interior, where $\overline{\text{conv}}$ denotes closed convex hull.

LEMMA 5.5. *Let* $\{\Delta_n\}$ *be a sequence of sets in* H *having full dimension. Let* $\{y^n\}$ *be a sequence in* H *such that*

$$0 < c \leq \|y^n\| \leq C .$$

Assume that

$$\langle y^n, z\rangle \geq -\epsilon_n \to 0 \quad (z \in \Delta_n, n = 1,2,\ldots) .$$

Then there exists a subsequence of $\{y^n\}$ *that converges weakly to an element* $y \in H$, $y \neq 0$.

For the proof (of a more general statement), see [4, Lemma 5.6].

We take advantage of (5.3) as follows. Given $\bar{t} > 0$, $u \in W(0,\bar{t},U)$ we define

$K(0,\bar{t},u;U) \subseteq E$, (following [4]), as the set of all elements of E of the form

$$\int_0^{\bar{t}} S(t,s;u)Bv(s)\,ds \qquad (v \in W(0,\bar{t};U)) .$$

THEOREM 5.6 (*The weak convergence principle*). *Assume that, for each* $\bar{t} > 0$ *and* $u \in W(0,\bar{t};U)$ *the set* $K(0,\bar{t},u;U)$ *has nonempty interior. Then the sequence* $\{y^n\}$ *in* (5.2) *has a subsequence weakly convergent to an element* $y \neq 0$.

The proof is achieved noting that the hypotheses and Lemmas 5.1 and 5.4 imply that the sequence

$$\{K(0,t_n,\bar{u}^n;U) - \Lambda\bar{u}^n(t_n)\}$$

has full dimension, and applying Lemma 5.5; observe that, assuming (as we may) that $\{\bar{u}^n\}$ is weakly convergent, Lemma 5.1 can be used to show that, in an obvious sense, $K(0,t_n,\bar{u}^n;U) \to K(0,\bar{t},\bar{u};U)$ and Lemma 5.4 implies that $\Lambda\bar{u}^n(t_n) \to \Lambda\bar{u}(\bar{t})$.

6. THE STRONG CONVERGENCE PRINCIPLE

Let Δ be an arbitrary set in a Hilbert space H. We say that a point y in H is Δ- *regular* if and only if there exists a hyperplane

$$\Gamma(y,\bar{y}) = \{z;\langle z - y,\bar{y}\rangle = 0\} \tag{6.1}$$

(the vector $\bar{y}$, called the *generator* of Γ, satisfies $\|\bar{y}\| = 1$), a number $\rho > 0$ and a map $\Pi : S(y,\rho) \cap \Gamma(y,\bar{y}) \to \Delta$ ($S(y,\rho)$ the closed sphere of center y and radius ρ) such that

$$\|\Pi(z) - z\| \leq r(\|z - y\|)\ (\|z - y\| \leq \rho) \tag{6.2}$$

with

$$r(\mu) = o(\mu) \text{ as } \mu \to 0 . \tag{6.3}$$

For instance, we check easily that if Δ is a sphere, every point y on Δ or on the boundary of Δ is regular.

Let $\{\Delta_n\}$ be a sequence of sets in H and let $\{y_n\}$ be a sequence in H. We say that $\{y_n\}$ is $\{\Delta_n\}$*-regular* if and only if each y_n is Δ_n-regular with ρ and $r(\mu)$ independent of n; although the Π_n may depend on n, (6.2) must be uniform with respect to n.

LEMMA 6.1. *Let* $\{\Delta_n\}$ *be a sequence of sets in* H, *and let* $\{y_n\}$ *be a* $\{\Delta_n\}$*-regular sequence. Assume the sequence* $\{\bar{y}_n\}$ *of generators of the cones* $\Gamma(y_n,\bar{y}_n)$ *in* (6.1) *is strongly convergent to* $\bar{y} \in H$. *Let* $\{y^n\}$ *be a sequence in* H *such that* $\|y^n\| = 1$ *and*

$$\langle y^n, z_n - y_n \rangle \geq -\epsilon_n \to 0 \qquad (z_n \in \Delta_n) .$$

Then

$$y^n \to \bar{y} \text{ strongly in } H .$$

For the proof, see [7].

Under the compactness assumption on $S(t)$ used in the previous section we obtain.

THEOREM 6.2 (*The strong convergence principle*). *Assume that, for every convergent sequence* $\{t_n\}$ *and every weakly convergent sequence* $\{\bar{u}^n\}$ *in* $W(0,t_n;U)$ *the sequence* $\{\Lambda\bar{u}^n(t_n)\}$ *is* $\{K(0,t_n,\bar{u}^n;U)\}$*-regular, with* $\bar{y}_n \to \bar{y}$. *Then the sequence* $\{y^n\}$ *in* (5.2) *is strongly convergent.*

The proof is an immediate consequence of Lemma 6.1.

7. QUASILINEAR ABSTRACT PARABOLIC EQUATIONS

The weak convergence principle (Theorem 5.3) is of very limited use; in fact, compactness of $S(t)$ (needed for Lemma 5.2) precludes the set $K(0,\bar{t},u;U)$ from having nonempty interior, except when E is finite dimensional. Thus, it must be modified to yield usable results. In this section, besides the compactness assumption we require $S(t)$ to be an *analytic* semigroup and consider again the system (4.6) defined by the initial value problem (4.2)-(4.3). Translating A if necessary we may assume that

$\|S(t)\| \leq Ce^{-\beta t}$ $(t \geq 0)$ so that fractional powers $(-A)^{\alpha}$ exist. The function $f(t,y,u)$ is of the form (5.1). The smoothness assumptions on $f(t,y)$ are now assumed to be satisfied instead by $(-A)^{\alpha} f(t,y)$ for some $\alpha > 0$.

The entire theory must be modified. We *assume* now that the target point $\bar{y}$ belongs to $D(A)$. A control $u(t)$ is $(\bar{t},\epsilon)$-*suboptimal* if

$$\|Ay(\bar{t},u) - A\bar{y}\| \leq \epsilon, \;\; y_0(\bar{t},u) \leq m + \epsilon \tag{7.1}$$

that is, we must "aim at the target" in the norm of $D(A)$ rather than in that of E. Given a sequence of (t_n,ϵ_n)-suboptimal controls we use instead of (3.11) the function

$$F_n(u) = \|Ay(t_n,u) - A\bar{y}\| \tag{7.2}$$

in the space $W(0,t_n; U)$; we define $F_n(u) = +\infty$ if $y(t_n,u)$ does not belong to $D(A)$. It is easily shown that the function $F_n(u)$ is lower semicontinuous ([2, Lemma 7.4]), thus Ekeland's theorem can be applied. We obtain in this way the following version of Theorem 3.1:

THEOREM 7.1 (*The modified sequence maximum principle*). *Let $\{u^n\}$ be a sequence of (t_n,u^n)-suboptimal controls with $\epsilon_n \to 0$. Then there exists a subsequence of $\{u^n\}$ (which we denote by the same symbol) such that*

$$t_n \to \bar{t}, \qquad y_0(t_n,u^n) \to m, \qquad Ay(t_n,u^n) \to A\bar{y}\,, \tag{7.3}$$

a second sequence $\{\bar{u}^n\}$ of controls with $\bar{u}^n \in W(-k,t_n; U)$ such that

$$F_n(\bar{u}^n) < F_n(u^n) < \infty\,, \tag{7.4}$$

$$d_n(u^n,\bar{u}^n) \to 0\,, \tag{7.5}$$

a sequence $\{y^n\}$ in $D(A)$ such that $\|Ay^n\|^2 = 1$ and a set e_n of full measure in $0 \leq s \leq t_n$ such that

$$\langle Ay^n, AS(t_n,s; u)B(v - \bar{u}^n(s))\rangle \geq -\delta_n \to 0 \qquad (v \in U, s \in e_n)\,. \tag{7.6}$$

The modified sequence maximum principle is exploited much in the same way as (5.2). We take $v = v(s)$ and integrate in $0 \le s \le \bar{t}$:

(7.7) $$\langle Ay^n, A\int_0^{t_n} S(t_n,s;\bar{u}^n)Bv(s)\,ds - A\int_0^{t_n} S(t_n,s;\bar{u}^n)B\bar{u}^n(s)\,ds\rangle \ge -\delta_n \to 0 .$$

It is easy to see, using (4.7), that

(7.8) $$\int_0^{t_n} S(t_n,s;\bar{u}^n)B\bar{u}^n(s)\,ds \in D(A) .$$

On the other hand, it is not necessarily true that

(7.9) $$\int_0^{t_n} S(t_n,s;\bar{u}^n)Bv(s)\,ds \in D(A) ,$$

thus we only claim (7.7) for those $v \in W(0,t_n;\,U)$ that satisfy (7.9). We can prove (again on the basis of (4.7)) that

$$A\int_0^{t_n} S(t_n,s;\bar{u}^n)B\bar{u}^n(s)\,ds$$

is strongly convergent in E. This makes it plausible that a result of the type of Theorem 5.6 exists; however, there are difficulties with the convergence of

$$\int_0^{t_n} S(t_n,s;\bar{u}^n)Bv(s)\,ds$$

thus we only treat the particular case where

$$B = I$$

and where 0 is an interior point of U. We show easily that if $y \in D(A)$ then $S(t,s;\,u)y$, as a function of s, is continuously differentiable in $0 \le s \le t$ and satisfies

$$(S(t,s;\,u)y)' = -S(t,s;\,u)(A + \partial_y f(s,y(s,u)))y .$$

Accordingly, if we define $v_n(s) = \{y - s(A + \partial_y f(s,y(s,\bar{u}^n)))y\}/t$, then

$$\int_0^{t_n} S(t_n,s;\bar{u}^n)v_n(s)\,ds = y .$$

Since $v(s) \in W(0,t_n;\,U)$ for sufficiently small $\|Ay\|$, it follows that the sets $A(K(0,t_n,\bar{u}^n;\,U \cap D(A))$ contain a common open set. We have then shown the following result.

THEOREM 7.2. *Let the assumptions above on* $S(t)$, $f(t,s;u)$, U *and* B *hold. Then the sequence* $\{y^n\}$ *in* (7.6) *has a subsequence weakly convergent in* $D(A)$ *to an element* $y \neq 0$.

The proof follows from Lemma 5.5.

8. CONVERGENCE OF SEQUENCES OF SUBOPTIMAL CONTROLS

We illustrate with an example how convergence principles can be translated into convergence results for suboptimal controls. Let $\{u^n(t)\}$ be a sequence of suboptimal controls and let $\{\tilde{u}^n(t)\}$ be the sequence in Theorem 7.1, satisfying (7.4), (7.5) and (7.6). Under the hypotheses in the last section, this last inequality becomes

$$\langle A^*S(t_n,s;\tilde{u}^n)^*Ay^n, v - \tilde{u}^n(s)\rangle \geq -\delta_n \to 0 \qquad (v \in U,\ s \in e_n)\ . \tag{8.1}$$

Using the compactness and uniform continuity properties of $A^*S(t,s;u)^*$ (which, in $t > s$ are essentially the same as those of $S(t,s;u)$ or $S(t,s;u)^*$) we deduce that

$$A^*S(t_n,s;\tilde{u}^n)^*Ay^n \to A^*S(t,s;\bar{u})^*A\bar{y} \tag{8.2}$$

strongly, where $\bar{y}$ is the weak limit of y^n in $D(A)$).

Let $z \neq 0$, $U(z,\delta)$ the set of all $u \in U$ such that

$$\langle z, v - u\rangle \geq -\delta \qquad (v \in U)$$

(for the geometry of the situation, see [5]). In view of (8.2), we have

THEOREM 8.1. *Assume that the control set* U *is such that*

$$\operatorname{diam} U(z,\delta) \to 0 \qquad (\delta \to 0)\ . \tag{8.3}$$

Then, if the time optimal control $\bar{u}$ *is unique,* d *is the set of all* s *in* $0 \leq s \leq \bar{t}$ *(* $\bar{t}$ *the optimal time) where*

$$A^*S(\bar{t},s,\bar{u})^*Ay \neq 0\ , \tag{8.4}$$

and $a > 0$, *any sequence* $\{u^n\}$ *of* (t_n,ϵ_n)*-suboptimal controls with* $\epsilon_n \to 0$ *converges in* $L^p(d \cap (0,\bar{t} - a); F)$, $(1 \leq p < \infty)$ *to* $\bar{u}$.

We note that the convergence statements refer to the controls $\tilde{u}^n$ (rather than to the u^n), but, in view of (7.5), they apply to the u^n as well. Of course, L^p convergence follows from pointwise convergence and the dominated convergence theorem. The fact that the *entire* sequence (not just a subsequence) converges to $\bar{u}$ results from uniqueness of $\bar{u}$ (see [5] for additional details). Naturally, in case the optimal control is not unique, we can only insure convergence of a subsequence.

Condition (8.3) will be satisfied if U has a smooth boundary (for instance, for a sphere). For remarks on the set d, see [5]. See also [5] for applications of the results above to the case where A is an uniformly elliptic operator (plus a boundary condition) in a domain in Euclidean space.

9. THE NONCOMPACT CASE

In systems such as those defined by quasilinear hyperbolic equations in a domain Ω of Euclidean space (see [6] for the necessary technical details) compactness of the solution $S(t,s;u)$ of the linearized equation is out of the question. However, the resolvent $R(\lambda;A)$ of the principal part is compact when Ω is bounded, and this is enough to generalize most of the theory with small modifications which we outline below.

Lemma 5.3 is false as it stands, but the following weaker conclusion can be guaranteed after (if necessary) passing to a subsequence:

$$\Lambda u^n(t) \to \Lambda u(t) \ \text{ in } \ L^2(0,T;E) \ . \tag{9.1}$$

Weak convergence principles such as Theorem 5.6 are not much good here, since the operator $S(t,s;u)^*$ is merely strongly continuous in t, s and u (u moving in the weak L^2-topology) and lacks any compactness properties. Thus, we must look for strong convergence principles like Theorem 6.2. We note, however, that the requirement that $\{\Lambda\tilde{u}^n(t_n)\}$ be $\{K(t_n,\tilde{u}^n; U)\}$-regular is difficult to verify. One instance where this can be done is that where $E = F$, U is the unit sphere of F, $B = I$ and $A + \partial_y f(t,y(t,u))$ is *skew adjoint* for all t and u. In fact, in this case each operator $S(t,s;u)$ is isometric and invertible, which is easily seen to imply that, for each n,

$$K(0,t_n,\bar{u}^n; U) = t_n U \ .$$

Now, $\Lambda\bar{u}^n(t_n) \in K(0,t_n,\bar{u}^n; U)$ and every point y in $\Delta = aU$ $(a \neq 0)$ is Δ-regular (with $\bar{y} = y/\|y\|$). Accordingly, Theorem 6.2 applies: convergence of suboptimal controls is achieved by the methods of §8.

10. GENERAL REMARKS

It is possible that Theorem 6.2 applies to systems described by quasilinear hyperbolic equations in bounded sets of n-dimensional space; however, we are as yet unable to prove this.

One (and by not means the least) fascinating feature about this Oberwolfach conference was to be next door to a meeting on Inverse Problems, and to participate in an evening free-for-all on the relation (if any) between optimal control problems and inverse problems. In the spirit of that discussion, I cannot help but remark that this paper might be titled "Stabilization of an Inverse Problem" (that problem being the notoriously ill-posed one of driving a system to a preassigned target) by means of a minimization requirement.

REFERENCES

1. I. Ekeland, Nonconvex minimization problems, Bull. Amer. Math. Soc. 1 (NS) (1979), 443-474.

2. H. O. Fattorini, The maximum principle for nonlinear nonconvex systems in infinite dimensional spaces, Proceedings of the 2nd. Conference on Control Theory of Distributed Parameter Systems, Vorau, 1984, Springer Lecture Notes in Control and Information Sciences 75 (1976), 162-178.

3. H. O. Fattorini, The maximum principle for nonlinear nonconvex systems with set targets, Proceedings of the 24th. IEEE Conference on Decision and Control, Fort Lauderdale, 1985.

4. H. O. Fattorini, A unified theory of necessary conditions for nonlinear nonconvex control systems, to appear in Appl. Math. Optimization.

5. H. O. Fattorini, Optimal control of nonlinear systems: convergence of suboptimal controls, I, to appear in Proceedings of Special Session on Operator Methods in Optimal Control Problems, Annual AMS Meeting, New Orleans, January 1986.

6. H. O. Fattorini, Optimal control of nonlinear systems: convergence of suboptimal controls, II, to appear in Proceedings of IFIP Workshop on Control Systems Described by Partial Differential Equations, Gainesville, February 1986.

7. H. O. Fattorini, Convergence of suboptimal controls: the point target case, to appear.

8. V. I. Plotnikov and M. I. Sumin, The construction of minimizing sequences in problems of control of systems with distributed parameters, Z. Vyčisl. Mat. i Mat. Fiz. 22 (1982), 49-56.

H. O. Fattorini
University of California
Department of Mathematics
Los Angeles, California 90024
U.S.A.

This research was supported in part by the National Science Foundation under grant DMS 82-00645.

International Series of
Numerical Mathematics, Vol. 78

ON STATE CONSTRAINED OPTIMAL SHAPE DESIGN PROBLEMS

J. Haslinger[1], P.Neittaanmäki[2] and D. Tiba[3]

[1]Faculty of Mathematics and Physics, Charles University, Czechoslovakia

[2]University of Jyväskylä, Department of Mathematics, Finland

[3]INCREST, Department of Mathematics, Romania

1. Introduction

This paper is concerned with the following optimal design problem with constraints both on the state and on the control:

$$\text{(P)} \qquad \text{Minimize } J(y,u)$$

subject to

$$A(u)y + \partial\varphi(y) \ni Bu + f \,, \tag{1.1}$$

$$y \in K \,, \tag{1.2}$$

$$u \in U_{ad} \,. \tag{1.3}$$

Above, we consider Banach spaces V, U with $U_{ad} \subset U$, $K \subset V$ convex, closed subsets, $f \in V^*$, $B : U \to V^*$ (the dual space) a linear continuous operator and $\varphi : V \to]-\infty, +\infty]$ a convex, lower semicontinuous, proper function.

For each $u \in U_{ad}$, $A(u) : V \to V^*$ is a linear, continuous operator. The precise hypothesis will be specified in the next sections, as needed.

Equation (1.1) is a variational inequality and we also use the variational inequality method [5], [7] in the treatment of the state constraints.

In order to motivate the study of the abstract control problem (P) we consider several examples which enter into this setting.

A) Let us define:

$$
\begin{aligned}
& V = H_0^2(0,1)\ ,\ U = C(0,1)\ ,\ B = 0\ ,\ \varphi = 0\ , \\
& U_{ad} = \{u \in W^{1,\infty}(0,1)\ ;\ 0 < \alpha \le u(x) \le \beta\ , |u'(x)| \le \gamma \text{ a.e. } [0,1]\}\ , \\
& K = \{y \in H_0^2(0,1)\ ;\ |y(x)| \le r\}\ , \\
& J(y,u) = \int_0^1 u(x)\,dx\ ,\ A(u)y = (uy'')''\ .
\end{aligned}
$$

This is the model of a beam with fixed end points, with load f and cross section $u(x)$, $x \in [0,1]$. We minimize the weight (equivalently, the volume) of the beam. The constraint $u \in U_{ad}$ is of a technological nature and, moreover, we require that the deflection of the beam remains within certain limits.

This type of problem is considered for example in [**6**].

B)

$$
\begin{aligned}
& V = \{y \in H^2(0,1)\ ;\ y(0) = y'(0) = 0\}\ ,\ U = C(0,1)\ , \\
& J(y,u) = \frac{1}{2}\,|y - y_0|_V^2\ ,\ y_0 \in V \text{ given,} \\
& U_{ad} = \{u \in W^{1,\infty}(0,1)\ ;\ 0 < \alpha \le u(x) \le \beta\ ,\ |u'(x)| \le \gamma \text{ a.e. } [0,1]\ ; \\
& \qquad \int_0^1 u(x)\,ds = M > 0\}\ , \\
& K = V \text{ (no state constraints)}\ , \\
& \varphi : V \to]-\infty, +\infty] \text{ given by} \\
& \qquad \varphi(y) = \begin{cases} 0 & y(1) \ge 0\ , \\ +\infty & \text{otherwise}\ , \end{cases} \\
& f,\ A(u),\ B \text{ are the same as above}\ .
\end{aligned}
$$

This is a beam fixed at 0 and simply supported at 1. The weight of the beam is prescribed and we require that the deflection y of the beam is close to a given deflection y_0.

An example of this type was considered by Hlaváček, Bock, Lovíšek [**3**].

C)

$$V = H_0^2(0,1)\ ;\ K = L^2(0,1)\ ,$$

$$U_{ad} = \{u \in L^\infty(0,1)\ ;\ \alpha \le u(x) \le \beta\ ;\ \int_0^1 u(x)\,dx = M\}\ ,$$

$\varphi : V \to]-\infty, +\infty]$ is given by

$$\varphi(y) = \begin{cases} 0 & y \ge -1 \text{ a.e. } [0,1]\ , \\ +\infty & \text{otherwise}\ , \end{cases}$$

$$J(y,u) = -\int_0^1 (1 + y(x))\,dx\ ,\ f \in V^*\ ,$$

$A(u)y = y^{(4)}$ is independent of u ,

$B : U \to H^{-2}(0,1)$ is the natural imbedding.

The beam is fixed at both end points and is not allowed to pass through the obstacle $y = -1$.

Parameter u is no longer the cross section, but rather a certain load. The significance of the problem is to maximize the area between the beam and the obstacle.

This type of example was solved by Gh. Morosanu, Zheng-Xu He [4].

D) Let Ω_u be the domain in $\mathbf{R}^3$ given by

$$\Omega_u = \{(x_1, x_2, x_3)\ ;\ 0 < x_3 < 1\ ;\ x_1^2 + x_2^2 < u(x_3)^2\}\ ,$$

where $u \in U_{ad} = \{u \in C^2(0,1)\ ;\ u(x) \ge 0,\ u(0) = 1,\ |u|_{C^2(0,1)} \le a\}$. Let us denote

$$\Gamma_1 = \{(x_1, x_2, 0)\ ;\ x_1^2 + x_2^2 \le 1\}\ ,$$

$$\Gamma_2 = \{(x_1, x_2, x_3)\ ;\ x_1^2 + x_2^2 = u(x_3)^2,\ x_3 \in [0,1]\}\ ,$$

$$\Gamma_3 = \{(x_1, x_2, 1)\ ;\ x_1^2 + x_2^2 \le u(1)^2\}\ .$$

We consider the optimization problem:

$$\text{Minimize} \int_0^1 u(z)\,dz$$

subject to:

$$\begin{aligned} &\Delta y = 0 && \text{in } \Omega_u\ , \\ &\frac{\partial y}{\partial n} = q_{in} && \text{in } \Gamma_1\ , \\ &\frac{\partial y}{\partial n} = 0 && \text{in } \Gamma_2\ , \\ &\frac{\partial y}{\partial n} + \alpha y = q_e && \text{in } \Gamma_3\ ,\ \alpha > 0\ , \end{aligned}$$

and the state constraints $y|_{\Gamma_1} \le y_f$.

This is the problem of the design of a space radiator and was studied by the penalization method by Delfour, Payre and Zolesio [**2**].

By scaling the domain Ω_u so that it becomes fixed, the optimization parameter u appears as a coefficient in the partial differential operator and we obtain a problem of type (P) with $A(u)$ generated by the bilinear form

$$a_u(y,v) = \int_\Omega \left(\frac{\partial y}{\partial x_1}, \frac{\partial y}{\partial x_2}, u\frac{\partial y}{\partial x_3} - \frac{\partial y}{\partial x_1}u'x_1 - \frac{\partial y}{\partial x_2}u'x_2\right)\cdot$$

$$\left(\frac{\partial v}{\partial x_1}, \frac{\partial v}{\partial x_2}, u\frac{\partial v}{\partial x_3} - \frac{\partial v}{\partial x_1}u'x_1 - \frac{\partial v}{\partial x_2}u'x_2\right) dx_1dx_2dx_3$$

$$+\alpha u^2(1) \int_{x_1^2+x_2^2\le 1} yv\, dx_1dx_2 \ ,$$

where "$\cdot$" is the scalar product in $\mathbf{R}^3$ and

$$\Omega = \{(x_1,x_2,x_3) \in \mathbf{R}^3 \ ; \ x_1^2 + x_2^2 < 1, \ x_3 \in]0,1[\} \ .$$

We remark that A does not depend linearly on u.

In this case we have $V = H^1(\Omega)$, $U = H^1(\Omega)$, $f = 0$, $B = 0$, $\varphi = 0$ and $K = \{y \in H^1(\Omega) \ ; \ y|_{\Gamma_1} \le y_f\}$.

The outline of the paper is as follows. In section 2 we discuss the existence of optimal pairs for problem (P). Section 3 is devoted to the discretization of (P), while in section 4 we apply the variational inequality approach to the finite dimensional problem.

2. Existence

We assume that $A(u) : V \to V^*$ is generated by a bilinear, continuous form

(2.1) $$[A(u)y, v] = a_u(y,v) \qquad \forall v \in V \ ,$$

which satisfies:

(2.2) $$a_u(y,y) \ge \omega\, |y|_V^2 \ , \ \omega > 0 \ , \ \forall u \in U_{ad} \ ,$$

(2.3) $$a_u(y,v) = a_u(v,y) \ ,$$

(2.4) $$A(u_n) \to A(u) \text{ in } L(V,V^*) \text{ for } u_n \to u \text{ in } U \ .$$

Here $[\cdot,\cdot]$ is the pairing between V and V^*.

Obviously $A(u) + \partial\varphi$ is maximal monotone in $V \times V^*$ and coercive, therefore (1.1) has a unique solution $y \in V$ for all $u \in U_{ad}$.

Let $J : V \times U \to]-\infty, +\infty]$ be a convex, lower semicontinuous, proper functional. The following existence result is quite standard.

Theorem 2.1. *Suppose that either a) or b) or c) is true:*

a) $U_{ad} \subset U$ *compact;*

b) $K \subset V$ *compact,* $U_{ad} \subset U$ *bounded and* $A(\cdot)$ *is linear, continuous in* u*,*

c) $a(\cdot,\cdot)$ *is independent of* u *and* U_{ad} *is bounded.*

Then $(\grave{P})$ *has at least one optimal pair* $\{y^*, u^*\}$ *if it has admissible pairs.*

Proof.

a) Let $\{u_n\} \subset U_{ad}$ be a minimizing sequence and $u_n \to u$ strongly in U.

Multiply (1.1) by y_n, the solution corresponding to u_n. From (2.2) we see that $\{y_n\}$ is bounded in V and $y_n \to y$ weakly in V, on a subsequence.

Obviously $y \in K$, $u \in U_{ad}$. We have

$$\begin{aligned}
&|[A(u_n)y_n, v] - [A(u)y, v]| \\
&\le |[A(u_n)y_n, v] - [A(u)y_n, v]| + |[A(u)y_n, v)] - [A(u)y, v]| \\
&\le |v|_V \; |A(u_n)y_n - A(u)y_n|_{V^*} + |[y_n - y, A(u)v]| \\
&\le |v|_V \; |A(u_n) - A(u)|_{L(V,V^*)} \; |y_n|_V + |[y_n - y, A(u)v]| \to 0 \text{ as } n \to \infty
\end{aligned}$$

since $y_n \to y$ weakly in V and $A(u_n) \to A(u)$ in $L(V, V^*)$. Therefore $A(u_n)y_n \to A(u)y$ weakly in V^*.

Furthermore, we obtain by (2.2)

$$\begin{aligned}
&\liminf\, [A(u_n)y_n, y_n - y] \ge \liminf\, [A(u_n)y, y_n - y] \\
&= \lim\, [A(u_n)y_n, y] - \lim\, [A(u_n)y, y] = 0\,.
\end{aligned}$$

We multiply (1.1) by $y_n - y$

$$[A(u_n)y_n, y_n - y] + \varphi(y_n) \le [Bu_n + f, y_n - y] + \varphi(y)\,.$$

Then

$$\limsup\, [A(u_n)y_n, y_n - y] \le \varphi(y) - \liminf\, \varphi(y_n) = 0\,.$$

We conclude that

$$\lim\ [A(u_n)y_n, y_n - y] = 0\ .$$

On the other hand, by (2.2)

$$[A(u_n)y_n - A(u_n)y, y_n - y] \geq \omega\, |y_n - y|_V^2$$

so $y_n \to y$ strongly in V. By the demiclosedness of $\partial\varphi$ we can pass to the limit and prove that y is the solution of (1.1) corresponding to u. Then $\{y, u\}$ is an optimal pair which we denote $\{y^*, u^*\}$.

b) Let $\{u_n\}$ be a minimizing sequence. Then, by hypothesis $\{u_n\}$ is bounded and $y_n \to y$ strongly in V. Moreover

$$\begin{aligned} &|[A(u_n)y_n - A(u)y, v]| \\ &\leq |[A(u_n)y_n - A(u_n)y, v]| + |[A(u_n)y - A(u_n)y, v]| \\ &\leq |A(u_n)|_{L(V,V^*)}\ |y_n - y|_V\ |v|_V + |[A(u_n)y - A(u)y, v]|\ . \end{aligned}$$

The operator $A : U \to L(V, V^*)$ is linear, continuous and therefore $\{A(u_n)\}$ is bounded in $L(V, V^*)$ and $[A(u_n)y - A(u)y, v] \to 0$ as $n \to \infty$.

The proof proceeds as for a). Part c) is a wellknown result.

3. Discretization

Let us assume that a) is valid, i.e. $U_{ad} \subset U$ is compact. We describe the discretization of problem (P) and we prove the convergence of the sequence of finite dimensional solutions as h, the discretization parameter, tends to zero. With any $h \in (0, 1)$ we associate:

- finite dimensional subspaces $V_h \subset V$, $U^h \subset U$;
- closed, convex subsets $K_h \subset V_h$ (the approximations of K);
- closed, convex subsets $U_{ad}^h \subset U^h$ (approximations of U_{ad});
- bilinear forms $a_{u_h}^h : V_h \times V_h \to \mathbf{R}$, $u_h \in U_{ad}^h$ (approximations of a_u);
- $\varphi_h : V_h \to]-\infty, +\infty]$ convex, lower semicontinuous, proper functions (approximations of φ);
- $f_h \in V_h^*$, $B_h \in L(U^h, V_h^*)$ (approximation of f and B);
- $J_h : V_h \times U_h \to \mathbf{R}$ convex, lower semicontinuous, proper functions (approximations of the cost functional J).

Let us note that we do not necessarily have $K_h \subset K$ and $U^h_{ad} \subset U_{ad}$. If, however this is true for any $h \in (0,1)$, we say that we have an internal approximation of K, respectively U_{ad}.

The approximation of the state equation (1.1) is now defined by means of the Ritz-Galerkin procedure:

$$
\begin{aligned}
&a^h_{u_h}(y_h, v_h - y_h) + \varphi_h(v_h) - \varphi_h(y_h) \\
&\geq [f_h + B_h u_h, v_h - y_h]_h\,, \qquad \forall v_h \in V_h\,,
\end{aligned}
\tag{3.1}
$$

where $u_h \in U^h_{ad}$ and $[\cdot,\cdot]_h$ means the pairing between V_h and V^*_h. Denote by

$$
\begin{aligned}
X &= \{u \in U_{ad} \mid y(u) \in K\}\,, \\
X_h &= \{u_h \in U^h_{ad} \mid y_h(u_h) \in K_h\}\,,
\end{aligned}
$$

where $y(u)$ is the solution of (1.1) corresponding to u and $y_h(u_h)$ is given similarly by (3.1). We assume that $X \neq \emptyset$, $X_h \neq \emptyset$ for any $h > 0$.

By the discretization of (P) we mean the problem:

$$
\min\ J_h(y_h(u_h), u_h) \tag{P_h}
$$

for $u_h \in X_h$ and $y_h(u_h)$ as above.

By $\{y^*_h, u^*_h\}$ we denote an optimal pair for (P_h) (the existence may be established as in §2). In what follows, we shall study the relation between optimal pairs of (P_h) and (P) as $h \to 0$.

First we analyze the relation between (3.1) and (1.1). We shall need the following hypotheses:

(H1) $\exists\tilde{\alpha} > 0 \; : \; a^h_{u_h}(v_h, v_h) \geq \tilde{\alpha}\,|v_h|^2_V \; , \; \forall v_h \in V_h \; , \; \forall u_h \in U^h_{ad} \; ;$

(H2) $\exists\tilde{M} > 0 \; : \; |a^h_{u_h}(y_h, v_h)| \leq \tilde{M}\,|y_h|_V \;\; |v_h|_V \; ,$

$\forall y_h, v_h \in V_h \; , \; \forall u_h \in U^h_{ad} \; , \; h \in (0,1) \; ;$

(H3) $u_h \to u \; , \; y_h \to y$ weakly in V , $v_h \to v$

$\Rightarrow \; a^h_{u_h}(y_h, v_h) \to a_u(y, v) \; ;$

(H4) $u_h \to u \; , \; y_h \to y$ weakly in V

$\Rightarrow \; \liminf_{h\to 0} \; a^h_{u_h}(y_h, y_h) \geq a_u(y, y) \; ;$

(H5) $v_h \to v \; \Rightarrow \; \varphi_h(v_h) \to \varphi(v) \; , \; v_h \in V_h \; ;$

(H6) $v_h \to v$ weakly in $V \; \Rightarrow \; \liminf_{h\to 0} \; \varphi_h(v_h) \geq \varphi(v) \; ;$

(H7) $\exists\lambda \in V^*$ and $\mu \in \mathbf{R}$ such that

$\varphi_h(v_h) \geq [\lambda, v_h] + \mu \quad \forall v_h \in V_h \; , \; \forall h \in (0,1) \; ;$

(H8) $\exists C > 0 \; : \; |[f_h, v_h]_h| \leq C\,|v_h|_V \; , \; \forall v_h \in V_h \; , \; \forall h \in (0,1) \; ;$

(H9) $v_h \to v$ weakly in $V \; \Rightarrow \; [f_h, v_h]_h \to [f, v]$ as $h \to 0$;

(H10) $u_h \in U^h_{ad} \; , \; |u_h|_U \leq c \; \Rightarrow$

$|[B_h u_h, v_h]_h| \leq C\,|v_h|_V \; , \; \forall v_h \in V_h \; , \; \forall h \in (0,1) \; ;$

(H11) $u_h \to u \; , \; v_h \to v$ weakly in V

$\Rightarrow \; [B_h u_h, v_h]_h \to [Bu, v]_h$ as $h \to 0$;

(H12) $\forall v \in V \; \exists v_h \in V_h \; : \; v_h \to v \; , \; h \to 0 \; .$

Proposition 3.1. *Under the above hypotheses, let $u_h \in U^h$ be such that $u_h \to u$ as $h \to 0$. Then $y_h(u_h) \to y(u)$ strongly in V.*

Proof. From (3.1) we see that $\{y_h(u_h)\}$ is bounded in V with respect to $h \in (0,1)$.

Let $y_h(u_h) \to y$ weakly in V on a subsequence and let $v \in V$ be arbitrary. By (H12) we find $v_h \in V_h$ such that $v_h \to v$ in V. Using (H6), (H5), (H3), (H4) we can pass to the limit in (3.1) and obtain:

$$a_u(y, v - y) + \varphi(v) - \varphi(u) \geq [f + Bu, v - y] \; , \; \forall v \in V \; ,$$

therefore $y = y(u)$ and $y_h(u_h) \to y(u)$ weakly in V.

To see that the convergence is strong we use (H1):

$$\begin{aligned}\tilde{\alpha}\,|y_h(u_h) - z_h|_V^2 &\le a^h_{u_h}(y_h(u_h) - z_h, y_h(u_h) - z_h)\\ &\le [f_h + B_h u_h, y_h(u_h) - z_h]_h + \varphi_h(z_h) - \varphi_h(y_h(u_h))\\ &\quad - a^h_{u_h}(z_h, y_h(u_h) - z_h)\ .\end{aligned} \tag{3.2}$$

Here $z_h \in V_h$ is chosen by (H12) such that $z_h \to y(u)$ in V.

By (3.2) and (H5), the proof is finished.

Now we are able to study the relation between optimal pairs of (P_h) and (P). We need some additional assumptions:

(K1) the family $\{U^h_{ad}\}$ is compact in the following sense: in any $\{u_h\}$, $u_h \in U^h_{ad}$ there is a subsequence $\{u_{h'}\} \subset \{u_h\}$ such that $u_{h'} \to u \in U_{ad}$;

(K2) $y_h \to y\ ,\ y_h \in K_h\ \Rightarrow\ y \in K$;

(K3) $\forall u \in X\ ,\ \exists u_h \in X_h\ :\ u_h \to u$;

(K4) $:\ y_h \to y\ ,\ y_h \in V_h\ ,\ u_h \to u\ ,\ u_h \in U^h\ \Rightarrow\ J_h(y_h, u_h) \to J(y,u)\ ,\ h \to 0$.

Theorem 3.2. *Let $\{y^*_h, u^*_h\}$ be an optimal pair of (P_h). Then there exists a subsequence $\{y^*_{h'}, u^*_{h'}\}$ such that $y^*_{h'} \to y^*$, $u^*_{h'} \to u^*$, where $\{y^*, u^*\}$ is an optimal pair of (P).*

Proof. From (K1), it follows that there exists a subsequence (denoted by $\{u^*_{h'}\}$) such that $u^*_{h'} \to u \in U_{ad}$. Applying Proposition 3.1 we see that $y^*_{h'} \to y(u)$ strongly in V. Moreover $y(u) \in K$ by (K2), that is $u \in X$. The definition of (P_h) yields:

$$J_{h'}(y^*_{h'}, u^*_{h'}) \le J_{h'}(y_{h'}(u_{h'}), u_{h'})\ ,\ \text{any } u_{h'} \in X_{h'}\ . \tag{3.3}$$

Let $\tilde{u} \in X$ be given. One can find a sequence $\tilde{u}_{h'} \in X_{h'}$ such that $\tilde{u}_{h'} \to \tilde{u}$ in U, by (K3). Again we have $y_{h'}(\tilde{u}_{h'}) \to y(\tilde{u})$ and, by (3.3) and (K4), we get:

$$J(y(u), u) \le J(y(\tilde{u}), \tilde{u})\ ,\ \forall \tilde{u} \in X$$

and the proof is finished.

Remark 3.3. Similar results may be obtained when conditions b) or c) from §2 are assumed.

We close this section with an example of the same type as A) in §1, which justifies the abstract setting considered above.

Let $V = H^2_0(0,1)$, $U = C(0,1)$ and

$$\begin{aligned}U_{ad} &= \{u \in W^{1,\infty}(0,1)\ ;\ 0 < \alpha \le u(x) \le \beta,\ |u'(x)| \le \gamma\}\ ,\\ K &= \{y \in V\ ;\ |y(x)| \le r \text{ in } [0,1],\ r > 0\}\ .\end{aligned}$$

Let $A(u)y = (uy'')''$, $B \equiv 0$, $\varphi \equiv 0$. The state equation becomes

$$A(u)y = f \ , \qquad f \in L^2(0,1) \ , \tag{3.4}$$

$$y(0) = y'(0) = y'(1) = y(1) = 0 \ . \tag{3.5}$$

Finally, let

$$J(y,u) = \int_0^1 u(x)\, dx \ . \tag{3.6}$$

Obviously U_{ad} is a compact subset of U, that is condition a) is fulfilled.

The optimum design problem (P), corresponding to this example, has at least one optimal pair $\{y^*, u^*\}$ if X is nonempty.

Let $D_h : 0 = a_0 < a_1 < \cdots < a_{n(h)} = 1$ be a partition of $(0,1)$ with norm h tending to zero. Moreover we assume that the family $\{D_h\}$ is regular, i.e. :

$$\exists \beta > 0 \text{ such that } \frac{h}{h_{min}} \le \beta \ ,$$

where $h_{min} = \min |a_i - a_{i-1}|$. Let

$$\begin{aligned} V_h &= \{v_h \in C^1(0,1) \ ; \ v_h|_{\overline{a_{i-1}a_i}} \in P_3 \ , \\ &\qquad v_h(0) = v_h'(0) = v_h(1) = v_h'(1) = 0\} \ , \\ U^h &= \{u_h \in C(0,1) \ ; \ u_h|_{\overline{a_{i-1}a_i}} \in P_1\} \ , \\ U_{ad}^h &= U^h \cap U_{ad} \ , \\ K_h &= \{v_h \in V_h \ ; \ |v_h(a_i)| \le r + h^q \ , \ \forall i\} \ , \end{aligned}$$

where $q \in (0,1)$ is given. It is easy to see that $K_h \not\subset K$. The approximation of the state equation reads as follows:

$$\int_0^1 u_h y_h'' v_h''\, dx = \int_0^1 f v_h\, dx \ , \ \forall v_h \in V_h \ . \tag{3.7}$$

Here we assume that $a_{u_h}^h \equiv a_{u_h}$, $[f_h, v_h]_h \equiv [f, v_h] \equiv \int_0^1 f v_h\, dx$, $J_h(y_h(u_h), u_h) = J(y_h(u_h), u_h)$, i.e. no numerical integration is used in the problem. The approximation of (P) is obvious now.

By the above choice (H1), (H2), (H8), (H9) are satisfied. Also (H5), (H6), (H7), (H10), (H11) are satisfied as $\varphi_h \equiv 0$, $B_h \equiv 0$, $h \in (0,1)$.

Let us check (H3), (H4). If $u_h \to u$ uniformly in $[0,1]$, $y_h \to y$ weakly in $H_0^2(0,1)$, $v_h \to v$ in $H_0^2(0,1)$ then

$$\begin{aligned}
&\int_0^1 u_h y_h'' v_h''\, dx \\
&= \int_0^1 (u_h - u) y_h'' v_h''\, dx + \int_0^1 u y_h'' (v_h'' - v'')\, dx + \int_0^1 u y_h'' v''\, dx \\
&\to \int_0^1 u y'' v''\, dx
\end{aligned}$$

and

$$\begin{aligned}
&\liminf_{h\to 0} \int_0^1 u_h y_h'' y_h''\, dx \\
&\geq \liminf_{h\to 0} \int_0^1 u y_h'' y_h''\, dx + \lim_{h\to 0} \int_0^1 (u_h - u) y_h'' y_h''\, dx \\
&\geq \int_0^1 u y'' y''\, dx
\end{aligned}$$

From the density of $\mathcal{D}(0,1)$ in $H_0^2(0,1)$ and wellknown properties of V_h we see that (H12) holds as well.

Arzela-Ascoli theorem and the definition of U_{ad}^h yield (K1). Also (K2) and (K4) are satisfied. The crucial point is to prove (K3).

Let $u \in X$ (assumed nonvoid) and $\overline{u}_h \in U^h$ be its piecewise linear Lagrange interpolate, i.e. a function from U^h such that

$$\overline{u}_h(a_i) = u(a_i) \ , \ \forall i \ .$$

Clearly $\overline{u}_h \in U_{ad}^h$ and

$$|u - \overline{u}_h|_{L^\infty(0,1)} \leq ch\, |u|_{W^{1,\infty}(0,1)} \leq ch \ . \tag{3.8}$$

Let $y(u) \in V$ be the solution of (1.1) and $y_h(\overline{u}_h) \in V_h$ be the solution of (3.1). Taking into account (3.8), a standard estimate gives

$$|y(u) - y_h(\overline{u}_h)|_{H^2(0,1)} \leq ch\, |y(u)|_{H^3(0,1)} \leq ch \ .$$

Therefore, as $y(u) \in K$, $y_h(\overline{u}_h) \in K_h$ for h sufficiently small and (K3) is proved.

4. The variational inequality approach

Let h be fixed, sufficiently small. Consider the discrete problem, in abstract form:

$$(\mathrm{P}_h) \qquad \min \; J_h(y_h, u_h)$$

subject to $u_h \in U_{ad}^h$, y_h given by:

$$(4.1) \qquad \begin{aligned} &a_{u_h}^h(y_h, v_h - y_h) + \varphi_h(v_h) - \varphi_h(y_h) \\ &\geq [f_h + B_h u_h, v_h - y_h]_h \quad, \forall v_h \in V_h \end{aligned}$$

(see (3.1)) and state constraints

$$(4.2) \qquad y_h \in K_h \; .$$

The notations are the same as in §3. Let ψ_h be the indicator function of K_h in V_h. We associate with (P_h) the unconstrained approximate problem

$$(\mathrm{P}_{h,\varepsilon}) \qquad \min \; \{J_h(y_h, u_h) + \frac{1}{2\varepsilon} |w|_{V_h}^2\} \; , \; \varepsilon > 0$$

subject to $u_h \in U_{ad}^h$, y_h given by

$$(4.3) \qquad \begin{aligned} &a_{u_h}^h(y_h, v_h - y_h) + \varphi_h(v_h) + \psi_h(v_h) - \varphi_h(y_h) - \psi_h(y_h) \\ &\geq [f_h + B_h u_h, v_h - y_h]_h \quad, \forall v_h \in V_h \; . \end{aligned}$$

Here $w \in \partial\psi_h(y_h)$ is just the section of $\partial\psi_h$ which occurs in (4.3).

If $\partial\varphi_h + \partial\psi_h = \partial(\varphi_h + \psi_h)$ (for instance under interiority assumptions, Aubin [**1**]) then $(\mathrm{P}_{h,\varepsilon})$ is a problem of the same type as (P_h). Moreover every $u \in U_{ad}^h$ is admissible for $(\mathrm{P}_{h,\varepsilon})$.

It follows easily that $(\mathrm{P}_{h,\varepsilon})$ has at least one optimal pair, which we denote by $\{y_\varepsilon, u_\varepsilon\}$. Denote by $w_\varepsilon \in \partial\psi_h(y_\varepsilon)$ the corresponding section and J_ε the cost functional of $(\mathrm{P}_{h,\varepsilon})$.

We remark that any admissible pair $\{\overline{y}_h, \overline{u}_h\}$ for (P_h) is admissible for $(\mathrm{P}_{h,\varepsilon})$ with the same cost since $\overline{y}_h \in K_h \;\Rightarrow\; 0 \in \partial\psi_h(\overline{y}_h)$ and $\overline{w}_h = 0$. Therefore

$$(4.4) \qquad J_\varepsilon(y_\varepsilon, u_\varepsilon) \leq J_\varepsilon(\overline{y}_h, \overline{u}_h) \leq J_h(\overline{y}_h, \overline{u}_h) \; .$$

We see that $\{w_\varepsilon\}$ is bounded in V_h with respect to $\varepsilon > 0$.

On the other hand $\{u_\varepsilon\}$ is bounded in U^h by $u_\varepsilon \in U^h_{ad}$. Then (4.1) shows that $\{y_\varepsilon\}$ is bounded in V_h with respect to $\varepsilon > 0$. By (4.4) this yields $w_\varepsilon \to 0$ in V_h as $\varepsilon \to 0$. Moreover $|w_\varepsilon|_{V_h} \leq c\varepsilon^{\frac{1}{2}}$.

Let $y_\varepsilon \to \hat{y}_h$, $u_\varepsilon \to \hat{u}_h$ on a subsequence. Passing to the limit in (4.3) we see that $\hat{y}_h$ is the solution of (4.1) corresponding to $\hat{u}_h$. Again by (4.4), we have that $\{\hat{y}_h, \hat{u}_h\}$ is an optimal pair for (P$_h$).

Denote by y^ε the solution of (4.1) corresponding to u_ε. The pair $\{y^\varepsilon, u_\varepsilon\}$ is not necessarily admissible for (P$_h$) since (4.2) may be violated. However, we have the following suboptimality result:

Theorem 4.1. *Under the hypotheses of Theorem 3.1 we have:*

i) *dist* $(y^\varepsilon, K_h)_{V_H} \leq c\varepsilon^{\frac{1}{2}}$ *with c a constant independent of* ε.

ii) *If* J_h *is continuous, then*

$$\lim_{\varepsilon\to 0} J_h(y^\varepsilon, u_\varepsilon) = J_h(y_h^*, u_h^*) \ .$$

Proof. Take $u_h = u_\varepsilon$ in (4.1) and in (4.3). Next choose $v_h = y^\varepsilon$ in (4.3) and $v_h = y_\varepsilon$ in (4.1) and add. We get:

$$-a^h_{u_\varepsilon}(y^\varepsilon - y_\varepsilon) + \psi_h(y^\varepsilon) - \psi_h(y_\varepsilon) \geq 0 \ .$$

By (H1) and the estimate on w_ε we obtain:

(4.5) $$|y^\varepsilon - y_\varepsilon|_{V_h} \leq c\varepsilon^{\frac{1}{2}} \ .$$

As $y_\varepsilon \in \mathrm{dom}\ \psi_h = K_h$, i) is proved.

We know that $y_\varepsilon \to \hat{y}$ and $u_\varepsilon \to \hat{u}$, and (4.5) shows that $y^\varepsilon \to \hat{y}$ also. Then, the continuity of J_h gives ii).

Remark 4.2. The continuity of J_h is a natural assumption as the constraints are considered independently.

Remark 4.3. For the example discussed in §3, by the definition of K_h and i), we have estimates of the distance between the computed solution y^ε and the set of constraints K.

References

1. J.P.Aubin : Méthodes explicites de l'optimisation. Paris. Dunod 1982

2. M.C. Delfour, G. Payre and J.P. Zolesio: Optimal parameter design of thermal diffusers for communication satellites. Optim. Contr. Appl. & Methods **7**, 163–184 (1986)
3. I.Hlaváček, I.Bock, J.Lovíšek: Optimal control of a variational inequality with applications to structural analysis. I. Optimal design of a beam with unilateral supports. Appl. Math. Optim. **11**, 111–143 (1984)
4. Gh. Morosanu, Zheng-Xu He: Optimal control of biharmonic variational inequalities. Preprint Univ. of Iasi, Romania (1985)
5. P. Neittaanmäki, D. Tiba: A variational inequality approach to constrained control problems. University of Jyväskylä, Dept. of Math., Preprint 51 (1986)
6. E. C. Renteria: Optimality necessary conditions for some structural design problems. (to appear)
7. D. Tiba: Une approche par inéquations variationnelles pour les problèmes de contrôle avec contraintes. C.R.A.S. Paris, t.302, Série I **no.1** (1986)

J. Haslinger, Faculty of Mathematics and Physics, Charles University, KAM MFF UK, Malostranské 2/25, CS-11800, Prague, Czechoslovakia

P. Neittaanmäki, University of Jyväskylä, Department of Mathematics, Seminaarinkatu 15, SF-40100 Jyväskylä, Finland

D. Tiba, INCREST, Department of Mathematics, Bd. Păcii 220, R-79622 Bucharest, Romania

International Series of
Numerical Mathematics, Vol. 78

AN APPLICATION OF QUASI NEWTON METHODS TO PSEUDOPARABOLIC OPTIMAL CONTROL PROBLEMS

C. T. Kelley and E. W. Sachs

Abstract We consider an infinite-dimensional version of the BFGS-method and investigate convergence properties for an implementable discretized version. This algorithm is taylored for an application to a boundary control problem with a pseudoparabolic differential equation. Numerical examples are given.

1. Introduction

In this paper we describe an application of quasi Newton methods to control problems for distributed parameter systems.

We use an infinite dimensional approach to analyze the convergence properties of the finite dimensional implemented algorithm. It is possible that an increase in the dimension of the discretized problem can lead to a deterioration in the convergence rate for quasi Newton methods, see e. g. Stoer [14]. However, recent results by Sachs [12] and Griewank [6] show that the choice of the starting operator which approximates the second derivative of the objective is crucial in the convergence behavior.

The authors investigated in [9] how these results can be used for a proper implementation of quasi Newton methods for unconstrained optimal control problems with ordinary differential equations. In this paper, we use the general framework of [9] and apply it to a class of optimal control problems without constraints where the system is described by a linear operator which occurs frequently in partial differential equations. We illustrate the results with an example from the optimal control of the pseudoparabolic differential equations.

Let H denote a Hilbert space and

$$F: H \to \mathbb{R}$$

is twice continuously Fréchet-differentiable on H. Instead of

$$\text{Min } F(u) \quad , \quad u \in H \, , \tag{P}$$

we search for critical points which satisfy the necessary condition $\nabla F(u) = 0$. Hence, we formulate quasi Newton methods for

$$\text{Solve } G(u) = 0 \quad , \quad u \in H \, , \tag{E}$$

where

$$G: H \to H$$

is continuously Fréchet-differentiable. Let L(H) be the space of invertible bounded linear operators on H. Then the BFGS-method which is due to Broyden [2], Fletcher [4], Goldfarb [5], and Shanno [13] and which is considered the most successful quasi Newton method, is formulated in Hilbert space as follows:

Given $u_i \in H \quad , \quad B_i \in L(H)$

(i) Solve $\quad B_i \, s_i = -G(u_i)$

(ii) Let $\quad u_{i+1} = u_i + s_i$

$$y_i = G(u_{i+1}) - G(u_i)$$

(iii) Let $\quad B_{i+1} = B_i + \dfrac{\langle y_i, \cdot \rangle}{\langle s_i, y_i \rangle} \, y_i - \dfrac{\langle B_i \, s_i, \cdot \rangle}{\langle s_i, B_i \, s_i \rangle} \, B_i \, s_i \, .$

The updated operators B_{i+1} maintain the invertibility and also the self-adjointness and positive definiteness if this is required for B_o. The important convergence result which can be shown for the finite dimensional case is that a superlinear rate of convergence holds locally, i. e. if u_o and B_o are sufficiently close to the solution u_* and $G'(u_*)$, then

$$\lim_{i\to\infty} \frac{\| u_{i+1} - u_* \|}{\| u_i - u_* \|} = 0 .$$

This result is not true in an arbitrary Hilbert-space. Griewank [6] showed that this result is salvaged if in addition

$$B_o - G'(u_*) \quad \text{is compact.}$$

This is an assumption which we can verify for various optimal control problems. If the structure of the cost function is of a special type, the update procedure can be connected to the secant method. This has the advantage that we retain the rate of convergence of the secant method for these infinite-dimensional problems. Numerical examples confirm this observation.

2. Discretized BFGS-method

In this section, we specialize some results the authors obtained in [9] for a setting which is more appropriate for our goals in this paper.

Let $H^N \subset H$ be a finite dimensional subspace of H. If we define for each N an operator

$$G^N : H^N \to H^N$$

which is continuously Fréchet-differentiable on H^N, we can apply a discretized version of the BFGS-method:

For given u_i^N and $B_i^N \in L(H^N)$

(i) Solve $B_i^N s_i^N = - G^N(u_i^N)$, $s_i^N \in H^N$

(ii) Let $u_{i+1}^N = u_i^N + s_i^N$

$$y_i^N = G^N(u_{i+1}^N) - G^N(u_i^N)$$

$$\text{(iii) Let } B_{i+1}^N = B_i^N + \frac{\langle y_i^N, \cdot\rangle}{\langle s_i^N, y_i^N\rangle}\, y_i^N - \frac{\langle B_i^N s_i^N, \cdot\rangle}{\langle s_i^N, B_i^N s_i^N\rangle}\, B_i^N s_i^N \;.$$

The only hypothesis we impose on the choice of G^N is the following

$$\text{(H 1) If } \lim_{N\to\infty} u^N = u \;,\; u^N \in H^N \;,\; u \in H \;,$$

$$\text{then } \lim_{N\to\infty} G^N(u^N) = G(u) \;.$$

In the algorithm we use as a stopping criterion the size of the norm of $G(u_i)$. Therefore, we define

$$i(\varepsilon) = \min\,\{i \in \mathbb{N} : \|G(u_i)\| < \varepsilon\}$$

$$i_N(\varepsilon) = \min\,\{i \in \mathbb{N} : \|G^N(u_i^N)\| < \varepsilon\}$$

which are the indices where the algorithm stops. We obtain the following theorem:

Theorem 2.1 Let H be a Hilbert space with inner product $\langle\cdot,\cdot\rangle$ and the corresponding norm denoted by $\|\cdot\|$. Let $H^N \subset H$ be a finite dimensional subspace of H, $G : H \to H$, $G^N : H^N \to H^N$ Lipschitz continuously Fréchet-differentiable on H and H^N, respectively, and $u_* \in H$ such that

$$G(u_*) = 0 \;,$$

$$G'(u_*) \text{ self-adjoint and positive definite.}$$

Select $B_0 \in L(H)$, $u_0 \in H$ such that

$$\|B_0 - G'(u_*)\| \quad\text{and}\quad \|u_0 - u_*\|$$

are sufficiently small to yield a linear convergence rate for the BFGS-iterates or if, in addition,

$$B_0 - G'(u_*) \text{ is compact ,}$$

to give a superlinear rate of convergence.

Choose $u_o^N \in H^N$ and $B_o^N \in L(H^N)$ such that

$$\lim_{N\to\infty} u_o^N = u_o \tag{2.1}$$

and

$$\lim_{N\to\infty} (B_o^N)^{-1} v^N = (B_o)^{-1} v \tag{2.2}$$

if

$$\lim_{N\to\infty} v^N = v \quad \text{for } v^N \in H, \ v \in H .$$

Then for each $\varepsilon > 0$ there exists $N_\varepsilon \in \mathbb{N}$ with

$$i(\varepsilon) - 1 \leq i_N(\varepsilon) \leq i(\varepsilon)$$

for all $N \geq N_\varepsilon$.

The proof follows from Section 2 in the authors' paper [9], if one sets $W = Z = H$,

$$\langle\cdot,\cdot\rangle_N = \langle\cdot,\cdot\rangle .$$

The theorem covers two cases: If the compactness condition is met, then the termination index $i_N(\varepsilon)$ is related to $i(\varepsilon)$ which itself is determined through the superlinear rate. On the other side, if $i(\varepsilon)$ is influenced by a linear rate only, this affects also $i_N(\varepsilon)$ and for high discretizations at least this influence should be noticeable.

3. Discretization

We want to consider optimal control problems with nonlinear objective function and a linear systems equation. Let C be a Banach space and let

$$S : H \to C$$

denote the solution operator for a linear partial differential equation with appropriate boundary conditions. Since we do not allow constraints we add a penalty term for the control in the cost function. In this paper the function F to be minimized in problem (P) is of the form

$$F(u) = f(Su) + \frac{a}{2}\|u\|^2 \qquad (3.1)$$

where a is a fixed constant and

a) $f : C \to \mathbb{R}$ is twice Lipschitz continuously Fréchet-differentiable

b) S is a linear and continuous map from H to C.

We denote the adjoint operator of S by

$$S^* : C^* \to H .$$

The equation to be solved is

$$G(u) = S^*(f'(Su)) + au = 0 . \qquad (3.2)$$

The derivative of G is

$$G'(u) = S^* f''(Su)S + aI \qquad (3.3)$$

where I is the identity operator on H and $f''(Su) : C \to C^*$.
We consider operators S which are expressed as

$$S = \sum_{k=0}^{\infty} c_k h_k , \qquad (3.4)$$

where $c_k \in C$ and $h_k \in H$ for $k \in \mathbb{N}$

and $S(u) = \sum_{k=0}^{\infty} c_k \langle h_k, u\rangle$.

Then $$S^* = \sum_{k=0}^{\infty} h_k c_k^{**} , \qquad (3.5)$$

where $c_k^{**} \in C^*$ is defined by

$$c_k^{**}(c^*) = c^*(c_k) , \quad c^* \in C^* .$$

We approximate G by truncating the series. For given $N \in \mathbb{N}$, let $m_N \in \mathbb{N}$ be such that

$$m_N < m_{N+1}$$

and $$S_N = \sum_{k=0}^{m_N} c_k h_k , \qquad (3.6)$$

$$H^N = \text{span}\,\{h_o,h_1,..,h_{m_N}\} \subset H\,.$$

Then
$$G_N(u^N) = S_N^*(f'(S_N u^N)) + au^N\,. \tag{3.7}$$

Furthermore, we suppose that

$$\lim_{i\to\infty} \| S_N - S\|_L = 0\,, \tag{3.8}$$

where $\|\cdot\|_L$ denotes the operator norm. This implies the compactness of the operator S, which is important because (3.3) shows that $G'(u_*)$ is the sum of a compact operator and a non-compact one, namely aI. Hence in the BFGS-method we should choose $B_o = aI$ so that the difference $B_o - G'(u_*)$ is compact.

The following lemma insures that (2.2) holds:

<u>Lemma 3.1</u> Let (3.6) and (3.8) hold.
If $A_o, A_o^N \in L(C,C^*)$, $N \in \mathbb{N}$, are such that

$$\| A_o^N - A_o\|_L \leq M \quad \text{for some } M > 0 \text{ and all } N \in \mathbb{N} \tag{3.9}$$

and
$$\lim_{N\to\infty} A_o^N c^N = A_o c \tag{3.10}$$

for all sequences $c^N \in C$ which converge to $c \in C$, then (2.2) is true with

$$B_o^N = S_N^* A_o^N S_N + aI \tag{3.11}$$

and
$$B_o = SA_oS + aI\,, \tag{3.12}$$

provided B_o^{-1} exists.

<u>Proof</u> Observe

$$B_o^N - B_o = (S_N^* - S^*)A_o^N S_N + S^*(A_o^N - A)S + S^*A_o^N(S_N - S)\,,$$

where the first and last term in the sum converge to zero in the operator norm because of (3.8) and (3.9). (3.10) and the compactness of S force the middle term also to converge to 0 in the operator norm, i. e.

$$\lim_{N\to\infty} \| B_o^N - B_o \|_L = 0 .$$

This implies that $(B_o^N)^{-1}$ exists for N sufficiently large and is uniformly bounded. Then (2.2) follows easily from the identity

$$B_o^{-1} - (B_o^N)^{-1} = B_o^{-1}(B_o^N - B_o)(B_o^N)^{-1} .$$

4. Pseudoparabolic Control Problem

Pseudoparabolic equations describe heat conduction problems where the material has a certain "memory". Control problems for these differential equations have been considered by L. White [15,16] and Baumeister, Jung, Scondo [1].

Let $y(t,x)$ denote the temperature at time $t \geq 0$ and at a point $x \in [0,1]$. The boundary value problem is given by

$$\begin{aligned}
&y_t(t,x) = y_{xx}(t,x) + \varepsilon y_{xtx}(t,x) , && x \in (0,1) , \ t \in (0,T)\\
&y(0,x) = 0 , && x \in (0,1)\\
&y_x(t,1) = 0 , && t \in (0,T]\\
&-y_x(t,0) - \varepsilon y_{xt}(t,0) = u(t) , && t \in (0,T] .
\end{aligned}$$

Here u is the control function and $\varepsilon > 0$ is a material constant.

For smooth input u we can express the solution with an infinite series. We define a generalized solution for $u \in L_2[0,T]$ in the same way (for a derivation see [1])

$$y(t,x) = \sum_{k=0}^{\infty} a_k^2 \, b_k \, \varphi_k(x)(e_k * u)(t) , \ x \in (0,1) , \ t \in (0,T)$$

where

$$\varphi_k(x) = \cos k\Pi x$$

$$\mu_k = k^2\Pi^2$$

$$b_k = \frac{1}{1+\varepsilon\mu_k}$$

$$\lambda_k = \frac{\mu_k}{1+\varepsilon\mu_k}$$

for $k = 0,1,2,..$ and

$$a_0 = 1, a_k = \sqrt{2} \quad \text{for } k \in \mathbb{N} ,$$

$$(e_k * u)(t) = \int_0^t e^{-\lambda_k(t-s)} u(s)ds .$$

In order to define S according to Section 3, we set

$$H = L_2[0,T] , \quad C = C[0,1]$$

and consider for fixed $T > 0$

$$Su = y(T,\cdot) .$$

With $c_k(\cdot) = a_k^2\, b_k\, \varphi_k(\cdot)$

and $h_k = e_k$,

we have
$$Su = \sum_{k=0}^{\infty} c_k \langle h_k, u\rangle .$$

In order to show (3.8) observe that

$$\| Su - S_N u \|_C \leq \sum_{k=m_N+1}^{\infty} a_k^2\, b_k \|\varphi_k\|_C \, |(e_k * u)(T)| .$$

Then by Hölder's inequality

$$|(e_k * u)(T)| \leq \left(\int_0^T e^{-2\lambda_k s} ds\right)^{1/2} \|u\|_H$$

$$\leq \left(\frac{1}{2\lambda_k}\right)^{1/2} \|u\|_H .$$

Since the sequence b_k tends to zero asymptotically like k^{-2} we obtain

$$\lim_{N\to\infty} \| S - S_N \|_C = 0 .$$

This proves that S is well-defined on the spaces indicated and is compact.

5. A Secant Method Update for a Class of Problems

The formula (3.12) in which B_o was chosen to be

$$B_o = S\,A_o\,S + aI$$

takes already the special structure of G' into account. However, for certain cost functionals one can extend the one-dimensional secant method in a way such that the R-order of the convergence is retained. This holds under the following assumption. We formulate it for the space of continuous functions C(D) , $D \in \mathbb{R}^n$ bounded, but this can be extended to many other function spaces.

Assumption (5.1): For every $y \in C = C(D)$ let $f'(y) \in C^*$ be representable by a Lipschitz continuously differentiable $\varphi : \mathbb{R} \to \mathbb{R}$ and

$$f'(y)(c) = \int_D \varphi(y(x))\ c(x)\ d\mu(x) \qquad (5.1)$$

holds for all $c \in C(D)$ and a measure μ on D.

This approach is also feasible, if f'(y) can be written as the sum of integrals of type (5.1).

This includes cost functions of the type

$$\int_D (Su(x) - z(x))^p dx + \frac{a}{2}\|u\|^2$$

and
$$\sum_{i=1}^{r} \rho_i (Su(x_i) - z(x_i)) + \frac{a}{2}\|u\|^2 \ , \quad x_i \in D \ ,$$

but not
$$\|Su - z\|_{L_p} + \frac{a}{2}\|u\|^2 \ .$$

With (5.1) we also know that the second derivative of F can be expressed in a much more detailed form than (3.3):

$$G'(u)(v)(w) = \int_D \varphi'(Su(x))Sv(x)Sw(x)\,dx + a\langle v,w\rangle. \quad (5.2)$$

Hence, similar to the secant method, we approximate $\varphi'(Su_{i+1}(x))$ by

$$\delta_{i+1}(x) = \begin{cases} \varphi'(Su_{i+1}(x)) & \text{if } S(u_{i+1}-u_i)(x) = 0 \\ \dfrac{\varphi(Su_{i+1}(x)) - \varphi(Su_i(x))}{S(u_{i+1} - u_i)(x)} & \text{otherwise} \end{cases}$$

and set

$$B_{i+1} = S^* A_{i+1} S + aI$$

with $\quad A_{i+1}(c)(c^*) = c^*(\delta_{i+1}(\cdot)\, c(\cdot))$.

For this method the following theorem holds:

Theorem 5.1 Let $C = C(D)$, $D \in \mathbb{R}^n$ bounded, H a Banach space with norm $\|\cdot\|$, $S : H \to C(D)$ linear and continuous, $f : C(D) \to \mathbb{R}$ twice Lipschitz continuously Fréchet-differentiable with assumption (5.1) to be true, $F : H \to \mathbb{R}$ defined by

$$F(u) = f(Su) + \frac{a}{2}\|u\|^2$$

attain its minimum at $u_* \in H$ and for some $\mu > 0$

$$F''(u_*)(v)(v) \geq \mu\|v\|^2 \quad \text{for all } v \in H.$$

If u_o and u_1 in H are chosen sufficiently close to $u_* \in H$, then there exists a sequence of numbers m_i which satisfy for some $c > 0$ and all i large enough

$$m_{i+1} \leq c\, m_i^p \quad, \; p = \frac{\sqrt{5}+1}{2} \quad,$$

and $\quad \|u_i - u_*\| \leq m_i$.

This is a statement on a convergence rate with an R-order of $(\sqrt{5}+1)/2$, which holds for the one-dimensional secant method.

For this class of control problems the proof carries over to the infinite-dimensional case, because the nonlinearity enters pointwise in a one-dimensional way. Pointwise quasi-Newton updates were also used for nonlinear elliptic boundary value problems [8] and optimal control problems with nonlinear ordinary differential equations [10]. A similar idea in the context of integral equations is discussed in Kelley and Northrup [7] where the nonlinearity has a substantially different structure than that considered in this paper.

The proof of the theorem can be obtained by checking the bounded deterioration property for the updates which implies the linear rate of convergence, see Dennis [3]. A comparison with Newton's method then yields for the updates the estimate for some constant $c_1 > 0$

$$\| B_i - G'(u_i) \| \leq c_1, \| u_i - u_{i-1} \| .$$

The quadratic convergence rate for Newton's method implies the inequality for some $c_2 > 0$

$$\| u_{i+1} - u_* \| \leq c_2 \| u_i - u_* \| \quad \| u_{i-1} - u_* \| .$$

This is the important estimate for the errors that will give the estimate for the R-order, see e. g. Ortega and Rheinboldt [11].

6. Numerical Example

We give a numerical example for the version of the secant method described in the previous section. The objective is to observe the R-order of convergence.

The infinite dimensional problem is approximated as follows:

Let $S_N = \sum_{k=0}^{m_N} c_k h_k$ as in Section 4.

The controls are chosen to be piecewise constant functions on each subinterval

$$0 = t_o < t, < \ldots < t_{\ell_N} = T .$$

The parameters are chosen as follows:

$$F(u) = \int_0^1 ((S_N u)(x) - z(x))^4 dx + \frac{a}{2} \int_0^T u(t)^2 dt$$
$$T = 0.2$$
$$\varepsilon = 0.1$$
$$\ell_N = 10 \quad \text{(discretization in time)}$$
$$k_N = 20 \quad \text{(discretization in space)}$$
$$m_N = 50$$
$$z(x) = \cos x$$
$$u_0(t) = 0$$

The first iterate u_1 was obtained by a steepest descent step. We give results for three different runs with $a = 1$, $a = 10^{-2}$ and $a = 10^{-4}$, so that the problem becomes less well-conditioned. The following values are tabulated

$$\gamma_i = \| G(u_i) \| = \| \nabla F(u_i) \|$$
$$\sigma_i = \| u_i - u_{i-1} \|$$
$$\Pi_i = \frac{\ln \| u_i - u_{i-1} \|}{\ln \| u_{i-1} - u_{i-2} \|} .$$

Π_i should approach the R-order of $(\sqrt{5} + 1)/2 \approx 1.618$ and is tabulated towards the end of the iteration. The iteration was stopped if γ_i was less than 10^{-16}.

Table 1: $a = 1$

i	γ_i	σ_i	Π_i
0	0.1312E+01		
1	0.9871E+00	0.5633E+00	
2	0.1245E+00	0.8141E-01	0.4370E+01
3	0.1392E-01	0.8186E-02	0.1916E+01
4	0.1765E-03	0.1025E-03	0.1911E+01
5	0.2468E-06	0.1436E-06	0.1715E+01
6	0.4385E-11	0.2551E-11	0.1694E+01
	0.2483E-16		

Table 2: $a = 10^{-2}$

i	γ_i	σ_i	Π_i
0	0.1312E+01		
1	0.3132E+00	0.1500E+01	
2	0.1596E+00	0.5068E+00	
3	0.6601E-01	0.4632E+00	0.1133E+01
4	0.3027E-01	0.4177E+00	0.1134E+01
5	0.8533E-02	0.1135E+00	0.2493E+01
6	0.4253E-03	0.2118E-01	0.1772E+01
7	0.1630E-04	0.2310E-03	0.2172E+01
8	0.3108E-07	0.4671E-06	0.1741E+01
9	0.6089E-12	0.5250E-10	0.1624E+01
	0.1869E-16		

Table 3: $a = 10^{-4}$

i	γ_i	σ_i	Π_i
0	0.1312E+01		
1	0.3261E+00	0.3021E+01	
2	0.1612E+00	0.1707E+01	
3	0.6543E-01	0.1319E+01	
4	0.2883E-01	0.7964E+00	
5	0.1240E-01	0.3770E+00	
6	0.5634E-02	0.2866E+00	
7	0.3072E-02	0.1300E+01	
8	0.9013E-03	0.7944E+00	
9	0.1146E-02	0.2241E+00	0.6497E+01
10	0.2821E-03	0.7364E-01	0.1744E+01
11	0.8819E-04	0.1843E-01	0.1531E+01
12	0.4430E-05	0.8669E-03	0.1765E+01
13	0.6526E-07	0.1291E-04	0.1597E+01
14	0.4916E-10	0.9732E-08	0.1639E+01
15	0.5444E-15	0.1074E-12	0.1619E+01
	0.2533E-18		

REFERENCES

1. Baumeister, J., Jung, W., Scondo, W., Über Rand-Kontrollprobleme aus der Wärmeleitung für Materialien mit Gedächtnis, in 'Optimal Control of Partial Differential Equations', eds. K.-H. Hoffmann and W. Krabs, Birkhäuser, Basel - Boston - Stuttgart, 75-91 (1984).

2. Broyden, C. G., A new double-rank minimization algorithm, AMS Notices 16, (1969).

3. Dennis, J. E. Jr., Towards a unified convergence theory for Newton-like methods, in 'Nonlinear Functional Analysis and Applications', ed. L. B. Rall, Academic Press, New York, 425-472 (1971).

4. Fletcher, R., A new approach to variable metric algorithms, Comput. J. 13, 317-322 (1970).

5. Goldfarb, D. G., A family of variable metric methods derived by variational means, Math. Comp. 24, 23-26 (1970).

6. Griewank, A., The superlinear convergence of secant methods on mildly nonlinear problems in Hilbert space, preprint (1984).

7. Kelley, C. T. and Northrup, J. I., Pointwise quasi-Newton methods and some applications, submitted to Proceedings of International Conference on Control and Identification of Distributed Systems, Vorau, Austria, July 1986.

8. Kelley, C. T. and Sachs, E. W., A quasi-Newton method for elliptic boundary value problems, SIAM J. Numerical Analysis (to appear).

9. Kelley, C. T. and Sachs, E. W., Quasi-Newton methods and unconstrained optimal control problems, preprint (1986).

10. Kelley, C. T. and Sachs, E. W., A pointwise quasi-Newton method for unconstrained optimal control problems, preprint (1986).

11. Ortega, J. M. and Rheinboldt, W. C., Iterative Solution of Nonlinear Equations in Several Variables, Academic Press, Orlando -...-Tokyo (1970).

12. Sachs, E. W., Broyden's method in Hilbert space, Math. Programming 35 (1986).

13. Shanno, D. F., Conditioning of quasi-Newton methods for function minimization, Math. Comp. 24, 647-657 (1970).

14. Stoer, J., Two examples on the convergence of certain rank-2 minimization methods for quadratic functionals in Hilbert space, Lin. Algebra Appl. 28, 217-222 (1979).

15. White, L. W., Controllability properties of pseudoparabolic boundary control problems, SIAM J. Contr. Optim. 18, 534-540 (1980).

16. White, L. W., Formulation of pseudo-parabolic boundary control problems, J. Math. Anal. Applic. 82, 284-291 (1981).

Carl T. Kelley
Department of Mathematics
North Carolina State University
Box 8205
Raleigh, NC 27695 - 8205
USA

Ekkehard W. Sachs
Universität Trier
FB IV - Mathematik
Postfach 3825
D-5500 Trier
West Germany

Acknowledgement: The research of the first author is supported by AFOSR grant # AFOSR - 86 -0074 and NSF grant # DMS - 8601139. The research of the second author was partially supported by AFOSR grant # AFOSR - 85 - 0214.

International Series of
Numerical Mathematics, Vol. 78

ASYMPTOTIC STABILITY OF SOLUTIONS TO A TWO-PHASE STEFAN PROBLEM WITH NONLINEAR BOUNDARY CONDITION OF SIGNORINI TYPE

Nobuyuki Kenmochi

Abstract. This paper is concerned with a two-phase Stefan problem, with time-dependent flux conditions of Signorini type on the fixed boundaries, in one dimensional space. Our main interest is the investigation of the periodic or almost periodic behavior of solutions with respect to time. We shall show that a periodic (resp. almost periodic) solution is unique and every solution asymptotically converges to it, provided that the flux conditions of Signorini type, given on the fixed boundaries, are periodic (resp. almost periodic) with respect to time.

1. Introduction

In the author's previous papers [18, 19] a two-phase Stefan problem, with flux control by means of time-dependent subdifferentials on the fixed boundaries, was studied, and a local existence and uniqueness theorem was established together with a comparison result for solutions. The problem is to find a function $u = u(t, x)$ on $J \times [0, 1]$, $J = [t_o, t_1]$ or $[t_o, t_1)$, and a curve $x = \ell(t)$, $0 < \ell(t) < 1$, on J such that

$$(1.1)\quad \rho(u)_t - u_{xx} = 0 \quad \text{in } Q^+_\ell(t_o, t_1) = \{(t,x);\ 0 < x < \ell(t),\ t_o < t < t_1\}$$
$$\text{and in } Q^-_\ell(t_o, t_1) = \{(t,x);\ \ell(t) < x < 1,\ t_o < t < t_1\},$$

$$(1.2)\quad u_x(t, 0+) \in \partial b^t_0(u(t, 0)) \quad \text{for a.e. } t \in J,$$

$$(1.3)\quad - u_x(t, 1-) \in \partial b^t_1(u(t, 1)) \quad \text{for a.e. } t \in J,$$

$$(1.4)\quad \begin{cases} u(t, \ell(t)) = 0 \quad \text{for } t \in J, \\ \ell'(t) \ (= \frac{d\ell(t)}{dt}) = - u_x(t,\ell(t)-) + u_x(t,\ell(t)+) \quad \text{for a.e. } t \in J, \end{cases}$$

and

$$(1.5)\quad \begin{cases} u(t_o, x) = u_o(x) \quad \text{for a.e. } x \in [0, 1], \\ \ell(t_o) = \ell_o, \end{cases}$$

where ρ: $R \to R$ is a given function with $\rho(0) = 0$ which is increasing and bi-Lipschitz continuous on R; for $t \in R$ and $i = 0, 1$, $b_i^t = b_i^t(.)$ is a proper l.s.c. convex function on R and ∂b_i^t stands for its subdifferential in R; u_o and ℓ_o are initial data which are respectively a function on [0, 1] and a number in the open interval (0, 1).

We are interested in the asymptotic behavior of solutions, which remains to be investigated as an interesting and important question. However it seems not to be easy to investigate it in the general setting. Therefore in the present paper we discuss this question in the case when flux conditions (1.2) and (1.3) are of the Signorini type, i.e.

$$(1.6)\qquad b_0^t(r)\ (\text{resp. } b_1^t(r)) = \begin{cases} 0 & \text{if } r \geqq g_o(t)\ (\text{resp. } r \leqq g_1(t)), \\ \infty & \text{if } r < g_o(t)\ (\text{resp. } r > g_1(t)), \end{cases}$$

where g_o, g_1 are given functions on R. Since

$$(1.7)\qquad \partial b_0^t(r)\ (\text{resp. } \partial b_1^t(r)) = \begin{cases} \{0\} \text{ if } r > g_o(t)\ (\text{resp. } r < g_1(t)), \\ (-\infty,0]\ (\text{resp.} [0,\infty)) \text{ if } r = g_o(t)\ (\text{resp. } g_1(t)), \\ \emptyset \quad \text{if } r < g_o(t)\ (\text{resp. } r > g_1(t)), \end{cases}$$

the boundary conditions (1.2) and (1.3) are respectively written in the forms:

$$(1.2)'\qquad \begin{cases} u(t, 0) \geqq g_o(t) & \text{for } t \in J, \\ u_x(t, 0+) \leqq 0 & \text{for a.e. } t \in J, \\ u_x(t, 0+) = 0 & \text{for a.e. } t \in J \text{ with } u(t, 0) > g_o(t), \end{cases}$$

and

$$(1.3)'\qquad \begin{cases} u(t, 1) \leqq g_1(t) & \text{for } t \in J, \\ u_x(t, 1-) \leqq 0 & \text{for a.e. } t \in J, \\ u_x(t, 1-) = 0 & \text{for a.e. } t \in J \text{ with } u(t, 1) < g_1(t). \end{cases}$$

Moreover, we restrict ourselves to the simplest case of ρ, i.e.

$$(1.8)\qquad \rho(r) = \begin{cases} c_o r & \text{for } r \geqq 0, \\ c_1 r & \text{for } r < 0, \end{cases}$$

where c_o, c_1 are positive constants. In this case, equation (1.1) has of the form:

$$(1.1)'\qquad c_o u_t - u_{xx} = 0 \ \text{ in } Q_\ell^+(t_o, t_1), \quad c_1 u_t - u_{xx} = 0 \ \text{ in } Q_\ell^-(t_o, t_1).$$

Throughout this paper we put

$$H = L^2(0, 1) \quad \text{and} \quad X = W^{1,2}(0, 1) \subset C([0, 1]),$$

and for any interval J in R denote by $SP(g_o, g_1)$ on J (resp. $SP(g_o, g_1; u_o, \ell_o)$ on $J = [t_o, t_1]$ or $[t_o, t_1))$ the problem (1.1)' - (1.3)' and (1.4) (resp. (1.1)' - (1.3)', (1.4) and (1.5)). It is said that a couple $\{u, \ell\}$ is a solution of $SP(g_o, g_1)$ (resp. $SP(g_o, g_1; u_o, \ell_o)$) on J, if

$$u \in W^{1,2}_{loc}(J; H) \cap L^{\infty}_{loc}(J; X), \quad \ell \in W^{1,2}_{loc}(J),$$

and (1.1)' - (1.3)' and (1.4) (resp. (1.1)' - (1.3)', (1.4) and (1.5)) hold.

The purpose of this work is to prove the existence of solutions to $SP(g_o, g_1; u_o, \ell_o)$ on $[t_o, \infty)$ and $SP(g_o, g_1)$ on R under some assumptions on g_o, g_1, and then to investigate the asymptotic behavior of the solutions in the following cases (i), (ii) and (iii):

(i) $g_o(t)$ and $g_1(t)$ converge as $t \to \infty$;
(ii) g_o and g_1 are periodic in t on R with same period;
(iii) g_o and g_1 are almost periodic in t on R.

Especially we are interested in the periodic and almost periodic behavior of solutions. It will be proved under (ii) (resp. (iii)) that there exists a unique periodic (resp. almost periodic) solution to $SP(g_o, g_1)$ on R, and that any solution of $SP(g_o, g_1)$ on $[t_o, \infty)$ asymptotically converges to the periodic (resp. almost periodic) solution as $t \to \infty$. In proving these behaviors of solutions the crucial step is to show the uniqueness of such a solution $\{u, \ell\}$ to $SP(g_o, g_1)$ on R that $u \in L^{\infty}(R \times [0,1])$ and $0 < \inf_{t\in R}\ell(t) \leqq \sup_{t\in R}\ell(t) < 1$.

So far as two-phase Stefan problems with usual Dirichlet and Neumann boundary conditions or nonlinear smooth flux conditions are concerned, the asymptotic stability of solutions has been studied by many authors. For example, see Cannon-Primicerio [3, 4], Friedman [9, 10, 11], Rubinstein [21] and Damlamian-Kenmochi [5] on the equilibrium stability; Štědrý-Vejvoda [23], Meirmanov [20] and DiBenedetto-Friedman [7] on the periodic stability; Ishii [15] and Damlamian-Kenmochi [6] on the almost periodic stability. Also, in case $b^t_i(.)$, i = 0, 1, are independent of time t, i.e. $b^t_i(.) = b_i(.)$, the global existence of a solution and the equilibrium stability were studied in detail by Yotsutani [24, 25] and these results completely cover the case of constant functions g_o, g_1 in our problem $SP(g_o, g_1)$.

Recently, Hoffmann and Sprekels [12, 13, 14] proposed an interesting problem of the free boundary control in two-phase Stefan problems. The free boundary control is especially important from the mechanical point of view, and it can be done by controlling the boundary fluxes $u_x(t, 0+)$ and $u_x(t, 1-)$ in some appropriate ways. In such a context the expressions (1.2) and (1.3) are also considered as simple models of boundary flux controls, though they are insufficient in some practical respects.

2. Existence of a solution to $SP(g_o, g_1; u_o, \ell_o)$ on $[t_o, \infty)$

Let us recall the results in [18] on the local existence, uniqueness, comparison and convergence of solutions, which are given in the following statements [I], [II] and [III]:

[I] Assume that $g_o, g_1 \in W^{1,2}_{loc}(R)$ and g_o (resp. g_1) is non-negative (resp. non-positive) on R, and let $t_o \in R$, $u_o \in X$ and $\ell_o \in (0, 1)$ such that

$$\left\{\begin{array}{ll} u_o \geqq 0 \text{ on } [0, \ell_o], & u_o \leqq 0 \text{ on } [\ell_o, 1], \\ u_o(0) \geqq g_o(t_o) \text{ and } & u_o(1) \leqq g_1(t_o). \end{array}\right. \tag{2.1}$$

Then there exists a solution $\{u, \ell\}$ to $SP(g_o, g_1; u_o, \ell_o)$ on a certain interval $[t_o, t_1]$ with $t_1 > t_o$.

Remark 2.1. The construction of a solution $\{u, \ell\}$ of $SP(g_o, g_1; u_o, \ell_o)$ is done in the framework of the theory of nonlinear evolution equations governed by time-dependent subdifferential operators in Hilbert spaces, and hence by its general theory (cf. [16; section 1.2]) the function $t \to |u_x(t,.)|^2_H$ is absolutely continuous on $[t_o, t_1]$.

[II] Let $g_o, \hat{g}_o$ be non-negative functions in $W^{1,2}_{loc}(R)$ such that $g_o \leqq \hat{g}_o$ on R, and let $g_1, \hat{g}_1$ be non-positive functions in $W^{1,2}_{loc}(R)$ such that $g_1 \leqq \hat{g}_1$ on R. Also, let $\{u, \ell\}$ and $\{\hat{u}, \hat{\ell}\}$ be respectively solutions of $SP(g_o, g_1)$ and $SP(\hat{g}_o, \hat{g}_1)$ on J, where J is an interval in R. Then, for any $s, t \in J$ with $s \leqq t$,

$$\begin{aligned} & |(\rho(u)(t)-\rho(\hat{u})(t))^+|_{L^1(0,1)} + (\ell(t)-\hat{\ell}(t))^+ + \\ & + \int_s^t (u_x(\tau,0+)-\hat{u}_x(\tau,0+))\sigma_o([u(\tau,0)-\hat{u}(\tau,0)]^+)d\tau - \\ & - \int_s^t (u_x(\tau,1-)-\hat{u}_x(\tau,1-))\sigma_o([u(\tau,1)-\hat{u}(\tau,1)]^+)d\tau \\ \leqq\ & |(\rho(u)(s)-\rho(\hat{u})(s))^+|_{L^1(0,1)} + (\ell(s)-\hat{\ell}(s))^+, \end{aligned} \tag{2.2}$$

where ρ is the function given by (1.8) and

$$\sigma_o(r) = \begin{cases} 1 & \text{for } r > 0, \\ 0 & \text{for } r = 0, \\ -1 & \text{for } r < 0. \end{cases}$$

From (2.2) it follows immediately that

(1) the function $\alpha(t) \equiv |(\rho(u)(t)-\rho(\hat{u})(t))^+|_{L^1(0,1)} + (\ell(t)-\hat{\ell}(t))^+$ is non-increasing in $t \in J$;

(2) if $u(s,.) \leqq \hat{u}(s,.)$ on [0, 1] and $\ell(s) \leqq \hat{\ell}(s)$ for $s \in J$, then $u(t,.) \leqq \hat{u}(t,.)$ on [0, 1] and $\ell(t) \leqq \hat{\ell}(t)$ for any $t \in J$ with $t \geqq s$; and

(3) the solution of $SP(g_o, g_1; u_o, \ell_o)$ on $J = [t_o, t_1)$ is unique.

[III] Let $\{u_n, \ell_n\}$, n = 1, 2,..., be a sequence of solutions of $SP(g_{o,n}, g_{1,n})$ on a fixed compact interval J in R. Suppose that $(-1)^i g_{i,n} \geqq 0$ on R and

$$g_{i,n} \to g_i \quad \text{weakly in } W^{1,2}(J) \text{ (as } n \to \infty), \ i = 0, 1,$$

and further suppose that $\{u_n\}$ is bounded in $W^{1,2}(J; H) \cap L^\infty(J; X)$ and $\{\ell_n\}$ is bounded in $W^{1,2}(J)$ with $\delta \leqq \ell_n \leqq 1 - \delta$ for a certain constant $\delta > 0$. If $u_n \to u$ in C(J; H) and $\ell_n \to \ell$ uniformly on J, then the limit $\{u, \ell\}$ is a solution to $SP(g_o, g_1)$ on J.

The first main result is concerned with the global existence of a solution to $SP(g_o, g_1; u_o, \ell_o)$.

<u>THEOREM 2.1</u>. Suppose the following condition (G) holds:

(G) $g_i \in W^{1,2}_{loc}(R)$, $s^{1,2}(g_i) \equiv \sup_{t\in R}|g_i|_{W^{1,2}(t,t+1)} < \infty$ for i = 0, 1, and

$$m \leqq g_o(t) \leqq M, \quad -M \leqq g_1(t) \leqq -m \quad \text{for } t \in R,$$

where m, M are positive constants.

Let $t_o \in R$, $u_o \in X$ and $\ell_o \in (0, 1)$ for which (2.1) holds. Then there exists one and only one solution $\{u, \ell\}$ to $SP(g_o, g_1; u_o, \ell_o)$ on $[t_o, \infty)$, and the following energy inequality holds:

$$(2.3)\quad \begin{aligned} &|u_x(t)|^2_H + 2c^*\int_s^t |\rho(u)'(\tau)|^2_H d\tau + \int_s^t |\ell'(\tau)|^2 d\tau \\ &\leqq |u_x(s)|^2_H + 2\int_s^t \{|u_x(\tau,0+)||g_o'(\tau)| + |u_x(\tau,1-)||g_1'(\tau)|\}d\tau \text{ for } t \geqq s \geqq t_o, \end{aligned}$$

where $u(t) = u(t,.)$, $u_x(t) = u_x(t,.)$, $\rho(u)' = \rho(u)_t$ and $c^* = \min\{1/c_o, 1/c_1\}$. Moreover, the following bounds hold:

(2.4) $$0 \leqq u \leqq L_o \quad \text{on } \overline{Q_\ell^+(t_o, \infty)}, \quad -L_o \leqq u \leqq 0 \quad \text{on } \overline{Q_\ell^-(t_o, \infty)}$$

and

(2.5) $$\delta_o \leqq \ell \leqq 1 - \delta_o \quad \text{on } [t_o, \infty),$$

where

$$L_o = L_o(|u_o|_{L^\infty(0,1)}) = \max\{M, |u_o|_{L^\infty(0,1)}\},$$

and

$$\delta_o = \delta_o(|u_{o,x}|_H) = \left(\frac{m}{m + M + |u_{o,x}|_H}\right)^2.$$

This theorem is proved after preparing some lemmas which hold under the same assumptions as in Theorem 2.1.

We denote by T^* the supremum of all $T > t_o$ such that $SP(g_o, g_1; u_o, \ell_o)$ has a solution on $[t_o, T]$, that is, the interval $[t_o, T^*)$ is the maximal interval of existence. First of all we show the inequality (2.3) for the solution $\{u, \ell\}$ on $[t_o, T^*)$.

LEMMA 2.1. Inequality (2.3) holds for any $s, t \in [t_o, T^*)$ with $s \leqq t$.

Proof. We first note from the classical results (cf. [2. 22]) that $\ell \in C^\infty((t_o, T^*))$, $u \in C^\infty(D^+(t_o,T^*))$ and $u \in C^\infty(D^-(t_o,T^*))$, where

$$D^\pm = \overline{Q_\ell^\pm(t_o,T^*)} \cap \{(t,x);\ 0 < x < 1,\ t_o < t < T^*\}.$$

Let T be any number with $t_o < T < T^*$ and choose a number $\delta > 0$ so that $\delta < \ell < 1 - \delta$ on $[t_o, T]$. We then observe that for any $t_o \leqq s < t \leqq T$

$$c_o\int_0^\delta u_t(t,x)(u(t,x)-u(s,x))dx = \int_0^\delta u_{xx}(t,x)(u(t,x)-u(s,x))dx$$

$$= -\int_0^\delta u_x(t,x)(u_x(t,x)-u_x(s,x))dx + u_x(t,\delta)(u(t,\delta)-u(s,\delta))$$

$$- u_x(t,0+)(u(t,0)-u(s,0))$$

and by (1.2)',

$$\begin{aligned} &u_x(t, 0+)(u(s, 0)-u(t, 0)) \\ &= u_x(t, 0+)(u(s, 0)-g_o(s)+g_o(s)-g_o(t)+g_o(t)-u(t, 0)) \\ &\leqq |u_x(t, 0+)||g_o(s)-g_o(t)|. \end{aligned}$$

Therefore,

$$(2.6)\qquad \begin{aligned} &c_o\int_0^\delta |u_t(t,x)|^2dx + \frac{1}{2}\frac{d}{dt}\int_0^\delta |u_x(t,x)|^2dx \\ &\leqq u_x(t,\delta)u_t(t,\delta) + |u_x(t,0+)||g_o'(t)| \qquad \text{for a.e. } t \in [t_o, T]. \end{aligned}$$

Similarly,

$$(2.7)\qquad \begin{aligned} &c_1\int_{1-\delta}^1 |u_t(t,x)|^2dx + \frac{1}{2}\frac{d}{dt}\int_{1-\delta}^1 |u_x(t,x)|^2dx \\ &\leqq - u_x(t,1-\delta)u_t(t,1-\delta) + |u_x(t,1-)||g_1'(t)| \quad \text{for a.e. } t\in[t_o, T]. \end{aligned}$$

Besides, just as in the proof of [24; Proposition 3.3] (or [8; Theorem 1]), we obtain

$$(2.8)\qquad \begin{aligned} &\{c_o\int_\delta^{\ell(t)} |u_t(t,x)|^2dx + c_1\int_{\ell(t)}^{1-\delta} |u_t(t,x)|^2dx\} + \frac{1}{2}\frac{d}{dt}\int_\delta^{1-\delta} |u_x(t,x)|^2dx \\ &+ \frac{1}{2}|\ell'(t)|^3 \leqq - u_x(t,\delta)u_t(t,\delta) + u_x(t,1-\delta)u_t(t,1-\delta) \text{ for a.e.} t\in[t_o,T]. \end{aligned}$$

It is easy to obtain (2.3) for any $t_o \leqq s < t \leqq T$ from (2.6) - (2.8). Q.E.D.

Next we compare $\{u, \ell\}$ on $[t_o, T^*)$ with the solutions of $(SP)_o = SP(m,-M; U_o, \xi_o)$ and $(SP)_1 = SP(M, - m; V_o, \zeta_o)$, where $0 < \xi_o < 1$, $0 < \zeta_o < 1$, $U_o \in X$ and $V_o \in X$ are given, and we assume that

$$U_o \geqq 0 \text{ on } [0, \xi_o],\quad U_o \leqq 0 \text{ on } [\xi_o, 1],\quad U_o(0) \geqq m,\quad U_o(1) \leqq - M,$$

and

$$V_o \geqq 0 \text{ on } [0, \zeta_o],\quad V_o \leqq 0 \text{ on } [\zeta_o, 1],\quad V_o(0) \geqq M,\quad V_o(1) \leqq - m.$$

According to the results in [24, 25], $(SP)_c$ and $(SP)_1$ have unique solutions $\{U, \xi\}$ and $\{V, \zeta\}$ on $[t_o, \infty)$, respectively, and the following asymptotic convergences hold:

$$(2.9)\qquad U(t,x) \to a_o(x) \equiv - (m+M)x + m \text{ in } C([0,1]),\ \xi(t) \to x_o \equiv \frac{m}{m+M} \text{ as } t \to \infty.$$

$$(2.10)\qquad V(t,x) \to a_1(x) \equiv - (m+M)x + M \text{ in } C([0,1]),\ \zeta(t) \to x_1 \equiv \frac{M}{m+M} \text{ as } t \to \infty.$$

<u>LEMMA 2.2</u>. $\xi \geqq (\frac{m}{|U_{o,x}|_H})^2$ and $\zeta \leqq 1- (\frac{M}{|V_{o,x}|_H})^2$ on $[t_o, \infty)$.

<u>Proof</u>. We prove the first inequality for the solution $\{U, \xi\}$. Since $|U_x(t)|_H \leqq |U_{o,x}|_H$ for any $t \geqq t_o$ (cf. (2.3) for $\{U, \xi\}$), we have

$$U(t, x) \geqq m + \int_0^x U_y(t, y)dy \geqq m - x^{1/2}|U_x(t)|_H \geqq m - x^{1/2}|U_{o,x}|_H,$$

so that

$$U(t, x) > 0 \quad \text{if } 0 \leqq x < \left(\frac{m}{|U_{o,x}|_H}\right)^2.$$

This shows that

$$\xi \geqq \left(\frac{m}{|U_{o,x}|_H}\right)^2 \quad \text{on } [t_o, \infty).$$

The second inequality is similarly obtained. Q.E.D.

<u>LEMMA 2.3</u>. For the solution $\{u, \ell\}$ to $SP(g_o, g_1; u_o, \ell_o)$ on $[t_o, T^*)$, suppose that for a constant $0 < \delta \leqq 1/2$

$$\delta \leqq \ell \leqq 1 - \delta \quad \text{on } [t_o, T^*). \tag{2.11}$$

Then,

$$\begin{aligned} &\sup_{t_o \leqq t \leqq t_o+\mu} (t-t_o)|u_x(t)|_H^2 + \sup_{t_o+\mu \leqq t < T^*} |u_x(t)|_H^2 + \int_{t_o}^{t_o+\mu} (\tau-t_o)|\rho(u)'(\tau)|_H^2 d\tau \\ &+ \sup_{t_o+\mu \leqq t < T^*-\mu} \int_t^{t+\mu} |\rho(u)'(\tau)|_H^2 d\tau + \int_{t_o}^{t_o+\mu} (\tau-t_o)|\ell'(\tau)|^3 d\tau \\ &+ \sup_{t_o+\mu \leqq t < T^*-\mu} \int_t^{t+\mu} |\ell'(\tau)|^3 d\tau \leqq L_1(|u_o|_{L^\infty(0,1)}, \mu, \delta), \end{aligned} \tag{2.12}$$

where $L_1(\cdot, \cdot, \cdot): R_+ \times (0, \infty) \times (0, 1/2] \to R_+$ is a bounded function on each compact subset of $R_+ \times (0, \infty) \times (0, 1/2]$.

<u>Proof</u>. We first show the estimate

$$\int_s^t |u_x(\tau)|_H^2 d\tau \leqq L_1'(|u_o|_{L^\infty(0,1)}, \delta, t-s) \quad \text{for any } t_o \leqq s \leqq t < T^*, \tag{2.13}$$

where $L_1'(\cdot, \cdot, \cdot): R_+ \times (0, 1/2] \times R_+ \to R_+$ is a bounded function on each compact subset of $R_+ \times (0, 1/2] \times R_+$. To get (2.13) we use the function

$$h(x) = \begin{cases} -(M/\delta)x + M & \text{for } 0 \leqq x < \delta, \\ 0 & \text{for } \delta \leqq x \leqq 1 - \delta, \\ -(M/\delta)x + M/\delta - M & \text{for } 1 - \delta < x \leqq 1. \end{cases}$$

We then compute for a.e. $\tau \in [t_o, T^*)$

$$\frac{d}{d\tau}|u(\tau)-h|_H^2 = 2\int_0^1 u_\tau(\tau,x)(u(\tau,x)-h(x))dx$$

$$= \frac{2}{c_o}\int_0^{\ell(\tau)} u_{xx}(\tau,x)(u(\tau,x)-h(x))dx + \frac{2}{c_1}\int_{\ell(\tau)}^1 u_{xx}(\tau,x)(u(\tau,x)-h(x))dx$$

$$= -\frac{2}{c_o}\int_0^{\ell(\tau)} u_x(\tau,x)(u_x(\tau,x)-h_x(x))dx - \frac{2}{c_1}\int_{\ell(\tau)}^1 u_x(\tau,x)(u_x(\tau,x)-h_x(x))dx$$

$$-\frac{2}{c_o}u_x(\tau,0+)(u(\tau,0)-M) + \frac{2}{c_1}u_x(\tau,1-)(u(\tau,1)+M)$$

$$\leqq -\frac{1}{c_o}\int_0^{\ell(\tau)} |u_x(\tau,x)|^2dx + \frac{1}{c_o}\int_0^{\ell(\tau)} |h_x(x)|^2dx - \frac{1}{c_1}\int_{\ell(\tau)}^1 |u_x(\tau,x)|^2dx$$

$$+ \frac{1}{c_1}\int_{\ell(\tau)}^1 |h_x(x)|^2dx;$$

we used above the estimates $u_x(\tau,0+)(u(\tau,0)-M) \geqq C$ and $u_x(\tau,1-)(u(\tau,1)+M) \leqq 0$, which follow from (1.2)' and (1.3)', to get the last inequality. Hence,

$$\frac{d}{d\tau}|u(\tau)-h|_H^2 + c^*|u_x(\tau)|_H^2 \leqq \max\{\frac{1}{c_o}, \frac{1}{c_1}\}|h_x|_H^2.$$

Integration of this inequality over $[s, t] \subset [t_o, T^*)$ yields

$$|u(t)-h|_H^2 + c^*\int_s^t |u_x(\tau)|_H^2 d\tau \leqq (t-s)\max\{\frac{1}{c_o}, \frac{1}{c_1}\}|h_x|_H^2 + |u(s)-h|_H^2.$$

Since $|h| \leqq M$, $|u| \leqq \max\{|u_o|_{L^\infty(0,1)}\}$ (cf. [17; Lemma 2.1]) and $|h_x|_H^2 \leqq 2M^2/\delta$, the estimate (2.13) is obtained for a suitable $L_1'(\ .,\ .,\ .)$ having the required property.

Next, we infer easily from (2.3) for any $t_o \leqq s \leqq t < T^*$ that

$$(2.14)\quad \begin{aligned} &(t-s)|u_x(t)|_H^2 + 2c^*\int_s^t (\tau-s)|\rho(u)'(\tau)|_H^2 d\tau - \int_s^t (\tau-s)|\ell'(\tau)|^3 d\tau \\ &\leqq \int_s^t |u_x(\tau)|_H^2 d\tau + 2\int_s^t (\tau-s)(|u_x(\tau,0+)||g_o'(\tau)| + |u_x(\tau,1-)||g_1'(\tau)|)d\tau. \end{aligned}$$

Also, we note by (2.1) that for a.e. $\tau \in [t_o, T^*)$

$$(2.15)\quad \begin{aligned} |u_x(\tau,0+)| &\leqq \varepsilon|u_{xx}(\tau)|_{L^2(0,1)} + C(\varepsilon,\delta)|u_x(\tau)|_{L^2(0,1)} \\ &\leqq \varepsilon|\rho(u)'(\tau)|_H + C(\varepsilon,\delta)|u_x(\tau)|_H \end{aligned}$$

and similarly

$$(2.16)\quad |u_x(\tau,1-)| \leqq \varepsilon|\rho(u)'(\tau)|_H + C(\varepsilon,\delta)|u_x(\tau)|_H,$$

where ε is an arbitrary positive number and $C(\varepsilon,\delta)$ is a number depending only on ε and δ. With an appropriate $\varepsilon > 0$, depending only on c^* and δ, we can obtain the following type of inequality from (2.14) - (2.16):

$$(t-s)|u_x(t)|_H^2 + 2c^*\int_s^t (\tau-s)|\rho(u)'(\tau)|_H^2 + \int_s^t (\tau-s)|\ell'(\tau)|^3 d\tau$$

$$\leqq k_1\int_s^t (1+\tau-s)|u_x(\tau)|_H^2 d\tau + k_2\int_s^t (\tau-s)(|g_0'(\tau)|^2+|g_1'(\tau)|^2)d\tau \tag{2.17}$$

for any $s, t \in [t_0, T^*)$ with $s \leqq t$,

where k_1, k_2 are positive constants depending only on c^* and δ. It is not difficult to deduce an estimate of the type (2.12) from (2.13) and (2.17). Q.E.D.

Proof of THEOREM 2.1. As initial data of $(SP)_0$ and $(SP)_1$ we take respectively

$$U_0 = \min\{a_0, u_0\}, \quad \xi_0 = \min\{x_0, \ell_0\},$$

and

$$V_0 = \max\{a_1, u_0\}, \quad \zeta_0 = \max\{x_1, \ell_0\},$$

where a_0, a_1, x_0, x_1 are as in (2.9) and (2.10). Applying (2) of result [II] for two solutions $\{u, \ell\}$ and $\{U, \xi\}$, we have

$$U \leqq u \quad \text{on } [t_0, T^*)\times[0, 1] \quad \text{and} \quad \xi \leqq \ell \quad \text{on } [t_0, T^*),$$

so that $\ell \geqq (m/|U_{0,x}|_H)^2$ on $[t_0, T^*)$ by Lemma 2.2. Therefore, noting that $|U_{0,x}|_H \leqq |a_{0,x}|_H + |u_{0,x}|_H = m + M + |u_{0,x}|_H$, we obtain that

$$\ell \geqq \delta_0 \quad \text{on } [t_0, T^*).$$

Also, by the comparison Lemma [17; Lemma 2.1],

$$0 \geqq u \geqq U \geqq -\max\{M, |u_0|_{L^\infty(0,1)}\} = -\max\{M, |u_0|_{L^\infty(0,1)}\} \quad \text{on } \overline{Q_\ell^-(t_0,T^*)}.$$

Comparing $\{u, \ell\}$ with $\{V, \zeta\}$, we see similarly that

$$\ell \leqq 1-\delta_0 \quad \text{on } [t_0, T^*), \quad 0 \leqq u \leqq V \leqq \max\{M, |u_0|_{L^\infty(0,1)}\} \quad \text{on } \overline{Q_\ell^+(t_0,T^*)}.$$

Thus (2.4) and (2.5) hold on the interval $[t_0, T^*)$.

In order to accomplish the proof of Theorem 2.1 it remains to show $T^* = \infty$. For a contradiction suppose $T^* < \infty$. Then, by Lemma 2.3,

$$u \in W^{1,2}(t_0, T^*; H) \cap L^\infty(t_0, T^*; X), \quad \ell \in W^{1,3}(t_0, T^*)$$

and

$$\lim_{t\uparrow T^*} u(t) \equiv u(T^*) \text{ weakly in } X, \quad \lim_{t\uparrow T^*} \ell(t) \equiv \ell(T^*)$$

exist. Moreover, $\delta_0 \leqq \ell(T^*) \leqq 1-\delta_0$, $u(T^*, .) \geqq 0$ on $[0, \ell(T^*)]$, $u(T^*, 0) \geqq g_0(T^*)$, $u(T^*, .) \leqq 0$ on $[\ell(T^*), 1]$ and $u(T^*, 1) \leqq g_1(T^*)$, which imply by the local existence result [I] that $\{u, \ell\}$ is extendable beyond the time T*. This contradicts the definition of T*, so $T^* = \infty$ holds true. Q.E.D.

3. Bounded solution of $SP(g_o, g_1)$ on R

Before discussing the periodic and almost periodic behavior of solutions to $SP(g_o, g_1; u_o, \ell_o)$, we consider a class of bounded solutions of $SP(g_o, g_1)$ on R.

<u>THEOREM 3.1</u>. Suppose (G) holds. Then, there exists one and only one solution $\{u, \ell\}$ to $SP(g_o, g_1)$ on R such that

(3.1) $$u \in L^\infty(R \times [0,1])$$

and

(3.2) $$0 < \inf_{t\in R} \ell(t) \leq \sup_{t\in R} \ell(t) < 1.$$

<u>Remark 3.1</u>. In case the boundary condition is of the usual Dirichlet type, the uniqueness of a solution satisfying (3.1) and (3.2) was proved by Ishii [15].

We denote by $Y(g_o, g_1)$ the class of all solutions $\{u, \ell\}$ to $SP(g_o, g_1)$ on R having properties (3.1) and (3.2), i.e.

$$Y(g_o, g_1) = \left\{ \{u, \ell\}; \begin{array}{l} \{u, \ell\} \text{ is a solution to } SP(g_o, g_1) \text{ on R such that} \\ u \in L^\infty(R \times [0,1]) \text{ and } 0 < \inf_{t\in R} \ell(t) \leq \sup_{t\in R} \ell(t) < 1 \end{array} \right\}.$$

The above theorem is equivalent to the fact that $Y(g_o, g_1)$ is non-empty and a singleton.

<u>LEMMA 3.1</u>. $Y(g_o, g_1) \neq \emptyset$.

<u>Proof</u>. For each n = 1, 2,..., let $\{u_n, \ell_n\}$ be the solution of $SP(g_o, g_1; z_n, x_n)$ on $[-n, \infty)$, where

$$z_n(x) = (1-x)g_o(-n) + xg_1(-n), \quad x \in [0,1],$$

and

$$x_n = \frac{g_o(-n)}{g_o(-n) - g_1(-n)}.$$

We note that $|z_n| \leq M$ on $[0,1]$, $m/(m+M) \leq x_n \leq M/(m+M)$ and $|z_{n,x}|_H \leq 2M$. Therefore it follows from Theorem 2.1 and Lemma 2.3 that

$$|u_n| \leqq M \quad \text{on } [-n, \infty) \times [0, 1],$$

$$\delta_1 \leqq \ell_n \leqq 1 - \delta_1 \quad \text{on } [-n, \infty), \quad \delta_1 = \frac{m^2}{(m+3M)^2},$$

and

$$\sup_{t \geqq -n+1} \{|u_{n,x}(t)|_H^2 + |\rho(u_n)'|^2_{L^2(t,t+1;H)} + |\ell'|^3_{L^3(t,t+1)}\} \leqq L_1(M, 1, \delta_1)$$

for $n = 1, 2, \ldots$, so that there is a subsequence $\{n_k\}$ of $\{n\}$ satisfying

$$u_{n_k} \to u \text{ in } C(J; H), \quad \ell_{n_k} \to \ell \text{ uniformly on } J \text{ as } k \to \infty$$

for each compact subinterval J of R. By result [III],the limit $\{u, \ell\}$ is a solution of $SP(g_o, g_1)$ on R and satisfies that $|u| \leqq M$ on $R \times [0, 1]$ and $\delta_1 \leqq \ell \leqq 1 - \delta_1$ on R. Thus $\{u, \ell\} \in Y(g_o, g_1) \neq \emptyset$. Q.E.D.

LEMMA 3.2. $Y(g_o, g_1)$ is a directed set with respect to the usual order, that is, for any $\{u_i, \ell_i\}$ in $Y(g_o, g_1)$, $i = 1, 2$, there are $\{u^*, \ell^*\}$, $\{u_*, \ell_*\}$ in $Y(g_o, g_1)$ such that

$$\text{(3.3)} \quad \begin{cases} u_* \leqq \min\{u_1, u_2\} \leqq \max\{u_1, u_2\} \leqq u^* & \text{on } R \times [0, 1], \\ \ell_* \leqq \min\{\ell_1, \ell_2\} \leqq \max\{\ell_1, \ell_2\} \leqq \ell^* & \text{on } R. \end{cases}$$

Proof. We note by assumption that

$$|u_i| \leqq K \quad \text{on } R \times [0, 1], \quad \delta \leqq \ell_i \leqq 1 - \delta \quad \text{on } R,\ i = 1, 2,$$

for certain constants $K \geqq 0$ and $\delta > 0$. Putting

$$z_n(x) = \min\{u_1(-n,x), u_2(-n,x)\}, \quad x_n = \min\{\ell_1(-n), \ell_2(-n)\}$$

for each $n = 1, 2, \ldots$, we consider problem $SP(g_o, g_1; z_n, x_n)$ on $[-n, \infty)$, and denote by $\{\tilde{u}_n, \tilde{\ell}_n\}$ its solution. Just as in the proof of Lemma 3.1, it can be seen that a suitable subsequence $\{\tilde{u}_{n_k}, \tilde{\ell}_{n_k}\}$ of $\{\tilde{u}_n, \tilde{\ell}_n\}$ converges in $C(J; H) \times C(J)$ for every compact $J \subset R$, and the limit $\{u_*, \ell_*\}$ belongs to $Y(g_o, g_1)$. Besides, from (2) of result [II] we see that

$$u_* \leqq \min\{u_1, u_2\} \quad \text{on } R \times [0, 1], \quad \ell_* \leqq \min\{\ell_1, \ell_2\} \quad \text{on } R.$$

By considering a sequence of problems $SP(g_o, g_1; w_n, y_n)$ on $[-n, \infty)$ associated with

$$w_n(x) = \max\{u_1(-n,x), u_2(-n,x)\}, \quad y_n = \max\{\ell_1(-n), \ell_2(-n)\},$$

we obtain similarly $\{u^*, \ell^*\} \in Y(g_o, g_1)$ satisfying the other inequalities in (3.3). Q.E.D.

LEMMA 3.3. Let $\{u_i, \ell_i\} \in Y(g_o, g_1)$, $i = 1, 2$, such that

(3.4) $\qquad u_1 \leqq u_2 \quad$ on $R \times [0, 1]$, $\quad \ell_1 \leqq \ell_2 \quad$ on R

and

(3.5) $\qquad |\rho(u_2)(t)-\rho(u_1)(t)|_{L^1(0,1)} + \ell_2(t) - \ell_1(t) \equiv \alpha_o$ (= const.) on R.

Then $\{u_1, \ell_1\} = \{u_2, \ell_2\}$.

Proof. We first show that

(3.6) $\quad u_{1,x}(t,0+) = u_{2,x}(t,0+), \quad u_{1,x}(t,1-) = u_{2,x}(t,1-) \quad$ for a.e. $t \in R$.

In fact, since $u_2 \geqq u_1$, we see with the help of the boundary conditions (1.2)' and (1.3)' that

(3.7) $\quad u_{2,x}(t,0+) \geqq u_{1,x}(t,0+), \quad u_{2,x}(t,1-) \leqq u_{1,x}(t,1-) \quad$ for a.e. $t \in R$.

Also, on account of (3.4) and (3.5), for a.e. $t \in R$,

$$
\begin{aligned}
0 &= \frac{d}{dt}\int_0^1 (\rho(u_2)(t,x)-\rho(u_1)(t,x))dx + \frac{d}{dt}(\ell_2(t)-\ell_1(t)) \\
&= \int_0^1 (\rho(u_2)_t(t,x)-\rho(u_1)_t(t,x))dx + \ell_2'(t) - \ell_1'(t) \\
&= \int_0^{\ell_2(t)} u_{2,xx}(t,x)dx + \int_{\ell_2(t)}^1 u_{2,xx}(t,x)dx - \int_0^{\ell_1(t)} u_{1,xx}(t,x)dx \\
&\qquad - \int_{\ell_1(t)}^1 u_{1,xx}(t,x)dx + \ell_2'(t) - \ell_1'(t) \\
&= - u_{2,x}(t,0+) + u_{1,x}(t,0+) + u_{2,x}(t,1-) - u_{1,x}(t,1-) + u_{2,x}(t,\ell_2(t)-) \\
&\quad - u_{2,x}(t,\ell_2(t)+) - u_{1,x}(t,\ell_1(t)-) + u_{1,x}(t,\ell_1(t)+) + \ell_2'(t) - \ell_1'(t) \\
&= - u_{2,x}(t,0+) + u_{1,x}(t,0+) + u_{2,x}(t,1-) - u_{1,x}(t,1-).
\end{aligned}
$$

The last equality together with (3.7) implies (3.6) for a.e. $t \in R$.

Between boundary values of u_1 and u_2 on $x = 0$, there are the following three possibilities (a), (b) and (c):

Case (a). $u_1(t, k) = u_2(t, k)$ for any $t \in R$ and for $k = 0, 1$.

Case (b). There are $t_o \in R$ and $k \in \{0, 1\}$ such that

$$u_1(t, k) < u_2(t, k) \quad \text{for any } t \geqq t_o.$$

Case (c). There are t_o, $t_1 \in R$ with $t_o < t_1$ and $k \in \{0, 1\}$ such that

$$u_1(t, k) < u_2(t, k) \quad \text{for any } t_o \leqq t < t_1, \; u_1(t_1, k) = u_2(t_1, k).$$

Case (a): In this case, taking account of (3.6), we see that $\{u_1, \ell_1\}$ and $\{u_2, \ell_2\}$ are solutions of two-phase Stefan problems with the same boundary values on $x = 0$ and $x = 1$, and hence it follows from [15; Theorem 3.3] that $u_1 = u_2$ and $\ell_1 = \ell_2$.

We show below that Cases (b) and (c) do not occur.

Case (b): We assume $k = 0$. Since $u_2(t,0) > u_1(t,0) \geqq g_o(t)$ for $t \geqq t_o$, it follows from (1.2)' and (3.6) that $u_{1,x}(t,0+) = u_{2,x}(t,0+) = 0$ for a.e. $t \geqq t_o$. Therefore, $\{u_1, \ell_1\}$ satisfies

$$\begin{cases} c_o u_{1,t} - u_{1,xx} = 0 \quad \text{in } Q^+_{\ell_1}(t_o, \infty), \\ u_1(t, \ell_1(t)) = 0 \quad \text{for } t > t_o, \\ u_{1,x}(t, 0+) = 0 \quad \text{for a.e. } t > t_o. \end{cases}$$

We now compare u_1 with the solution W of the following problem:

$$\begin{cases} c_o W_t - W_{xx} = 0 \quad \text{in } (t_o, \infty) \times (0, 1), \\ W(t, 1) = 0 \quad \text{for } t > t_o, \\ W_x(t, 0+) = 0 \quad \text{for } t > t_o, \\ W(t_o, x) = u_1^+(t_o, x) \quad \text{for } x \in [0, 1]. \end{cases}$$

Then, by the comparison result for the heat equations,

$$0 \leqq u_1 \leqq W \quad \text{on } Q^+_{\ell_1}(t_o, \infty),$$

and by the stability result [9; Chapter 6], $W(t, x) \to 0$ uniformly in $x \in [0, 1]$ as $t \to \infty$. This implies that $u_1(t, 0) \to 0$ as $t \to \infty$, which contradicts that $u_1(t, 0) \geqq g_o(t) \geqq m$. In the case of $k = 1$ we have similarly a contradiction. Thus Case (b) never occurs.

Case (c): We may assume $k = 0$. Now, choose a positive number δ so that $\delta \leqq \ell_i \leqq 1 - \delta$ on R, $i = 1, 2$, and put $D = (t_o, t_1+1) \times (0, \delta)$. Then, by (3.6) and by assumptions, $Z = u_2 - u_1$ satisfies

$$\begin{cases} c_o Z_t - Z_{xx} = 0 \quad \text{in } D, \\ Z \geqq 0 \quad \text{on } \overline{D}, \quad Z(t, 0) > 0 \quad \text{for } t_o \leqq t < t_1, \\ Z_x(t, 0+) = 0 \quad \text{for } t_o < t < t_1 + 1. \end{cases}$$

Therefore $Z > 0$ on D and Z attains the minimum 0 at $(t_1, 0)$, and hence $Z_x(t_1, 0+)$ is strictly positive by the Friedman's result [9; Chapter 2, Theorem 14]. This is a contradiction. Thus Case (c) never occurs. Q.E.D.

LEMMA 3.4. $Y(g_o, g_1)$ is a singleton.

Proof. Let $\{u_i, \ell_i\}$, $i = 1, 2$, be two elements in $Y(g_o, g_1)$. In showing $\{u_1, \ell_1\} = \{u_2, \ell_2\}$ we may assume by virtue of Lemma 3.2 that $u_1 \leqq u_2$ and $\ell_1 \leqq \ell_2$. Put

$$\alpha_o = \lim_{t\to-\infty} \{|\rho(u_2)(t)-\rho(u_1)(t)|_{L^1(0,1)} + \ell_2(t) - \ell_1(t)\},$$

and choose a constant $\delta > 0$ with $\delta \leqq \ell_i \leqq 1 - \delta$ on R, $i = 1, 2$. By Lemma 2.3, we then observe that for $i = 1, 2$,

$$|u_i|^2_{L^\infty(R;X)} + \sup_{t\in R} |u_i|^2_{W^{1,2}(t,t+1;H)} + \sup_{t\in R} |\ell_i|^3_{W^{1,3}(t,t+1)} < \infty,$$

so that we can take a sequence $\{t_n\}$ with $t_n \to -\infty$ such that as $n \to \infty$,

$$u_i(\cdot+t_n) \to \hat{u}_i \quad \text{in } C_{loc}(R;H), \quad \ell_i(\cdot+t_n) \to \hat{\ell}_i \quad \text{in } C_{loc}(R)$$

as well as

$$g_i(\cdot+t_n) \to \hat{g}_i \quad \text{weakly in } W^{1,2}_{loc}(R)$$

for $i = 1, 2$. Besides it follows from result [III] that $\{\hat{u}_i, \hat{\ell}_i\}$, $i = 1, 2$, are solutions of $SP(\hat{g}_o, \hat{g}_1)$ on R. Clearly, $\hat{u}_i \in L^\infty(R\times[0,1])$, $i = 1, 2$, $\hat{u}_1 \leqq \hat{u}_2$ and $\delta \leqq \hat{\ell}_1 \leqq \hat{\ell}_2 \leqq 1 - \delta$. Hence $\{\hat{u}_i, \hat{\ell}_i\} \in Y(\hat{g}_o, \hat{g}_1)$, $i = 1, 2$. Moreover,

$$|\rho(\hat{u}_2)(t)-\rho(\hat{u}_1)(t)|_{L^1(0,1)} + \hat{\ell}_2(t) - \hat{\ell}_1(t) = \alpha_o \quad \text{for any } t \in R.$$

From Lemma 3.3 with g_o, g_1 replaced by $\hat{g}_o$, $\hat{g}_1$, we see that $\hat{u}_1 = \hat{u}_2$ and $\hat{\ell}_1 = \hat{\ell}_2$, which implies $\alpha_o = 0$. Consequently, (1) of result [II] implies that $u_1 = u_2$ and $\ell_1 = \ell_2$. Q.E.D.

The above lemmas complete the proof of Theorem 3.1.

4. Stability of solutions

In this section we study the stability of the equilibrium solution, the periodic solution and the almost periodic solution.

THEOREM 4.1. Suppose (G) holds and

$$g_i(t) \to g_{i,\infty} \quad \text{as } t \to \infty, \quad i = 0, 1.$$

Let $t_o \in R$ and $\{u, \ell\}$ be the solution of $SP(g_o, g_1)$ on $[t_o, \infty)$. Then

(4.1) $u(t, x) \to u_\infty(x) \equiv (1-x)g_{o,\infty} + xg_{1,\infty}$ uniformly in $x \in [0,1]$ as $t \to \infty$

and

(4.2) $$\ell(t) \to \ell_\infty \equiv \frac{g_{o,\infty}}{g_{o,\infty} - g_{1,\infty}} \text{ as } t \to \infty.$$

<u>Proof</u>. For each small $\varepsilon > 0$ we put

$$g_{i,\pm\varepsilon}(t) = g_{i,\infty} \pm \varepsilon, \quad t \in R, \quad i = 0, 1,$$

and choose a positive number $t_\varepsilon \geqq t_o$ such that

$$g_{i,\infty} - \varepsilon \leqq g_i(t) \leqq g_{i,\infty} + \varepsilon, \quad t \geqq t_\varepsilon, \quad i = 0, 1.$$

Now, denote by $\{u_{\pm\varepsilon}, \ell_{\pm\varepsilon}\}$ the solutions of $SP(g_{o,\pm\varepsilon}, g_{1,\pm\varepsilon}; z_{\pm\varepsilon}, \ell_{o,\pm\varepsilon})$ on $[t_\varepsilon, \infty)$, respectively, where

$$z_\varepsilon(x) = \max\{u_\infty(x)+\varepsilon, u(t_\varepsilon,x)\}, \quad \ell_{o,\varepsilon} = \max\{\frac{g_{o,\infty}+\varepsilon}{g_{o,\infty}-g_{1,\infty}}, \ell(t_\varepsilon)\},$$

$$z_{-\varepsilon}(x) = \min\{u_\infty(x)-\varepsilon, u(t_\varepsilon,x)\}, \quad \ell_{o,-\varepsilon} = \min\{\frac{g_{o,\infty}-\varepsilon}{g_{o,\infty}-g_{1,\infty}}, \ell(t_\varepsilon)\}.$$

Then, by the comparison result [II],

(4.3) $$u_{-\varepsilon} \leqq u \leqq u_\varepsilon \quad \text{on } [t_\varepsilon, \infty) \times [0, 1]$$

and

(4.4) $$\ell_{-\varepsilon} \leqq \ell \leqq \ell_\varepsilon \quad \text{on } [t_\varepsilon, \infty).$$

Also, according to [25; Theorem 4] on the asymptotic convergence in the time-independent case, we see that

(4.5) $u_{\pm\varepsilon}(t, x) \to u_\infty(x) \pm \varepsilon$ uniformly in $x \in [0, 1]$ as $t \to \infty$

and

(4.6) $$\ell_{\pm\varepsilon}(t) \to \ell_{\infty,\pm\varepsilon} \equiv \frac{g_{o,\infty}\pm\varepsilon}{g_{o,\infty}-g_{1,\infty}} \quad \text{as } t \to \infty.$$

It follows from (4.3) - (4.6) that (4.1) and (4.2) hold. Q.E.D.

The above theorem says that the asymptotic convergence of solutions to $SP(g_o, g_1)$ on $[t_o, \infty)$ is just the same as in the case of problems with the usual Dirichlet boundary conditions.

Next, we consider the almost periodic behavior of solutions. A solution $\{u, \ell\}$ of $SP(g_o, g_1)$ on R is called almost periodic, if u is almost periodic as a function from R into $C([0,1])$ and ℓ is also almost periodic as a function from R into itself. For the definition of almost periodicity and for general properties of almost periodic functions we refer to the book of Amerio-Prouse [1].

THEOREM 4.2. Suppose (G) holds and g_i, $i = 0, 1$, are almost periodic from R into itself. Then we have:

(a) $SP(g_o, g_1)$ has one and only one almost periodic solution $\{u_{ap}, \ell_{ap}\}$ on R;

(b) a solution $\{u, \ell\}$ of $SP(g_o, g_1)$ on R is almost periodic if and only if $u \in L^\infty(R\times[0,1])$ and there is a positive constant δ such that

$$\delta \leqq \ell \leqq 1 - \delta \quad \text{on } R;$$

(c) for any solution $\{u, \ell\}$ of $SP(g_o, g_1)$ on $[t_o, \infty)$ it holds that

$$u(t, x) - u_{ap}(t, x) \to 0 \quad \text{uniformly in } x \in [0, 1] \text{ as } t \to \infty$$

and

$$\ell(t) - \ell_{ap}(t) \to 0 \quad \text{as } t \to \infty.$$

Proof. By Theorem 3.1, there exists one and only one solution $\{u, \ell\}$ to $SP(g_o, g_1)$ on R such that $u \in L^\infty(R\times[0,1])$ and $\delta \leqq \ell \leqq 1 - \delta$ on R for a certain constant $\delta > 0$. We are going to show that $\{u, \ell\}$ is almost periodic. For the contrary suppose that u is not almost periodic as a function from R into $C([0,1])$. Then there would be a sequence $\{\tau_n\}$ in R such that the sequence $\{u(\cdot+\tau_n)\}$ does not contain any uniformly convergent subsequence of functions from R into $C([0,1])$, so that there would be two subsequences $\{s_n\}$ and $\{t_n\}$ of $\{\tau_n\}$, a sequence $\{\theta_n\}$ in R and a positive number ε_o such that

$$|u(\theta_n + s_n) - u(\theta_n + t_n)|_{C([0,1])} \geqq \varepsilon_o \quad \text{for all } n. \tag{4.7}$$

Also, by taking subsequences if necessary, we may assume from the almost periodicity of g_i that

$$g_i(\cdot + \tau_n) \to \hat{g}_i \quad \text{uniformly on } R \text{ (as } n \to \infty\text{)}, \ i = 0, 1, \tag{4.8}$$

for some almost periodic functions $\hat{g}_i$ on R, and from Lemma 2.3 that

$$u(\cdot + \theta_n + s_n) \to u_1 \quad \text{in } C(J; H), \ \ell(\cdot + \theta_n + s_n) \to \ell_1 \quad \text{in } C(J)$$

and

$$u(\cdot + \theta_n + t_n) \to u_2 \quad \text{in } C(J; H), \ \ell(\cdot + \theta_n + t_n) \to \ell_2 \quad \text{in } C(J)$$

for every compact interval J in R. We note from (4.8) that $g_i(\cdot + \theta_n + s_n)$ and $g_i(\cdot + \theta_n + t_n)$ converge uniformly on R as $n \to \infty$ to the same limit function g_i^*, $i = 0, 1$. Therefore $\{u_i, \ell_i\}$, $i = 1, 2$, are solutions of $SP(g_o^*, g_1^*)$ on R such that $u_i \in L^\infty(R\times[0,1])$ and $\delta \leqq \ell_i \leqq 1 - \delta$ on R, so that it follows from

Theorem 3.1 that $u_1 = u_2$ and $\ell_1 = \ell_2$. On the other hand, (4.7) implies $u_1(0) \neq u_2(0)$, which is a contradiction. Similarly the almost periodicity of ℓ is seen. Thus (a) and (b) are obtained. In order to prove (c), let $\{u, \ell\}$ be any solution to $SP(g_o, g_1)$ on $[t_o, \infty)$. Put

$$\alpha_o \equiv \lim_{t\to\infty} \{|\rho(u)(t)-\rho(u_{ap})(t)|_{L^1(0,1)} + |\ell(t)-\ell_{ap}(t)|\}.$$

Now, using Lemma 2.3 and the almost periodicity of g_i, we can extract a sequence $\{t_n\}$ with $t_n \to \infty$ (as $n \to \infty$) such that

$$g_i(\cdot + t_n) \to g_i \quad \text{uniformly on } R,\ i = 0, 1,$$

$$u_{ap}(\cdot + t_n) \to u_{ap} \quad \text{in } C([0, 1]) \text{ uniformly on } R,$$

$$\ell_{ap}(\cdot + t_n) \to \ell_{ap} \quad \text{uniformly on } R$$

and

$$u(\cdot + t_n) \to \hat{u} \quad \text{in } C(J; H),$$

$$\ell(\cdot + t_n) \to \hat{\ell} \quad \text{in } C(J)$$

for every compact interval J in R. Then, by Theorem 2.1 and result [III], $\{\hat{u}, \hat{\ell}\}$ is a solution to $SP(g_o, g_1)$ on R, $\hat{u} \in L^\infty(R \times [0,1])$ and $\delta \leqq \hat{\ell} \leqq 1 - \delta$ on R for some constant $\delta > 0$. Therefore, by (b), $\{\hat{u}, \hat{\ell}\} = \{u_{ap}, \ell_{ap}\}$, and hence $\alpha_o = 0$. This implies (c), since $\{u(t);\ t \geqq t_o\}$ is bounded in X. Q.E.D.

Finally we give a result on the periodic behavior of solutions. A solution $\{u, \ell\}$ of $SP(g_o, g_1)$ on R is called T_o-periodic, if $u(t + T_o) = u(t)$ in H and $\ell(t + T_o) = \ell(t)$ for any $t \in R$.

<u>THEOREM 4.3</u>. Suppose (G) holds and g_i, $i = 0, 1$, are T_o-periodic on R for a positive number T_o. Then we have:

(d) $SP(g_o, g_1)$ has one and only one T_o-periodic solution $\{u_p, \ell_p\}$ on R;

(e) a solution $\{u, \ell\}$ of $SP(g_o, g_1)$ on R is T_o-periodic if and only if $u \in L^\infty(R \times [0,1])$ and there is a positive constant δ such that

$$\delta \leqq \ell \leqq 1 - \delta \quad \text{on } R;$$

(f) for any solution $\{u, \ell\}$ of $SP(g_o, g_1)$ on $[t_o, \infty)$ it holds that

$$u(t, x) - u_p(t, x) \to 0 \quad \text{uniformly in } x \in [0, 1] \text{ as } t \to \infty$$

and

$$\ell(t) - \ell_p(t) \to 0 \quad \text{as } t \to \infty.$$

<u>Proof</u>. First we show the existence of a T_o-periodic solution. To this end we need a more general existence result [19; Theorem 2.4] for $SP(g_o, g_1; u_o,$

ℓ_o). According to it with Theorem 2.1, if initial data u_o, ℓ_o satisfy, instead of (2.1) with $t_o = 0$, that $0 < \ell_o < 1$, $u_o \in H$, $u_o \geqq 0$ a.e. on $[0, \ell_o]$ and $u_o \leqq 0$ a.e. on $[\ell_o, 1]$, then $SP(g_o, g_1; u_o, \ell_o)$ admits one and only one solution $\{u, \ell\}$ on R_+ in the following sense that $u \in C(R_+; H)$, $\ell \in C(R_+)$, $u(0) = u_o$, $\ell(0) = \ell_o$ and $\{u, \ell\}$ is a solution of $SP(g_o, g_1)$ on $[\varepsilon, \infty)$ in the sense mentioned in the Introduction for every $\varepsilon > 0$; it is easily seen that comparison result [II] holds for solutions in this weak sense. Now, consider the functions a_o, a_1 and numbers x_o, x_1 as given by (2.9) and (2.10), and let $\{u, \ell\}$ be the solution of $SP(g_o, g_1; a_o, x_o)$ on R_+ in the above weak sense. Also,note that the couples $\{a_o, x_o\}$ and $\{a_1, x_1\}$ are time-independent solutions to $SP(m, - M; a_o, x_o)$ and $SP(M, - m; a_1, x_1)$ on R_+, respectively. Therefore it follows from result [II] that

$$(4.9) \qquad a_o \leqq u \leqq a_1 \quad \text{on } R_+ \times [0, 1], \quad x_o \leqq \ell \leqq x_1 \quad \text{on } R_+$$

and that

$$(4.10) \qquad \begin{cases} u(t + nT_o, x) \leqq u(t + (n+1)T_o, x) & \text{on } [0, T_o] \times [0, 1], \\ \ell(t + nT_o) \leqq \ell(t + (n+1)T_o) & \text{on } [0, T_o] \end{cases}$$

for $n = 1, 2, \ldots$. We see from (4.9) and (4.10) and from the estimates in Lemma 2.3 that

$$u(\cdot + nT_o) \to \tilde{u} \quad \text{in } C([0, T_o]; H) \quad \text{as } n \to \infty$$

and

$$\ell(\cdot + nT_o) \to \tilde{\ell} \quad \text{in } C([0, T_o]) \text{ as } n \to \infty.$$

Besides, $\{\tilde{u}, \tilde{\ell}\}$ is a solution to $SP(g_o, g_1)$ on $[0, T_o]$ satisfying

$$\tilde{u}(0) = \tilde{u}(T_o) \text{ in } H \quad \text{and} \quad \tilde{\ell}(0) = \tilde{\ell}(T_o).$$

Therefore, the T_o-periodic extension of $\{\tilde{u}, \tilde{\ell}\}$ onto the whole line R is a T_o-periodic solution to $SP(g_o, g_1)$ on R. The uniqueness of T_o-periodic solution is a consequence of Theorem 3.1, and thus (d) and (e) hold. Finally (f) is a special case of (c). Q.E.D.

REFERENCES

1. L. Amerio and G. Prouse, Almost Periodic Functions and Functional Equations, Van Nostrand Reinhold, NewYork-Cincinati-Toronto-London-Melbourne, 1971.
2. J. R. Cannon and C. D. Hill, On the infinite differentiability of the free boundary in a Stefan problem, J. Math. Anal. Appl. 22(1967), 385-397.

3. J. R. Cannon and M. Primicerio, A two-phase Stefan problem with temperature boundary conditions, Ann. Mat. Pura Appl. 88(1971), 177-192.

4. J. R. Cannon and M. Primicerio, A two-phase Stefan problem with flux boundary conditions, Ann. Mat. Pura Appl. 88(1971), 193-205.

5. A. Damlamian and N. Kenmochi, Asymptotic behavior of solutions to a multiphase Stefan problem, to appear in Japan J. Appl. Math. (1986).

6. A. Damlamian and N. Kenmochi, Periodicity and almost periodicity of solutions to a multi-phase Stefan problem in several space variables, Tech. Reports Math. Sci. No.13, Chiba Univ., 1985.

7. E. DiBenedetto and A. Friedman, Periodic behavior for the evolutionary dam problem and related free boundary problems, to appear in J. Diff. Eq..

8. L. C. Evans and D. B. Kotlow, One-dimensional Stefan problems with quasilinear heat conduction, unpublished.

9. A. Friedman, Partial Differential Equations of Parabolic Type, Prentice-Hall, Englewood Cliffs, N. J., 1964.

10. A. Friedman, The Stefan problem in several space variables, Trans. Amer. Math. Soc. 133(1968), 51-87.

11. A. Friedman, One dimensional Stefan problems with nonmonotone free boundary, Trans. Amer. Math. Soc. 133(1968), 89-114.

12. K.-H. Hoffmann and J. Sprekels, Real-time control of the free boundary in a two-phase Stefan problem, Numer. Funct. Anal. Optimiz. 5(1982), 47-76.

13. K.-H. Hoffmann and J. Sprekels, Automatic delay-control in a two-phase Stefan problem, Intern. Ser. Numer. Math. 62, Differential-Difference Equations, ed. Collatz and al. Birkhauser Verlag, Basel, 1983.

14. K.-H. Hoffmann and J. Sprekels, Real-time control in a free boundary problem connected with the continuous casting of steel, preprint, Math. Inst. Univ. Augsburg, 1983.

15. H. Ishii, Asymptotic stability and existence of almost periodic solutions for one-dimensional two-phase Stefan problem, Math. Japonica 25(1980), 379-393.

16. N. Kenmochi, Solvability of nonlinear evolution equations with time-dependent constraints and applications, Bull. Fac. Education, Chiba Univ. 30 (1981), 1-87.

17. N. Kenmochi, Asymptotic behavior of solutions to a Stefan problem with obstacles on the fixed boundary, Hiroshima Math. J. 14(1984), 1-13.

18. N. Kenmochi, Two-phase Stefan problems with nonlinear boundary conditions described by time-dependent subdifferentials, Tech. Reports Math. Sci. No.18, Chiba Univ., 1985.

19. N. Kenmochi, Global existence of solutions of two-phase Stefan problems with nonlinear flux conditions described by time-dependent subdifferentials, Tech. Reports Math. Sci. No.9, Chiba Univ., 1986.

20. A. L. Meirmanov, The structure of a generalized solution of the Stefan problem, periodic solutions, Soviet Math. Dokl. 28(1983), 440-443.

21. L. I. Rubinstein, The Stefan problem, Transl. Math. Monographs 27, Amer. Math. Soc., Providence R. I., 1971.

22. D. G. Schaeffer, A new proof of the infinite differentiability of the free boundary in the Stefan problem, J. Diff. Eq. 20(1976), 266-269.

23. M. Štědrý and O. Vejvoda, Time periodic solutions of a one-dimensional two-phase Stefan problem, Ann. Mat. Pura Appl. 129(1981), 67-78.

24. S. Yotsutani, Stefan problems with the unilateral boundary condition on the fixed boundary II, Osaka J. Math. 20(1983), 803-844.

25. S. Yotsutani, Stefan problems with the unilateral boundary condition on the fixed boundary IV, Osaka J. Math. 21(1984), 149-167.

Nobuyuki KENMOCHI

Department of Mathematics
Faculty of Education
Chiba University
1-33 Yayoi-chō, Chiba-shi
Japan

International Series of
Numerical Mathematics, Vol. 78

ON THE CONTROL OF THE SECONDARY COOLING IN THE CONTINUOUS CASTING PROCESS

Pekka Neittaanmäki

University of Jyväskylä, Department of Mathematics, Finland

1. Introduction

Continuous casting is today replacing ingot casting as the major process for the production of steel in the form of slabs, blooms, billets etc. The complexity of this process is such that until recently innovations to machine design could only be tested by full scale runs on the production machine. This is extremely costly and in many cases production cannot be delayed for such tests to occur. For offering alternative means of testing new designs, numerical simulation models of the continuous casting process have been developed, especially during the last decade. We refer to conference proceedings [3], [5], [6] [16]. Furthermore we mention articles [4], [9], [13], [23], [24] concerning heat transfer models and FE-method, [12], [29] on numerical modelling of material properties in mushy zone, [10], [30] on boundary element method, [11], [24] on FE-modelling of thermal stresses, [2], [9], [13], [17]–[20], [25]–[28] on control of secondary cooling and [1], [7], [8], [31] concerning real-time control problems.

This contribution is the continuation of papers [17]–[20]. Our goal is to determine an optimal cooling strategy for the secondary cooling of billets, in order to achieve good productivity and to cast defect-free products.

In continuous casting cooling is used to accelerate steel solidification and to strengthen the solified shell. However, improper water quality or distribution changes rapidly the surface temperature and this may cause different kind of surface and internal defects. To avoid these defects, the strand has to be cooled down according to the pattern which depends on steel quality, product size, casting speed and machine design.

The schematic representation of the continuous casting machine of billets used in numerical simulations is shown in Figure 1.1. The secondary cooling system is assumed to comprise

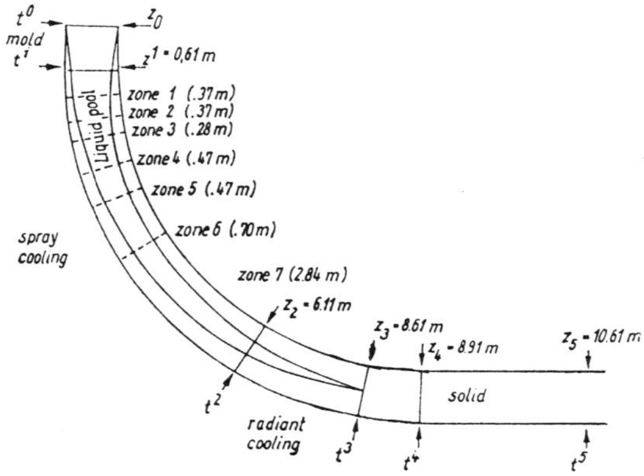

Figure 1.1 The continuous casting machine used in the calculations; curved billet caster.

seven cooling zones. The length of each zone is given in Figure 1.1. The unbending point is 8.91 meters from the meniscus.

The molten steel is fed from a ladle into a water cooled mold. The product is supported by rolls after mold and cooled by water sprays during the secondary cooling region (zones 1–7 in Figure 1.1). After the end of the secondary cooling (point z_2 in Figure 1.1) the product is cooled only by radiation. The unbending point and the cutting point are at the distance of z_4 and z_5 meters from the meniscus, respectively.

In our mathematical model we shall assume that the casting speed V is constant (in fact it could be optimized as well). Consequently $t_i = z_i/V$, where t_i is time and z_i distance from the meniscus (see Figure 1.1). In order to define the water cooling strategy and the spray system design, the heat flow and solidification rate must be known. Two different models are presented. The first method (chapter 3) is based on a heat conduction equation (2.1) with a Dirichlet boundary data (with desired surface temperature) and on the use of the heat flow equation (2.4) in the secondary cooling region. The aid of this method is to define the heat transfer coefficient (or in fact water flux) corresponding to the desired surface temperature along and across the secondary cooling region. By this model the surface temperature cannot be controlled after the secondary cooling region.

The second method (chapter 4), which is based on the optimal control theory, is more sophisticated ([**2**], [**14**], [**17**], [**18**], [**19**], [**20**]). In this method the problem for finding the optimal cooling strategy for water spray cooling leads us to an optimal control problem with constraints in state and control (see Problem 4.2). The state is governed by a nonlinear parabolic-type equation with phase changes (eq. (2.1)) and nonlinear boundary conditions (eq. (2.4)). A penalty method is used to eliminate the state constraints. The obtained nonlinear (nonsmooth) programming problem is solved by the bundle algorithm [15]. By this model the heat transfer coefficients along and across the strand surface can be calculated in order to get a desirable temperature distribution in the strand surface and to meet metallurgical cooling criteria determined beforehand. The model gives thereby an improved basis for the design of the secondary cooling system and to define the maximum casting speed to produce defect-free products.

2. The heat transfer model

The heat transfer model is based on the numerical solution of the unsteady heat conduction equation, which describes the heat transfer from the interior of the strand to the external surface (equation (2.1))

$$\frac{\partial}{\partial t} H(T) = \triangle K(T) \qquad in\ \Omega \times (0, t_5). \tag{2.1}$$

H(T) and K(T) are the enthalpy and the Kirchhoff transformation, respectively. They are defined by the following equations:

$$H(T) = \int_0^T [\rho(s)c(s) + \frac{\rho(s)L}{T_l - T_s}]ds \tag{2.2}$$

$$K(T) = \int_0^T k(s)ds. \tag{2.3}$$

The specific heat c(T) and the thermal conductivity k(T) of steel are defined separately for three temperature regions, inside which they are assumed to be constant. These regions are the liquid region, the mushy region and the solid shell. The density ρ of the steel is assumed to be independent on temperature. These assumptions imply by equations (2.2)-(2.3) that H(T) and K(T) are piecewise linear functions of T as indicated in Figure 2.1.

The list of symbols used is given in Table 2.2.

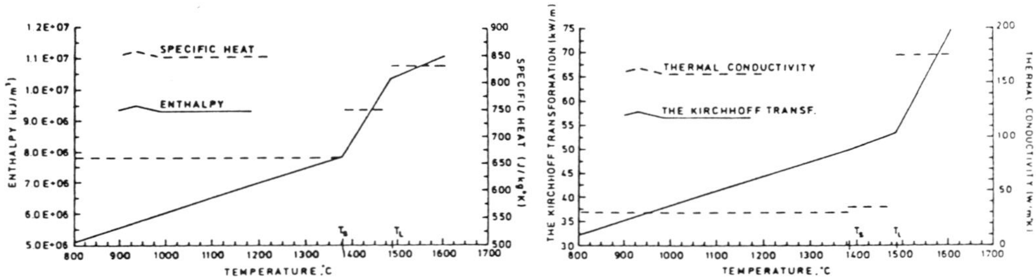

Figure 2.1 H(T) and K(T)

Table 2.2 - List of symbols.

t	time	k(T)	thermal conductivity
T	temperature	c(T)	specific heat
T_l	liquidus temperature	σ	Stefan-Bolzmann const.
T_s	solidus temperature	ε	emissity
T_{mold}	ambient mold temp.	ϱ	density
T_{H_2O}	spray water temperature	L	latent heat
$\frac{\partial}{\partial n}T$	temperature gradient	V	casting speed
	to strand surface	x^+	the positive part of x;
H	enthalpy		$x^+ = x, \ for \ x > 0$ and
h_{mold}	heat transfer coefficient		$x^+ = 0, \ for \ x \leq 0$
	in the mold	Ω	cross-section of a billet
h	water heat transfer	Γ	boundary of Ω
	coefficient	W	water flux

The model is simplified to a two-dimensional one, because in the continuous casting of steel the heat conduction in the withdrawal direction is minute and can be neglected. The convective heat flow in the liquid pool is quite complex due to the turbulent mixing imparted by the input metal stream. It is taken into account in the model by defining an effective liquid thermal conductivity, which includes the effects of convective mixing. It is assumed to be roughly six times greater than the normal value for the liquid thermal conductivity. For models of analysing the metallurgical solidification processes we refer to [**3**],[**12**],[**29**].

In order to solve equation (2.1) for the transient temperature distribution, boundary conditions as well as an initial condition must be specified. We have two possibilities to define the boundary conditions (Neumann or Dirichlet type), depending on what we know about the heat extraction on the boundary Γ.

If we assume that the heat transfer from the strand surface to the environment takes place by convection and by radiation, the boundary conditions are constituted as:

$$-k(T)\frac{\partial}{\partial n}T = \begin{cases} h_{mold}(T - T_{mold}), & \text{in mold region;} \\ h(T - T_{H_2O}) + \sigma\epsilon(T^4 - T^4_{ext}), & \text{in sec. cool. region;} \\ \sigma\epsilon(T^4 - T^4_{ext}), & \text{in radiant cool. region;} \end{cases} \tag{2.4}$$

Secondly, we can assume that the surface temperature has a given temperature distribution $T_g(x,t)$. Thus, the boundary condition is constituted as:

$$T(x,t) = T_g(x,t) \qquad on\ \Gamma \times (t_1,t_2) \quad (in\ sec.\ cooling\ region) \tag{2.5}$$

For $t = 0$ we assume that the temperature distribution at the meniscus is uniform and equal to the liquidus temperature of the incoming metal stream:

$$T(x,t) = T_l(x) \qquad t = t_0 = 0\ and\ x \in \Omega \tag{2.6}$$

The problem (2.1), (2.6) is called the multiphase Stefan problem with a Neumann (eq. (2.4)) or Dirichlet (eq. (2.5)) type boundary condition. The unknown term is the temperature field $T(x,t)$ (the state variable). The solvability of a similar system is discussed in [**22**], for example.

The heat extraction in the mold region is very complicated due to the air cap formation between the billet surface and the mold wall. In numerical simulations we have used the following approximation for h_{mold}

$$h_{mold}(x,t) = \begin{cases} 2.0 - 0.2\sqrt{max(0,t-6)}\frac{kW}{m^2\,{}^\circ K}; & x\ lies\ in\ the\ midface \\ 2.0 - 0.5\sqrt{max(0,t-3)}\frac{kW}{m^2\,{}^\circ K}; & x\ lies\ in\ the\ corner \\ interpolant\ of\ the\ above\ values\ for\ other\ x\ and\ t \end{cases}$$

where x refers to the boundary Γ of Ω. The above approximation is based on practical fitting (see also [**3**], [**9**], [**24**]). The air gap formation reduces the heat transfer coefficient in the corner.

2.2 The discrete model for the Neuman type problem (2.1),(2.4),(2.5).

Discretizing the spatial domain by finite elements, and applying the Euler method, the following nonlinear system of equations is obtained:

$$\begin{cases} M\dfrac{H(T^{i+1})-H(T^{i})}{\Delta t}+AK(T^{i+1})+B(h^{i+1}_{mold})T^{i+1}=B(h^{i+1}_{mold})T^{i+1}_{mold};\ t^{i+1}\in(0,t_1] \\ M\dfrac{H(T^{i+1})-H(T^{i})}{\Delta t}+AK(T^{i+1})+B(h^{i+1})T^{i+1}+\sigma\epsilon B[T^{i+1}]^4=B(h^{i+1})T^{i+1}_{H_2O} \\ \qquad +\sigma\epsilon B[T^{i+1}_{ext}]^4; \qquad t^{i+1}\in(t_1,t_2] \\ M\dfrac{H(T^{i+1})-H(T^{i})}{\Delta t}+AK(T^{i+1})+\sigma\epsilon B[T^{i+1}]^4=\sigma\epsilon B[T^{i+1}_{ext}]^4;\ t^{i+1}\in(t_2,t_5] \\ T^0=T_l \end{cases} \tag{2.7}$$

We have denoted by T^i the nodal value vector of the temperature field at time level $t^i=i\Delta t$: $T^i=T(t^i)=(T_1(t^i),...,T_n(t^i))$; $[T^i]^4=(T_1(t^i)^4,...,T_n(t^i)^4)$. The typical components of matrices M (mass matrix) and A (stiffness matrix) are defined by

$$M_{ij}=\int_\Omega \varphi_i\varphi_j\,dx \qquad A_{ij}=\int_\Omega \nabla\varphi_j\cdot\nabla\varphi_j\,dx. \tag{2.8}$$

Here φ_i denotes the finite element shape function assosiated with the node i of the triangular finite element mesh.

Suppose that the nodes of Γ have been numbered first p = number of boundary nodes. Then $B=(b_{ij})$ is the $(n\times n)$ matrix defined as follows: $b_{ii}=d$, $i=1,...,p$; $b_{ij}=0$ otherwise, where d denotes the mesh parameter on the boundary Γ, (a trapezoidal rule is applied in numerical integration). Moreover, the notation $B(h)$ denotes the diagonal matrix with components $B(h)_{ii}=dh_i$, $i=1,...,p$ and $B(h)_{ij}=0$ otherwise.

In order to solve eq. (2.7) an iterative method is used. On such boundary nodes where the nonlinear boundary condition, Stefan condition, is assumed, the Newton-Raphson method with assumption that the nodes are in a solid state is used. At other nodes we use the modified SOR method which takes into account the phase change temperatures. For details see [**13**].

3. The first method. The billet with the desired surface temperature

Suppose that during the secondary cooling we want to have the surface temperature distribution T_g $(=T_g(x,t))$. In order to find the water spray cooling W $(\frac{l}{m^2s})$ which gives this surface temperature field, we apply the boundary condition (2.4) and the relation between the spray heat transfer coefficients and the water flux. This relation is linear or nonlinear [3], depending on the model (strand size, machine design). Suppose for example that

$$h = 0.14W + 0.1\ . \tag{3.1}$$

The algorithm for finding an "optimal" h is given below:

Algorithm 3.1

Step 1. For a given surface temperature T_g solve the problem (2.1),(2.6) with the Dirichlet boundary data

$$T = T_g \qquad on \qquad \Gamma \times (t_1, t_2). \tag{3.2}$$

Step 2. Determine the spray heat transfer coefficient h from the relation

$$-k(T)\frac{\partial}{\partial n}T = h(T - T_{H_2O}) + \sigma\epsilon(T^4 - T_{ext}^4) \quad on \quad \Gamma \times (t_1, t_2). \tag{3.3}$$

Step 3. Determine the water flux W from the relation (3.1) (or from some other related relation).

In fact, we can solve the relation between water flux W and heat transfer coefficient h with this Dirichlet type problem using the surface temperature measured in the factory as a boundary condition. The Algorithm 3.1 is useful as well in calculating of special control relations between the heat transfer coefficients and residence time in dynamic control model. For details we refer to a forthcoming paper.

We shall illustrate the usefulness of the above algorithm by an example.

Example 3.1. Consider the case of billet casting. The schematic representation of the continuous casting machine is shown in Figure 1.1. The numerical values of material and casting data are shown in Table 3.1 and in Figure 2.1.

Table 3.1 - Material and casting data used.

Carbon content	0.5 %	ρ	7200 $\frac{kg}{m^3}$
$T_l = T_0$	1485 °C	L	272 $\frac{kJ}{kg}$
T_s	1377 °C	σ	$5.67\times10^{-8}\frac{W}{m^2K^4}$
T_{mold}	80 °C	ϵ	0.8
T_{H_2O}	27 °C	Cross-section: 100×100 mm^2	
T_{ext} spray z.	97 °C	Casting speed 2.80 $\frac{m}{min}$	
T_{ext} rad. z.	437 °C	Mold lenght 0.61 m	

The desired surface temperature T_g is given on the corner and midface by the equation

$$T_g(x,t) = \begin{cases} 0.54 \times t + 904.43, & t \in (t_1, t_4) \quad \text{(corner)}; \\ -0.16 \times 10^{-3} \times t + 1100.03, & t \in (t_1, t_4) \quad \text{(midface)}. \end{cases} \tag{3.4}$$

For the other points of Γ T_g is given by the parabolic fitting.

In Figure 3.2 (a) we see the water spray heat transfer coefficients obtained by Algorithm 3.1 at corner and midface. Figure 3.2 (b) and (c) show the surface temperature and shell thickness obtained from (2.1), (2.4), (2.6) (Neumann type problem) with a boundary data like Figure 3.2 (a). In [13] similar results are reported also in the case of slab casting.

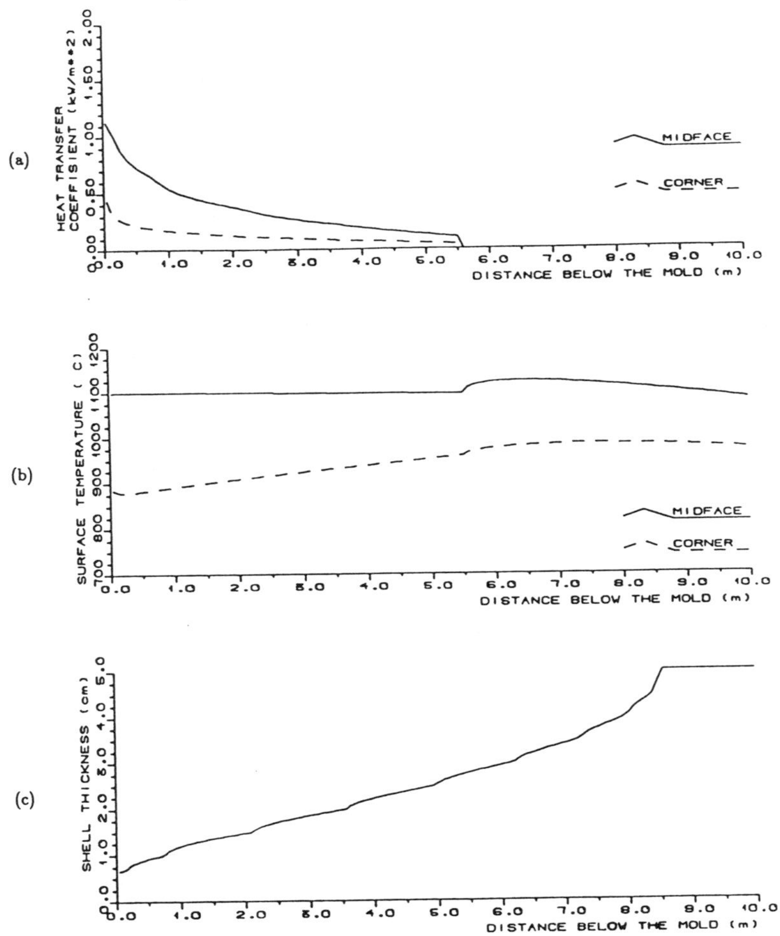

Figure 3.2

4. The second method. Optimization of water heat transfer coefficient

4.1 The problem.

As we can see in Example 3.1 the surface temperature cannot be controlled after the end of the secondary cooling zone and some important metallurgical constraints are not satisfied. Suppose we want to have the average surface temperature as near as possible to a given temperature T_g and moreover the following metallurgical constraints (state constraints) must be satisfied:

(1) The surface temperature along the caster must be between the lower bound T_{min} and the upper bound T_{max}.

(2) The temperature variation along the surface must lie in the range $[CN, CP]$; CN<0 and CP>0 some given constants.

(3) The surface temperature at the unbending point must be over T_{duc}.

For a constant casting speed 2.8 $\frac{m}{min}$ the above constraints show that the length of the liquid pool is less than 8.3 m.

Again we are led to the control problem of finding optimal heat transfer coefficients in the boundary condition (2.4). The relation (3.1) then gives information about the corresponding water flux.

Let U_{ad} denote the set of admissible controls (heat transfer coefficients):

$$U_{ad} = \{h(x,t) | h^i_{min} \leq h(x,t) \leq h^i_{max}; \qquad i = 1, ..., 7\}, \tag{4.1}$$

where h^i_{min} and h^i_{max} are the minimum and maximum possible heat transfer coefficients in the cooling zone i. For the metallurgical constraints (1)–(3) we apply the penalty technique with the nonmeeting of the constraints. Thence our control problem reads

$$\min_{h \in U_{ad}} J(T(h); h), \tag{4.2}$$

subject to the state problem (2.1), (2.4),(2.5).

The cost function J is a sum of partial costs $J = J_0 + J_1 + J_2 + J_3$, where

$$J_0(T(h);h) = \frac{1}{2}\int_{t_1}^{t_4}\int_\Gamma [(T(x,t) - T_g)]^2 d\Gamma dt \ ,$$

$$J_1(T(h);h) = \frac{c_1}{2}\int_{t_1}^{t_5}\int_\Gamma \{[(T_{min} - T(x,t))^+]^2 + [(T(x,t) - T_{max})^+]^2\} d\Gamma dt \ ,$$

$$J_2(T(h);h) = \frac{c_2}{2}\int_{t_1}^{t_5-\Delta t}\int_\Gamma \Big\{[(\frac{T(x,t+\Delta t) - T(x,t)}{\Delta t} - CP)^+]^2 + [(CN - \frac{T(x,t+\Delta t) - T(x,t)}{\Delta t})^+]^2\Big\} d\Gamma dt \ ,$$

$$J_3(T(h);h) = \frac{c_3}{2}\int_\Gamma [(T_{duc} - T(x,t_4))^+]^2 d\Gamma \ .$$

Above, c_i are constants which express the relative importance of criterion J_i, i=1,...,3, with respect to the other ones. For the analysis of state constrained control problems (penalty or variational inequality approach) we refer to [**21**] and references therein.

4.2 The discretization of Problem (4.2).

We use the same discretization by the finite element method in space and by the finite difference method in time as in Chapter 2.2. Furthermore we denote by $k_1, ..., k_5$ the indices of the time levels at distances $z_1, ..., z_5$ (see Fig. 1.1) from the meniscus, respectively.

When an appropriate numerical quadrature is used to compute the cost functional (4.2) we are led to a finite dimensional problem

$$\min_{h\in U_{ad}} J_d(T(h);h); \ \ J_d(T(h);h) = J_{0,d} + J_{1,d} + J_{2,d} + J_{3,d} \tag{4.3}$$

subject to the state system (2.7). Above, the partial costs $J_{i,d}$, i=0,...,3 are defined as follows:

$$J_{0,d}(T(h);h) = \frac{\Delta t}{2}\sum_{i=k_1}^{k_4}(T^i - T_g^i, BT^i - BT_g^i))$$

$$J_{1,d}(T(h);h) = \frac{c_1\Delta t}{2}\sum_{i=k_1}^{k_5}[((T^i - T_{max}^i)^+, B(T^i - T_{max}^i)^+) + ((T_{min}^i - T^i)^+, B(T_{min}^i - T^i)^+)]$$

$$J_{2,d}(T(h);h) = \frac{c_2\Delta t}{2}\sum_{i=k_1}^{k_5-1}[((\frac{\partial T^i}{\partial t} - CP)^+, B(\frac{\partial T^i}{\partial t} - CP)^+) + ((CN - \frac{\partial T^i}{\partial t})^+, B(CN - \frac{\partial T^i}{\partial t})^+)]$$

$$J_{3,d}(T(h);h) = \frac{c_3\Delta t}{2}((T_{duc} - T^{k_4})^+, B(T_{duc} - T^{k_4})^+)$$

For short, we have used the abbreviation $\frac{\partial}{\partial t}T^i(x,t)$ for the difference $\frac{T^{i+1}-T^i}{\Delta t}$.

4.3 Method for solving Problem (4.3).

The three main steps in the minimization of the cost function (4.3) for a given casting speed are:

- The calculation of the temperature map inside the strand for given settings of the secondary cooling.
- The calculation of the gradient of the cost function.
- The calculation of the new solution by some gradient (or subgradient) method with projection on the constraints.

The directional (direction s) gradient of the cost function $J_d(T(h);h)$ can be expressed as:

$$\nabla J_d(T(h);h)s = \sum_{k=k_1+1}^{k_2} (p^{k-1}, s^k(T^k - T^k_{H_2O}) \tag{4.4}$$

where p^k is the solution of the following adjoint system.

$$\begin{cases} -M(\frac{\partial}{\partial T}H^{k+1})\frac{p^{k+1}-p^k}{\Delta t} + A(\frac{\partial}{\partial T}K^{k+1})p^k + B(h^{k+1})p^k + 4\epsilon\sigma B([T^{k+1}]^3)p^k \\ \qquad = F_0^k + F_1^k + F_2^k + F_3^k; \qquad k = k_1, ..., k_2 - 1 \\ -M(\frac{\partial}{\partial T}H^{k+1})\frac{p^{k+1}-p^k}{\Delta t} + A(\frac{\partial}{\partial T}K^{k+1})p^k + 4\epsilon\sigma B([T^{k+1}]^3)p^k \\ \qquad = F_0^k + F_1^k + F_2^k + F_3^k; \qquad k = k_2, ..., k_5 - 1 \\ p^{k_5} = 0, \end{cases} \tag{4.5}$$

where the nonzero elements of F_i^k are

$$F_0^k = \Delta t[(B(T^k - T_g^k)^+)] \qquad ,k = k_1, ..., k_4$$

$$F_1^k = c_1 \Delta t[B(T^k - T_{max})^+ + B(T_{min} - T^k)^+] \qquad ,k = k_1, ..., k_5 - 1$$

$$\begin{aligned} F_2^k = c_2[&B(\frac{\partial T^{k-1}}{\partial t} - CP)^+ + B(CN - \frac{\partial T^{k-1}}{\partial t})^+) \\ &+ B(\frac{\partial T^k}{\partial t} - CP)^+ + B(CN - \frac{\partial T^k}{\partial t})^+)] \qquad ,k = k_1, ..., k_5 - 1 \end{aligned}$$

$$F_3^k = c_3 \Delta t[B(T_{duc} - T^k)^+] \qquad ,k = k_4$$

and where $M(\cdot)$ and $A(\cdot)$ are the weighted variants of the matrix M and of the stiffness matrix A in (2.8). Note that $\frac{\partial}{\partial T}H^{k+1}$ and $\frac{\partial}{\partial T}K^{k+1}$ are not defined everywhere without modifications (cf Fig 2.1).

Equation (4.5) is a linear system in an implicit form and it can be solved for instance by the normal S.O.R.-method at every time step $k = k_1, ..., k_5 - 1$.

4.4 Algorithm for solving Problem (4.3).

Algorithm 4.1

Let $h_0 \in U_{ad}$, ϵ, η be given. Denote by ∂J the ϵ-subdifferential of J. Set i=n=0, p_i=0. (i=number of iterations, n=number of subgradients in the bundle)

Step 1. For given h_n solve the state problem (2.7) in order to obtain $T(h_n)$ and the adjoint state problem (4.5) in order to obtain $g_n \in \partial J_d$.

Step 2. Calculate s_n (search direction) being the projection of origin onto the convex hull of $G_n := \{-g_{p_i}, ..., -g_n\}$. Test if $|s_n| < \eta$, then STOP.

Step 3. Calculate ρ_n such, that

$$J_d(h_n + \rho_n s_n) \le J_d(h_n + \rho s_n), \qquad \forall \rho > 0.$$

Set $h_{n+1} := h_n + \rho_n s_n$. Take the projection of h_{n+1} onto the constraints.

Step 4. Determine $g_{n+1} \in \partial J_d(h_{n+1})$ such that $(g_{n+1}, s_n) = 0$. Set n:=n+1.

Step 5. If $(g_n, h_n - h_{p_i}) \le \epsilon$, then go to Step 2.

Step 6. Set i:=i+1, p_i:=n, then go to Step 1. (new iteration begins)

The analysis of the above type algorithm is given in [**14**].

Example 4.2

Let us consider the same situation as in the previous Example 3.1. The cooling criteria used this time can be seen at Table 4.1.

Table 4.1 - Cooling criteria used.

Criterion	Aimed value
The desired surface temperature T_g	as in eq. (3.4)
Maximum reheating rate on the surface	$+0.5\frac{°C}{sec}$
Minimum cooling rate on the surface	$-0.5\frac{°C}{sec}$
Surface temperature at the unbending point (8.3 m) T_{duc}	$> 1000\ °C$
Minimum surface temperature along the secondary cooling zones T_{min}	900 $°C$
Maximum surface temperature along the secondary cooling zones T_{max}	1200 $°C$

Figure 4.2 shows analogues results to Figure 3.2 which now are obtained by Algorithm 4.1 as an initial guess a rough approximation for h resulting by Algorithm 3.1. After optimization of the heat transfer coefficients (water flux) the surface temperature is very near to the desired temperature T_g and moreover the state constraints are accomplishing in a satisfactory way. This situation is presented in Figure 4.2. The information in Figure 4.3 consists of the whole face of the billet. Therein the contour plot of the control (water spray heat transfer coefficients), the surface temperature and the centre plane are given. The transverse profiles of the water spray heat transfer coefficients, (averaged values) as well as the upper (h^i_{max}) and lower (h^i_{min}) bounds for the control are presented in Figure 4.4.

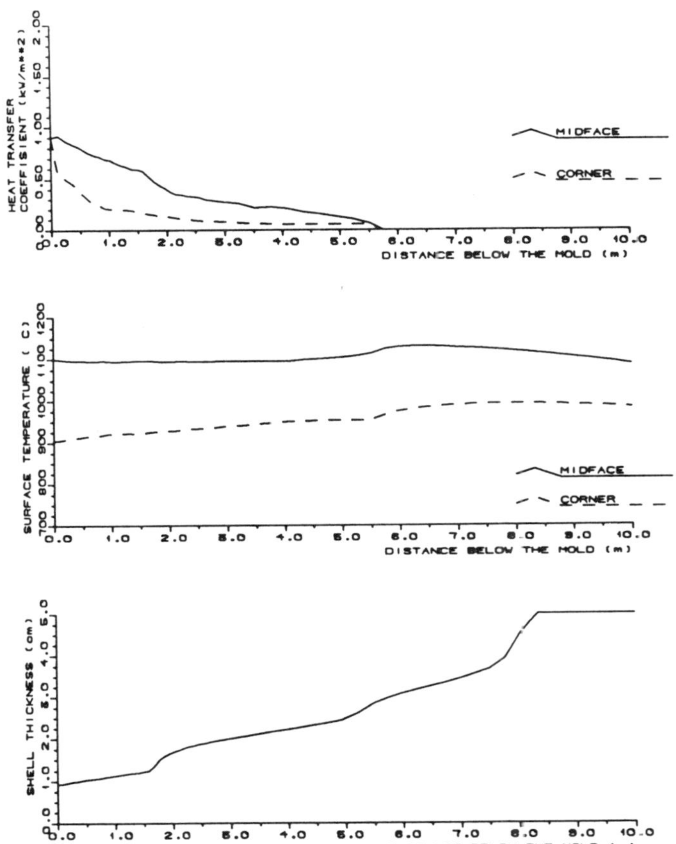

Figure 4.2

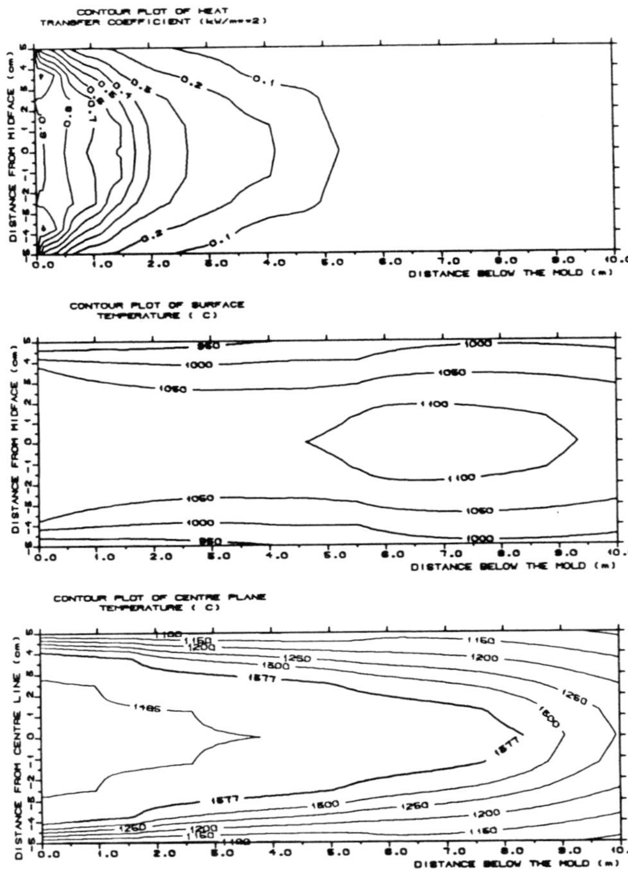
CONTOUR PLOT OF HEAT TRANSFER COEFFICIENT (kW/m**2)
DISTANCE FROM MIDFACE (cm)
DISTANCE BELOW THE MOLD (m)
CONTOUR PLOT OF SURFACE TEMPERATURE (C)
DISTANCE FROM MIDFACE (cm)
DISTANCE BELOW THE MOLD (m)
CONTOUR PLOT OF CENTRE PLANE TEMPERATURE (C)
DISTANCE FROM CENTRE LINE (cm)
DISTANCE BELOW THE MOLD (m)

Figure 4.3

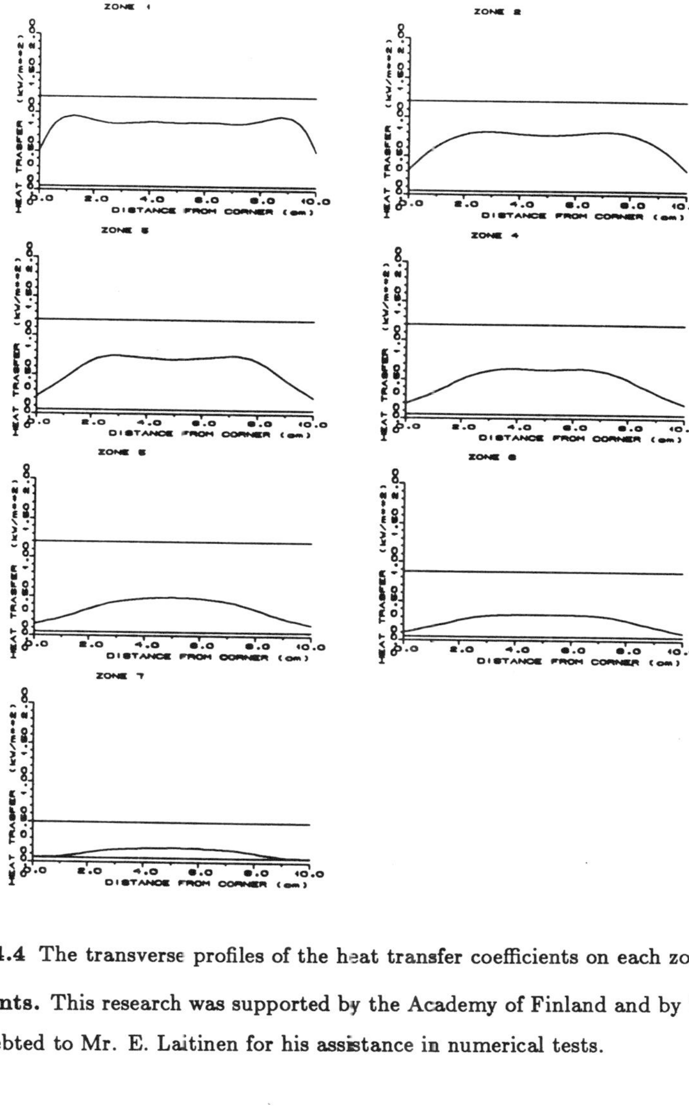

Figure 4.4 The transverse profiles of the heat transfer coefficients on each zone.

Acknowledgements. This research was supported by the Academy of Finland and by TEKES. The author is indebted to Mr. E. Laitinen for his assistance in numerical tests.

References

1. Baptista, L.A.: Control of spray cooling in the continuous casting of steel. Theses of University of British Columbia (1979)
2. Birat, J.P., Larrecq, M., Le Bon, A., Jeanneau, M., Poupon, M. and Senaneuch, D.: Control of secondary cooling in continuous casting of plate grades. IRSID, ACI 83 RE 1009, Août 1983

3. Brimacombe, J.K., Samarasekera, I.V. and Lait, J.E.: Continuous Casting. Vol 2, Book Crafters, Ins., Chelsea, MI (1984)
4. Elliot, C.M. and Ockendon, J.R.: Weak and variational methods for moving boundary problems. Research Notes in Mathematics, 59. Pitman 1982
5. Fasano, A. and Primicerio, M. (Eds.): Free boundary problems, theory and applications. Vol I–II, Research Notes in Mathematics, 78 and 79. Pitman 1983
6. Gorenflo, R. and Hoffmann, K.-H. (Eds.): Applied Nonlinear Functional Analysis. Frankfurt am Main. Peter Lang Verlag 1983
7. Hoffmann, K.-H. and Sprekels, J.: Real-time control of the free boundary value in a two-phase Stefan problem. Numer. Funct. Anal. and Optimiz. **5**, 47–66 (1982)
8. Hoffmann, K.-H. and Sprekels, J.: Real-time control in a free boundary problem connected with the continuous casting of steel. In: Proc. of Conference on Optimal Control of Partial Differential Equations, Oberwolfach December 5–11, 1982. K.-H. Hoffmann and W. Krabs (Eds.), ISNM 68. Birkhauser 1984
9. Holappa, L., Louhenkilpi, S., Laitinen, E. and Neittaanmäki, P.: Optimization of the secondary cooling in the continuous casting of billets. In: Proc. of 24th Annual Conference of Metallurgists, 18.–21. August 1985, Vancouver
10. Hong, C.P., Umeda, T. and Kimura, Y.: Numerical models for casting solidification: Part I. The coupling of the boundary element and finite difference methods for solidification problems. Metallurgical transactions **Vol. 15B**, 91–99 (1984)
11. Koikkalainen, P., Laitinen, E., Louhenkilpi, S., Neittaanmäki, P. and Holappa, L.: FE-modelling of continuous casting problems. In: Proc. of Int. Confr. on Computational Mechanics, Tokyo 25.–29. May, 1986 pp. III 29–III 36. Springer Verlag 1986
12. Koikkalainen, P., Asano, N. and Neittaanmäki, P.: Numerical modelling of material properties in mushy zone. (in Japanese). To appear
13. Laitinen, E.: Numerical Approximation of Heat Transfer Problems. Licenciate thesis at University of Jyväskylä, Department of Mathematics, 1986
14. Larrecq, M., Birat, J.P., Saques, C. and Henry, J.: Optimization of casting and cooling conditions on steel continuous casters; Implementation of optimal strategies on slap and bloom casters. IRSID, ACI 83 RE 1004, Jullet 1983
15. Lemarechal, C., Strodiot J.J. and Bihain, A.: On a bundle algorithm for nonsmooth optimization. In: Nonlinear Programming 4 p. 245. Academic Press 1981
16. Lewis, R.W. and Morgan, K. (Eds.): Proc. of the 4th Int. Confr. on Numerical Methods in Thermal Problems, July 15–18, 1985 in Swansea. Vol I and II. Pineridge Press 1986
17. Neittaanmäki, P.: On the control of cooling during continuous casting. In [**16**], pp. 240–249
18. Neittaanmäki, P. and Laitinen, E.: Optimization of cooling conditions in continuous casting. In: Proceedings of the summer school in numerical analysis at Jyväskylä 17.–10.6.1985. University of Jyväskylä, report 31, ed. by P. Neittaanmäki, (1985)
19. Neittaanmäki, P. and Laitinen, E.: Determination of water heat transfer coefficients and their control in continuous casting of steel billets. In: Proceeding of Lappeenranta Summerschool on heat transfer 1985, 12.–15.8.1985. Lappeenranta University of Technology, (1985)
20. Neittaanmäki, P. and Laitinen, E.: Temperature distribution and its control. GAMM, ZAMM, Band 66 **Heft 4/6**, T387–T390 (1986)
21. Neittaanmäki, P. and Tiba, D.: A variational inequality approach to constrained control problems. University of Jyväskylä, Dept. of Math., Preprint 51 (1986)
22. Niezgódka, M., Pawlow, I. and Visintin, A.: On multi-phase Stefan type problems with nonlinear flux at the boundary in several space variables. Pubb. N. 293, Pavia 1981

23. Pawlow, I., Shindo, Y. and Sakawa, Y.: Numerical solution of multidimensional two-phase Stefan problem. Numer. Funct. Anal. Optimiz. **8**, 55–84 (1985)

24. Rogberg, B.: High temperature properties of steel and their influence on the formation of defects in continuous casting. Dissertation, The Royal Institute of Technology, Department of Casting of Metals (1982)

25. Saguez, C.: Contrôle optimal de systemès à frontiere libre. Thèse, Univ. Technologique Compiegne (1980)

26. Saguez, C.: Optimal control of free-boundary problems. in 12th IFIP-conference on system modelling and optimization, Budapest, September 2–6, 1985

27. Saguez, C.: Optimal control of free-boundary problems. In: Proceedings of 12th IFIP-conference on System Modelling and Optimization, Budapest September 2–6, 1985, to appear in LN in Control and Information Sciences. Springer Verlag 1986

28. Saguez, C.: Optimal control for minimization of default domain. In: Proceedings of the IFIP WG 7.2 Working Conference on Boundary Control and Boundary Variations, Nice, June 10–13, 1986. To appear

29. Woller, V.R., Moore, J.J. and Shah: Simple techniques for the analysis of metallurgigal solidification processes. in [**16**], pp. 229–239

30. Tiba, M.: The boundary element method in two-phase Stefan problems. To appear

31. Yamasaki, J., Miyakara, S., Kodama, M., Matsukawa, T., Matsumo, J. and Suzuki, K.: The control of the surface temperature in the continuous slab casting machine by on-line digital computer. In: Proc. of 8th Triennial World Congress, Kyoto, Japan. IFAC Control Science and Technology, 2639–2644, 1981

Pekka Neittaanmäki, University of Jyväskylä, Department of Mathematics, Seminaarinkatu 15, SF-40100 Jyväskylä, Finland

International Series of
Numerical Mathematics, Vol. 78

OPTIMAL CONTROL OF TWO-PHASE STEFAN PROBLEMS - NUMERICAL SOLUTIONS

Irena Pawlow

Abstract. A method of constructing optimal controls for two-phase Stefan problems is proposed. The control action is performed via boundary conditions of the mixed type. An elliptic degeneration of the Stefan problems is admitted. Discrete approximations to the optimal control problems are constructed. A discussion of the results of some corresponding numerical experiments is given.

1. INTRODUCTION

We are concerned with boundary control of two-phase Stefan problems. More precisely, we are interested in the multidimensional problems, possibly of mixed elliptic-parabolic type.

Such problems arise, in particular, from the mathematical modelling of various thermal and diffusive phase transition processes of the type solid-liquid, as well as some two-phase flows with saturation in porous media and electrochemical processes. A control action in the class of problems under consideration is often performed via conditions imposed on the fixed boundary of the appropriate geometric domain (cf., [3]) what has delivered an origin of our study.

A complete state of systems governed by the Stefan problems comprises two components:

(i) a field function, typically temperature or mass concentration in thermal and diffusive problems, respectively (pressure head for flows in porous media, electric potential for electrochemical processes, etc.),

(ii) a free boundary between different phases.

In higher dimensions, in view of the troubling lack of any

regularity of the free boundary (cf., [4]), the second component can be only indirectly observed and controlled. Whenever possible, the Stefan problems are then reformulated to some weak form (cf., [7]). There are two basic classes of the suitable weak formulations:

(i) variational equation in terms of the internal energy (enthalpy) and temperature,

(ii) variational inequality in terms of the freezing index.

Characteristic for both is their fixed-domain form, with the free boundary no longer explicitly present (this is the case as long as dynamic conditions holding on the free boundary are in a relevant Rankine-Hugoniot form, cf. [11]).

Although both weak formulations are nearly equivalent, the variational inequality approach seems to be preferable to some extent in as much the corresponding field function, freezing index, is continuously related to temperature allover the domain whereas the relevant relation between temperature and internal energy is usually multi-valued (cf., [4 ,7]). This preference becomes of special importance at the numerical treatment of the problems.

In this paper we exploit the variational inequality formulation of the two-phase Stefan problem (cf., [7]). We develop an algorithm for numerical solving a related problem of boundary control. Since the most typical characterizations of the control objectives for the problems under consideration consist in approaching an imposed pattern of the state trajectory (either the complete distributed state or its terminal and boundary traces) and in assuring a desired movement of the free boundary, we have constructed the cost functionals to be minimized so as to express these goals.

Our construction of the algorithm splits into two stages:

(i) regularization of the variational inequality, comprising a parabolic regularization and smoothing; the first is of basic importance in the problems of elliptic-parabolic type, the second provides differentiability of state observation mappings and consequently differentiability of the cost functional,

(ii) discretization of the resulting regularized optimal control problems in space and time.

It is to be noted that similar classes of control problems were also studied in [1,5,6,12,13]. The authors of those papers dealt, however, exclusively with strongly parabolic two-phase Stefan problems and exploited their enthalpy formulation combined with smoothing of the multi-valued graph temperature-enthalpy (which represents the relation temperature-internal energy).

We develop an alternative apprcach, equally applicable to the optimal control of parabolic and degenerate, elliptic-parabolic two-phase Stefan problems. In doing so we proceed along the lines of [10] where a complete numerical analysis is offered, in particular including results on stability, convergence of discrete approximations and rate of this convergence.

Here, in turn, we rather focus on an assessment of the practical efficiency of the algorithm. To illustrate its performance, we summarize results of some numerical tests.

Acknowledgment. The numerical experiments presented in this paper were carried out at the Institute of Mathematics, University of Augsburg, due to invitation of the author by Prof. Karl-Heinz Hoffmann, what is to be gratefully acknowledged. Special gratitude of the author is to Mr. Klaus Bernt, for an expert technical assistance, especially at producing graphic outputs.

2. ELLIPTIC-PARABOLIC TWO-PHASE STEFAN PROBLEM AND ITS VARIATIONAL INEQUALITY FORMULATION

We shall consider a class of controlled phase transition processes governed by a multidimensional two-phase Stefan problem, possibly of mixed elliptic-parabolic type. For reference purposes we introduce now its classical form.

Let Ω be an open bounded domain in $\mathbb{R}^N$, $N \geq 1$ ($N \leq 3$ in applications), with a sufficiently regular boundary Γ. For a finite time interval $(0,T)$, denote $Q = \Omega \times (0,T)$, $\Sigma = \Gamma \times (0,T)$. To determine are a function $\vartheta(x,t)$ and a surface S defined by

$$S = \{ (x,t) \in Q \mid \Phi(x,t) = 0 \} ,$$

representing the free boundary, which satisfy the system:

$$\begin{cases} c(\vartheta)\,\vartheta' - \nabla (k(\vartheta)\nabla\vartheta) = \lambda & \text{in } Q \setminus S , & (1) \\ \vartheta = 0 & \text{on } S , & (2) \\ [k(\vartheta)\nabla\vartheta|_{0+} - k(\vartheta)\nabla\vartheta|_{0-}] \circ \nabla\Phi = L\,\Phi' & \text{on } S , & (3) \\ \vartheta(x,0) = \vartheta_o(x) & \text{for } x \in \Omega , & (4) \\ k(\vartheta)\,\partial_\nu\vartheta + p\int_0^\vartheta k(s)ds = u & \text{on } \Sigma . & (5) \end{cases}$$

Above, $\vartheta' = \frac{\partial\vartheta}{\partial t}$, $\partial_\nu\vartheta$ denotes the outward normal derivative on Γ , $c = c(\vartheta) \geqq 0$, $k = k(\vartheta) > 0$, $\lambda = \lambda(x,t)$, $u = u(x,t)$, $\vartheta_o = \vartheta_o(x)$, $p = p(x) \geqq 0$ are given functions of their arguments and L is a given nonnegative constant.

The coefficients c and k are given as piecewise smooth functions of ϑ with possible singularities at the critical point $\vartheta = 0$ of the phase transition, moreover, k is assumed strictly positive throughout while c only nonnegative, possibly vanishing at some values of ϑ . Equation (1) may be therefore of mixed type (elliptic-parabolic). Function u will be treated as representing a control action.

System (1)-(5), referred to as the two-phase Stefan problem in its classical form, can be considered as a mathematical model of some thermal phase transitions solid-liquid, saturated-unsaturated flows in porous media or quasisteady electrochemical processes (cf., [2,10]), in particular. These processes, among many others, due to their applicational character give rise to numerous control problems. The objectives of the control usually refer to assuring a desired dynamics of the state of process, i.e., some space- and time-dependent distribution of ϑ and a desired movement of the free boundary S .

In the phase transition processes under consideration the control action is usually performed by means of data imposed on the fixed boundary Γ or some its part, for instance with the use of the flux function u in system (1)-(5).

In order to guarantee global in time existence of a solution to the above formulated Stefan problem and simultaneously to fit typical frames of the related control problems in, the corresponding weak (variational) formulations are to be introduced. Here we shall use the variational inequality formulation of system (1)-(5). To construct this formulation, we proceed in a standard way (cf., [7]). The following sequence of transformations and resulting new variables is to be introduced:

- Kirchhoff transformation

$$\Theta = K(\vartheta) = \int_0^{\vartheta} k(s)ds \; ,$$

- enthalpy graph (multi-valued)

$$\gamma_o(r) = \tilde{\gamma}_o(r) + L\,\mathrm{sign}^+(r) \; , \qquad r \in \mathbb{R} \; ,$$

where

$$\tilde{\gamma}_o(r) = \int_0^{r} \rho(s)ds \; , \qquad \rho(r) = \frac{c(K^{-1}(r))}{k(K^{-1}(r))} \; ,$$

K^{-1} is the inverse to K (well-defined since $k > 0$),

$$\mathrm{sign}^+(r) = \begin{cases} 0 & , \text{ if } r < 0 \\ [0,1] & , \text{ if } r = 0 \\ 1 & , \text{ if } r > 0 \; , \end{cases}$$

- Baiocchi-Duvaut transformation

$$y(x,t) = \int_0^{t} \Theta(x,s)ds \; , \qquad (x,t) \in Q \; ,$$

with y - freezing index.

Formally, in terms of y and the enthalpy γ_o, problem (1)-(5) takes the form (cf., [7])

$$\begin{cases} \gamma_o(y') - \Delta y \ni f_o & \text{in } Q \; , \quad \text{(6a)} \\ \partial_\nu y + py = g & \text{on } \Sigma \; , \quad \text{(6b)} \\ y(0) = 0 & \text{in } \Omega \; , \quad \text{(6c)} \end{cases}$$

where

$$f_o(x,t) = \int_0^t \lambda(x,s)ds + w_o(x) , \quad g(x,t) = \int_0^t u(x,s)ds,$$

and w_o which represents the initial enthalpy of the system at $t = 0$ is given compatible with initial temperature Θ_o , i.e.,

$$w_o \in \gamma_o(\Theta_o) \qquad \text{a.e. in } Q .$$

Note that in the parabolic case (c strictly positive) the graph γ_o is strictly monotone; in the degenerate elliptic-parabolic case (c nonnegative) γ_o remains only monotone (without being strictly monotone).

Problem (6) can be formulated as the following evolution variational inequality (cf., [7,10]):

Problem (VI). Determine a function $y : [0,T] \to H^1(\Omega)$, such that

$$\begin{cases} y \in H^1(0,T;H^1(\Omega)) , \\ (\tilde{\gamma}_o(y'(t))-f_o(t),z-y'(t)) + a(y(t),z-y'(t)) - \\ \quad - (g(t),z-y'(t))_\Gamma + \Psi_o(z) - \Psi_o(y'(t)) \geq 0 \\ \qquad \text{for all } z \in H^1(\Omega) , \text{ a.a. } t \in [0,T] , \\ y(0) = 0 \quad \text{in } \Omega , \end{cases}$$

where $(\cdot,\cdot)$, $(\cdot,\cdot)_\Gamma$ are the standard inner products in $L^2(\Omega)$ and $L^2(\Gamma)$, respectively,

$$a(y,z) = (\nabla y, \nabla z) + (p\, y , z)_\Gamma ,$$

$$\Psi_o(z) = L \int_\Omega \psi_o(z(x))dx , \quad \psi_o(z) = \max\{0,z\} .$$

Definition. By the weak solution of the elliptic-parabolic two--phase Stefan problem (1)-(5) we understand a function y (freezing index) which satisfies variational inequality (VI).

According to this definition, since $y' = \Theta$ a.e. in Q , the free boundary S can be recovered only a posteriori as the level set $\{ (x,t) \mid y'(x,t) = 0 \}$.

Let us remark that every classical solution of problem (1)-(5) satisfies (VI) and, conversely, provided y is sufficiently regular, the function $\vartheta = K^{-1}(y')$ can be shown to satisfy problem (1)-(5) in the classical sense.

The solution y of (VI) exists and is unique under some regularity assumptions on the data (cf., [7,10]).

3. STATEMENT OF THE OPTIMAL CONTROL PROBLEM

The solution y of (VI) is considered as the state corresponding to the boundary control $u \in \mathcal{U}$. The control space $\mathcal{U}$ is alternatively assumed as either of

$$\mathcal{U} = \mathcal{U}^o \equiv L^2(\Sigma) \qquad \text{or} \qquad \mathcal{U} = \mathcal{U}^1 = H^1(0,T;L^2(\Gamma)) ,$$

equipped with the norms

$$\|u\|_{\mathcal{U}^o} = \|u\|_{L^2(\Sigma)} \quad , \quad \|u\|_{\mathcal{U}^1} = \|u(0)\|_{L^2(\Gamma)} + \|u'\|_{L^2(\Sigma)}$$

(the last equivalent to the standard norm of $H^1(0,T;L^2(\Gamma))$), respectively.

We consider the following optimal control problem with distributed observation of $\Theta = y'$ (for instance corresponding to the observation of temperature, pressure head or electric potential field, in dependence on nature of the problem):

<u>Problem (CP)</u>. $\inf\limits_{u \in \mathcal{U}} \{ J(y',u) = \frac{1}{2} \|y' - \Theta_d\|^2_{L^2(Q)} + \frac{\alpha}{2} \|u\|^2_{\mathcal{U}} \}$

subject to y being the solution of (VI) corresponding to control u.

Here $\Theta_d \in L^2(Q)$ is a given reference function and α is a given positive constant.

Let $\Xi : \mathcal{U} \to L^2(Q)$ denote the state observation mapping defined by $\Xi(u) = y'$ where y is the relevant solution of (VI). The control problem (CP) can be then completely formulated in the control space as

$$\inf_{u \in U} \{ I(u) = J(\Xi(u),u) \} .$$

Due to continuity properties of the mapping Ξ , problem (CP) admits at least one solution $\hat{u} \in U$ (cf., [8,10]).

Apart from problem (CP) we have treated numerically also some other control problems which involve an observation of the evolution of either of the phases by means of its characteristic function (see Section 6).

4. DISCRETE APPROXIMATIONS TO OPTIMAL CONTROL PROBLEM (CP)

The proposed discrete approximation to problem (CP) comprises: (i) regularization of (VI) , (ii) discretization of the regularized variational inequality, (iii) discretization of the corresponding control problem.

(i) *Regularization*. This stage is optional; if performed, the regularization comprehends a *parabolic regularization* (this only in the degenerate elliptic-parabolic case) and some *smoothing* procedure (cf., [7]). The parabolic regularization of (VI) consists in approximating the graph γ_o (possibly multi-valued) by a family of strictly monotone graphs γ_μ , $\mu \in (0,1]$. The smoothing, in turn, relies upon approximating the graph γ_μ by some smooth functions $\gamma_{\mu\varepsilon}$, $\varepsilon \in (0,1]$ (single-valued, see Fig. 1).

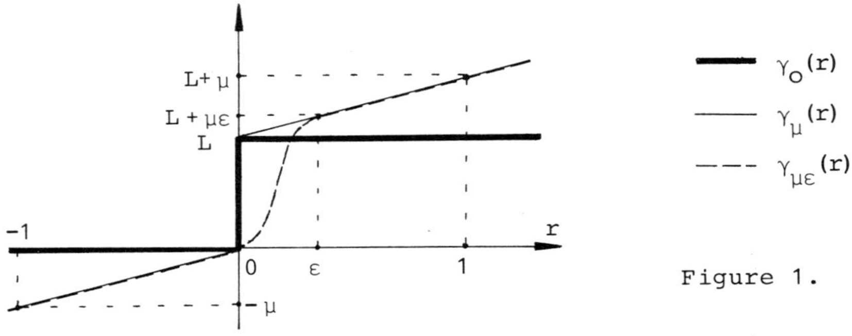

Figure 1.

The regularized problem corresponding to (6) has the form

$$\begin{cases} \gamma_{\mu\varepsilon}(y'_{\mu\varepsilon}) - \Delta y_{\mu\varepsilon} = f_{\mu\varepsilon} & \text{in } Q , & \text{(7a)} \\ \partial_\nu y_{\mu\varepsilon} + p\, y_{\mu\varepsilon} = g & \text{on } \Sigma , & \text{(7b)} \\ y_{\mu\varepsilon}(0) = 0 & \text{in } \Omega , & \text{(7c)} \end{cases}$$

where $\gamma_{\mu\varepsilon}(r) = \tilde{\gamma}_{\mu\varepsilon}(r) + L\,\chi_\varepsilon(r)$,

$\tilde{\gamma}_{\mu\varepsilon}(r) = \int_0^r \rho_\varepsilon(s)ds + \mu\, r$,

$\chi_\varepsilon \in C^2(\mathbb{R})$ is an approximation of the Heaviside graph $\text{sign}^+(r)$, for instance in a polynomial form, cf., [7],

ρ_ε is a compatible approximation of the coefficient ρ ,

$f_{\mu\varepsilon}(x,t) = \int_0^t \lambda(x,s)ds + w_{\mu\varepsilon}(x)$,

$w_{\mu\varepsilon}(x) = w_{o\varepsilon}(x) + \mu\,\Theta_o$, $w_{o\varepsilon} = \gamma_{o\varepsilon}(\Theta_o)$.

The corresponding variational inequality formulation of problem (7) is given by

Problem $(VI)^\mu_\varepsilon$, $\mu,\varepsilon \in [0,1]$.

$$\begin{cases} y_{\mu\varepsilon} \in H^1(0,T;H^1(\Omega)) , \\ (\tilde{\gamma}_{\mu\varepsilon}(y'_{\mu\varepsilon}(t)) - f_{\mu\varepsilon}(t), z - y'_{\mu\varepsilon}(t)) + a(y_{\mu\varepsilon}(t), z - y'_{\mu\varepsilon}(t)) - \\ \quad - (g(t), z - y'_{\mu\varepsilon}(t))_\Gamma + \Psi_\varepsilon(z) - \Psi_\varepsilon(y'_{\mu\varepsilon}(t)) \geq 0 \\ \qquad \text{for all } z \in H^1(\Omega) , \text{ a.a. } t \in [0,T] , \\ y_{\mu\varepsilon}(0) = 0 \quad \text{in } \Omega , \end{cases}$$

where $\Psi_\varepsilon(z) = L \int_\Omega \psi_\varepsilon(z(x))dx$,

$\psi_\varepsilon \in C^3(\mathbb{R})$ is the corresponding approximation of ψ_o , compatible with χ_ε .

Remark. Problem $(VI)^\mu_\varepsilon$ with $\mu = \varepsilon = 0$ (without any regularization) is to be identified with (VI).

(ii) *Discretization of the regularized variational inequality.*

Now we introduce a discrete approximation to $(VI)^{\mu}_{\varepsilon}$. We shall assume for simplicity that Ω is a convex polygon in the plane.

We introduce a regular triangulation $\mathcal{T}_h$ of Ω with the characteristic parameter $h \in (0,1]$ which corresponds to the mesh size. Let V_h be a finite-dimensional subspace of $H^1(\Omega)$, defined by

$$V_h = \{ v_h \in H^1(\Omega) \cap C^0(\bar{\Omega}) \mid v_h \text{ is a polynomial of the first order over any } T \in \mathcal{T}_h \} .$$

Assume the time interval $[0,T]$ be divided into M equal subintervals $[t_i, t_{i+1}]$ of the length k , where $t_i = ik$, $i=0,..,M$ with $k = T/M$. We shall use the standard notations

$$y^i(x) = y(x,t_i) \quad , \qquad y^i = \frac{y^{i+1} - y^i}{k} \quad ,$$

$$y^{i+\varkappa} = \varkappa y^{i+1} + (1-\varkappa) y^i \quad , \qquad \varkappa \in [0,1] \, .$$

Eventually, (VI) is approximated by

Problem $(VI)^{\mu}_{\varepsilon,hk}$, $\mu, \varepsilon \in [0,1]$ arbitrary parameters, $h,k > 0$.

$$\left\{ \begin{array}{l} \text{Determine} \quad y^i = y^i_{\mu\varepsilon hk} \in V_h \, , \quad i=0,\dots,M \, , \quad \text{such that} \\ y^{i+1} = y^i + k\,\delta y^i \quad , \\ (\tilde{\gamma}_{\mu\varepsilon}(\delta y^i) - f^i_{\mu\varepsilon h}, z_h - \delta y^i) + a(y^{i+\varkappa}, z_h - \delta y^i) - \\ \quad - (g^i, z_h - \delta y^i)_{\Gamma} + \Psi_{\varepsilon}(z_h) - \Psi_{\varepsilon}(\delta y^i) \geqq 0 \\ \qquad \text{for all} \quad z_h \in V_h \quad , \quad i=0,\dots,M-1 \, , \\ y^0 = 0 \quad \text{in} \quad \Omega \quad , \end{array} \right.$$

where $\varkappa \in [0,1]$ is an arbitrary parameter which specifies type of the numerical scheme (from explicit up to fully implicit).

(iii) *Discretization of the control problem.* Let U_h be the space generated by traces of the elements of V_h on Γ, endowed with the $L^2(\Gamma)$-norm; $\mathcal{U}^o_{hk}$ the space of functions $u : [0,T] \to U_h$ piecewise constant on $[t_i, t_{i+1})$, $i=0,\dots,M-1$, equipped with the norm of $\mathcal{U}^o$; $\mathcal{U}^1_{hk}$ the space of functions $u : [0,T] \to U_h$, piecewise linear on $[t_i, t_{i+1})$, equipped with the norm of $\mathcal{U}^1$.

Let $\Xi^\mu_{\varepsilon,hk} : \mathcal{U} \to L^2(Q)$ denote the discrete state observation mapping defined by

$$[\Xi^\mu_{\varepsilon,hk}(u)](t) = \delta y^i_{\mu\varepsilon hk} \qquad \text{for } t \in [t_i, t_{i+1}),\ i=0,\dots,M-1$$

where $y_{\mu\varepsilon hk}$ is the relevant solution of $(VI)^\mu_{\varepsilon,hk}$. The discrete control problem corresponding to (CP) takes the form

<u>Problem $(CP)^\mu_{\varepsilon,hk}$</u>, $\mu, \varepsilon \in [0,1]$, $h,k > 0$.

$$\inf_{u \in \mathcal{U}_{hk}} \{ I^\mu_{\varepsilon hk}(u) = J_k(\Xi^\mu_{\varepsilon,hk}(u), u) \equiv \frac{1}{2} \| \Xi^\mu_{\varepsilon,hk}(u) - \Theta_{dk} \|^2_{L^2(Q)} + \frac{\alpha}{2} \|u\|^2_{\mathcal{U}} \},$$

where $\mathcal{U}_{hk} = \mathcal{U}^o_{hk}$ or $\mathcal{U}_{hk} = \mathcal{U}^1_{hk}$, Θ_{dk} is a piecewise constant approximation of the reference element Θ_d. .

Let us note that since $(VI)^\mu_\varepsilon$ at $\mu = \varepsilon = 0$ is identical with (VI), the control problem $(CP)^\mu_\varepsilon$ for $\mu = \varepsilon = 0$ can be identified with (CP), correspondingly.

The functional $I^\mu_{\varepsilon,hk}$ is weakly l.s.c. and radially unbounded on $\mathcal{U}_{hk}$. Hence, for any fixed $\mu, \varepsilon \in [0,1]$ and $h,k > 0$, problem $(CP)^\mu_{\varepsilon,hk}$ admits at least one optimal solution $\hat{u}_{\mu\varepsilon hk} \in \mathcal{U}_{hk}$ (cf., [10]).

It has been also proved in [10] that the discrete control problems $(CP)^\mu_{\varepsilon,hk}$ approximate problem (CP) both in the sense of a convergence of the minimal values of the cost functionals and the relevant optimal solutions. The results of [10] guarantee:

(i) iterative convergences (equally at $\mathcal{U}_{hk} = \mathcal{U}^o_{hk}$ and $\mathcal{U}^1_{hk}$): first at $k \to 0$ (for any fixed μ,ε,h; μ and ε possibly equal zero), then at $\mu,\varepsilon,h \to 0$;

(ii) joint convergences (only in the case of $\mathcal{U}_{hk} = \mathcal{U}^1_{hk}$) at μ,

$\varepsilon, h, k \to 0$, simultaneously.

In the case of $\mathcal{U}_{hk} = \mathcal{U}^1_{hk}$, the convergence rate of the minimal values of the discrete functionals has been proved to be of order $O(h^{1/2})$, cf., [10] .

5. ALGORITHM FOR SOLVING THE OPTIMAL CONTROL PROBLEM

In this section we present a gradient-type algorithm for numerical solving the control problem (CP). To specify the situation, we shall assume that the smoothing parameter ε is positive, and in the degenerate elliptic-parabolic case also that μ is positive.

For the regularized control problem $(CP)^{\mu}_{\varepsilon,hk}$ necessary conditions of optimality can be given in an explicit form. To this purpose, let us introduce the relevant adjoint problem:

Problem $(AP)^{\mu}_{\varepsilon,hk}$ - , $\mu, \varepsilon, h, k > 0$ ($\mu = 0$ in the parabolic case).

$$\begin{cases} \text{Determine } p^i \in V_h \text{ , } i=0,\dots,M \text{ , which satisfy the system of equations} \\ (D\gamma_{\mu\varepsilon}(\delta y^i)\,\delta p^i , z_h) - a(p^{i+1-\varkappa}, z_h) = (\delta y^i - \Theta^i_d, z_h) \\ \qquad \text{for all } z_h \in V_h \text{ , } i=0,\dots,M-1 \text{ ,} \\ p^M = 0 \quad \text{in } \Omega \text{ ,} \end{cases}$$

where y^i is the solution of $(VI)^{\mu}_{\varepsilon,hk}$, $D\gamma_{\mu\varepsilon}$ denotes the Gateaux differential of the mapping $\gamma_{\mu\varepsilon}$.

With the use of problem $(AP)^{\mu}_{\varepsilon,hk}$, the gradient of the functional $I^{\mu}_{\varepsilon,hk}$ can be given the following characterization:

(i) for $u, v \in \mathcal{U}^o_{hk}$

$$DI^{\mu}_{\varepsilon,hk}(u)\,v = \sum_{i=0}^{M-1} k\,(-p^{i+1} + \alpha u^i , v^i)_{\Gamma} \quad ;$$

(ii) for $u, v \in \mathcal{U}^1_{hk}$

$$DI^{\mu}_{\varepsilon,hk}(u)\,v = \sum_{i=0}^{M-2} k\,\left(-\frac{k}{2} p^{i+1} - \sum_{\ell=i+2}^{M} k\,p^{\ell} + \alpha\,\delta u^i , \delta v^i\right)_{\Gamma} +$$

$$+ \quad k \left(-\frac{k}{2} p^M + \alpha \delta u^{M-1}, \delta v^{M-1}\right)_\Gamma + \left(-\sum_{i=1}^{M} k p^i + \alpha u^0, v^0\right)_\Gamma .$$

According to the above characterization of $DI^{\mu}_{\varepsilon,hk}$, the following gradient-type algorithm for solving the control problem (CP) can be proposed.

Algorithm. Let $\mu \geqq 0$, $\varepsilon,h,k > 0$ be fixed. Assume that $\mu > 0$ in the elliptic-parabolic case. Let n denote the iteration index.

Step 0. Set $n = 0$, take an arbitrary starting point $u^{(0)} \in \mathcal{U}_{hk}$ ($\mathcal{U}_{hk} = \mathcal{U}^{o}_{hk}$ or $\mathcal{U}_{hk} = \mathcal{U}^{1}_{hk}$).

Step 1. Compute $\delta y^{(n)}$ by solving $(VI)^{\mu}_{\varepsilon,hk}$.

Step 2. Compute $I^{\mu}_{\varepsilon hk}(u^{(n)})$ and check whether $u^{(n)}$ satisfies any of the stop criteria. If YES then STOP, otherwise proceed to Step 3.

Step 3. Compute adjoint state $p^{(n)}$ by solving problem $(AP)^{\mu}_{\varepsilon,hk}$.

Step 4. Compute new control $u^{(n+1)}$ from the relations:

in the case $\mathcal{U}_{hk} = \mathcal{U}^{o}_{hk}$

$$u^{i,(n+1)} = u^{i,(n)} - \beta_n \left[\alpha u^{i,(n)} - p^{i+1,(n)}|_\Gamma\right] ,$$

$$\text{for } i = 0,\dots,M-1 ;$$

in the case $\mathcal{U}_{hk} = \mathcal{U}^{1}_{hk}$

$$\delta u^{i,(n+1)} = \delta u^{i,(n)} - \beta_n \left[\alpha \delta u^{i,(n)} - \frac{k}{2} p^{i+1,(n)}|_\Gamma - \sum_{\ell=i+2}^{M} k p^{\ell,(n)}|_\Gamma\right], \quad i = 0,\dots,M-2 ,$$

$$\delta u^{M-1,(n+1)} = \delta u^{M-1,(n)} - \beta_n \alpha \delta u^{M-1,(n)} ,$$

$$u^{0,(n+1)} = u^{0,(n)} - \beta_n \left[\alpha u^{0,(n)} - \sum_{i=1}^{M} k p^{i,(n)}|_\Gamma\right],$$

where β_n is an appropriately chosen real parameter, for instance according to the line minimization.

Step 5. $n := n+1$ and return to Step 1.

The stop criterion in Step 2 can be in particular expressed in terms of:

(i) the difference of cost functional values in two subsequent iterations,

(ii) the gradient norm,

(iii) the difference of the values of control norms in two subsequent iterations.

6. NUMERICAL RESULTS

To verify the practical efficiency of the algorithm proposed in Section 5, we have carried out a series of numerical experiments. The control action was performed via mixed type boundary condition (5), with u as the control variable. Here we present results of three experiments corresponding to different types of the state observation.

Experiment (E1) is related to an observation of the evolution of one of the phases (say, the liquid phase, for instance), i.e., of the set $Q_2 = \{ (x,t) \in Q \mid \Theta(x,t) > 0 \}$, where $\Theta = y' = \Xi(u)$ and y is the solution of (VI) corresponding to the control u . The observation is realized by means of the characteristic function χ of the set Q_2 in Q ,

$$\chi(x,t;u) = \begin{cases} 1 , & \text{for } (x,t) \in Q_2 \\ 0 , & \text{for } (x,t) \in Q \setminus Q_2 . \end{cases}$$

The actual characteristic function $\chi(u)$ is compared with a given reference χ_T which corresponds to a desired form of the liquid phase $\Omega_2(T)$ at the terminal time moment $t = T$; $\chi_T(x) = 1$ for $x \in \Omega_2(T)$ and $\chi_T(x) = 0$ for $x \in \Omega \setminus \Omega_2(T)$.

Implicitly, this case refers to an observation of the free boundary movement, with a given reference - a desired terminal form of the free boundary. This reflects the possibility of treating the boundary of the supports of the functions $\chi(u)$ and χ_T as the relevant actual and reference free boundaries between different phases, respectively.

We have solved the optimal control problem with the following cost functional to be minimized:

$$\inf_{u \in \mathcal{U}^1} \{ I(u) = \frac{1}{2} \|\chi(u) - \chi_T\|^2_{L^2(Q)} + \alpha_o \|u(0)\|^2_{L^2(\Gamma)} + \alpha_1 \|u'\|^2_{L^2(\Sigma)} \} ,$$

with α_o, α_1 given positive constants. Here the objective of control is to stabilize the free boundary at a given time-independent reference.

It is to be remarked that in numerical computations we have alternatively used controls from the spaces $\mathcal{U}^o = L^2(\Sigma)$ and $\mathcal{U}^1 = H^1(0,T;L^2(\Gamma))$. As we could observe in the course of experiments the choice of $\mathcal{U}^1$ as the control space turned out preferable, providing as a rule a better performance of the process of computations (faster practical convergence of that process). For this reason we restrict our exposition here to such a case.

In the experiments it was of principal importance to adjust properly the weight coefficients α_o, α_1 so as to avoid a possible overbalancing which would give favour to controls with a minimal norm rather than to ensure an accurate reproduction of the desired state.

In numerical computations we have taken $\Omega = (-1,1) \times (-1,1)$ and $T = 0.256$. The uniform triangulation $\mathcal{T}_h$ of Ω has been constructed (see Fig. 2) with the number of all nodes $q = 81$ (the corresponding number of boundary nodes on Γ is 32). The time interval $[0,T]$ has been uniformly discretized with 33 nodes ($M = 32$). The resulting dimension of the discrete optimal control problem to be solved is $33 \times 32 = 1056$ (the control action is imposed at all boundary nodes).

The model problem has been assumed as elliptic-parabolic, with the parameters $\rho(\Theta) = 0.8$ if $\Theta < 0$ and $\rho(\Theta) = 0$ if $\Theta > 0$, $L = 1$, $p = 1$. The control problem has been solved in the regu-

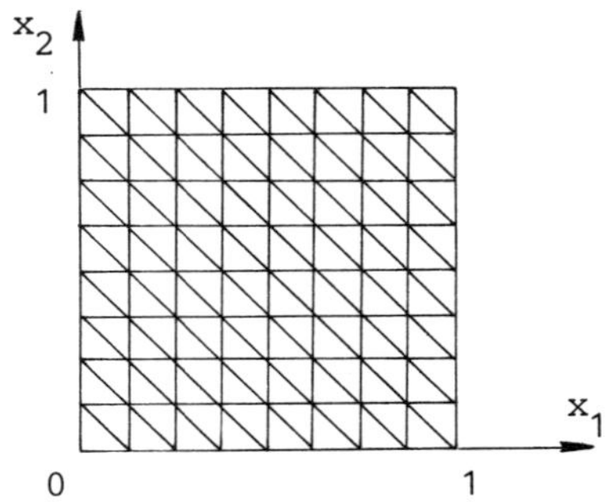

Figure 2.

larized form, with parameters $\mu = 0.2$, $\varepsilon = 0.01$, $\varkappa = 1$, $\alpha_o = 0.5$ and $\alpha_1 = 0.1$.

Fig. 3a displays the distribution of Θ and the form of free boundary at the initial time moment $t = 0$. On the left, also the resulting initial value of the control function u on the boundary Γ is shown. Observe that the initial shape of the actual free boundary is visibly different from the assumed reference corresponding to χ_T . The reference is symmetric in (x_1, x_2) and time-independent. At $t = 0.072$ the situation becomes entirely different (see Fig. 3b); except for the corners, the recovery of the reference free boundary is already quite accurate. At $t = 0.168$ (see Fig. 3c) and finally at $t = 0.232$ (see Fig. 3d), some further improvement of the recovery is still observed. Because of the symmetric reference, optimal controls are symmetric on Γ , too.

Let us note that due to imposing the observation with time-independent reference χ_T allover the time interval $[0,T]$ we have ensured stabilization of the resulting free boundary at the reference, avoiding the danger of numerical instabilities which might arise when one is dealing with a cost functional entirely reduced to the terminal state (and terminal time instant).

Experiment (E2) is related with an observation of the whole distribution of (x,t), $(x,t) \in Q$ corresponding to the control u . This distribution is compared with a given terminal reference distribution $\Theta_T(x)$ for $x \in \Omega$. The corresponding control problem is

$$\inf_{u \in \mathcal{U}^1} \{ I(u) = \frac{1}{2} \| \Theta(u) - \Theta_T \|^2_{L^2(Q)} + \alpha_o \| u(0) \|^2_{L^2(\Gamma)} + \alpha_1 \| u' \|^2_{L^2(\Sigma)} \}$$

FIGURE 3, A-B : Experiment (E1)

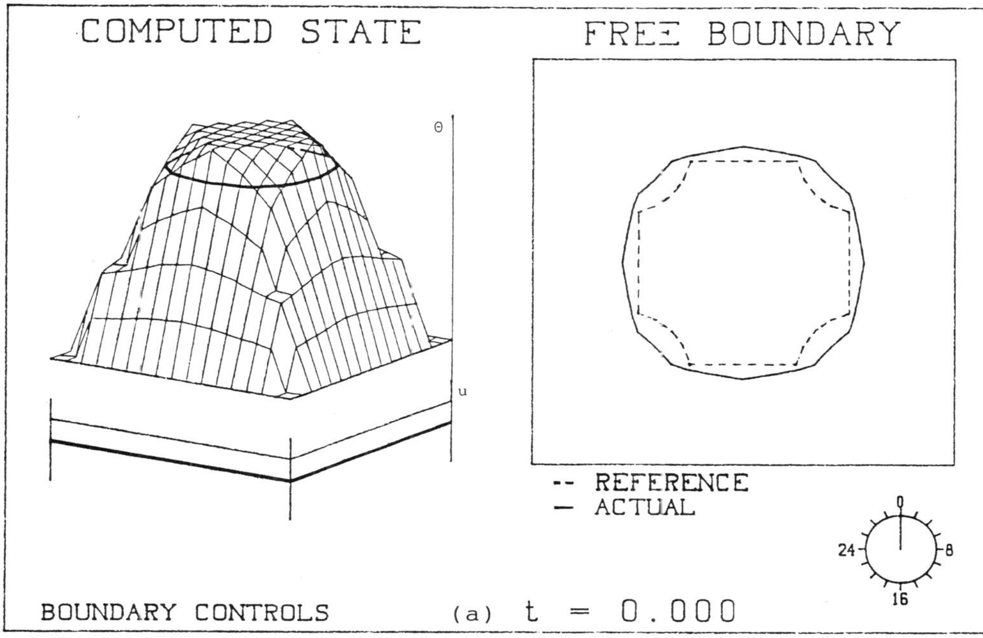

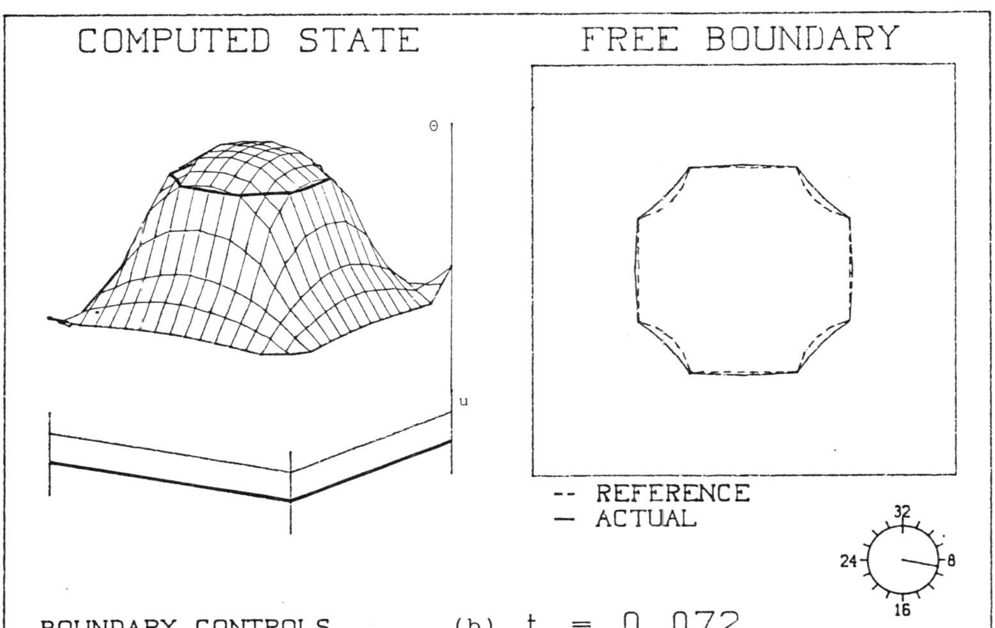

FIGURE 3, C-D : Experiment (E1) - continuation

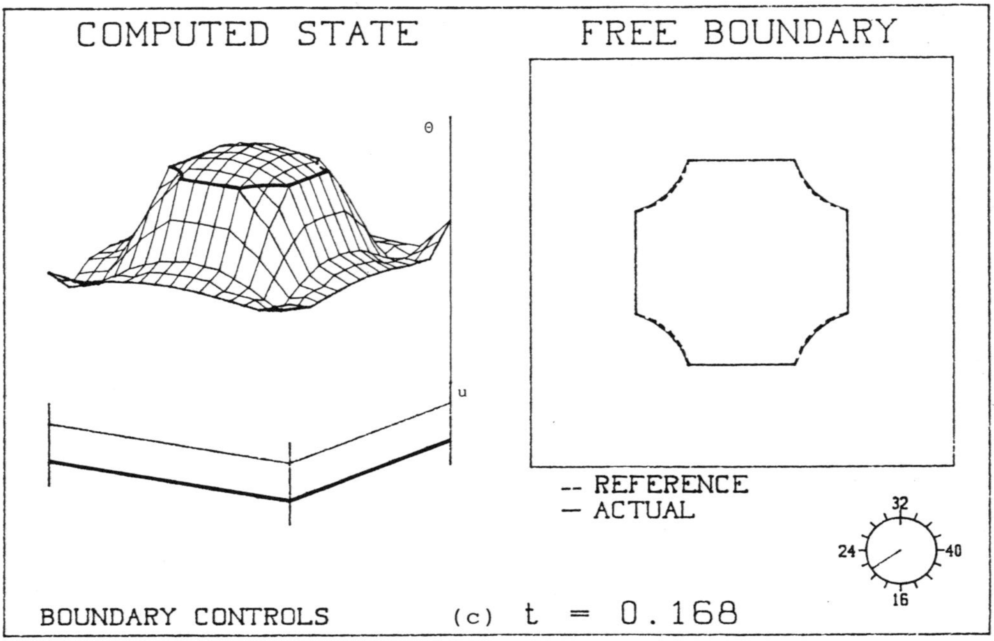

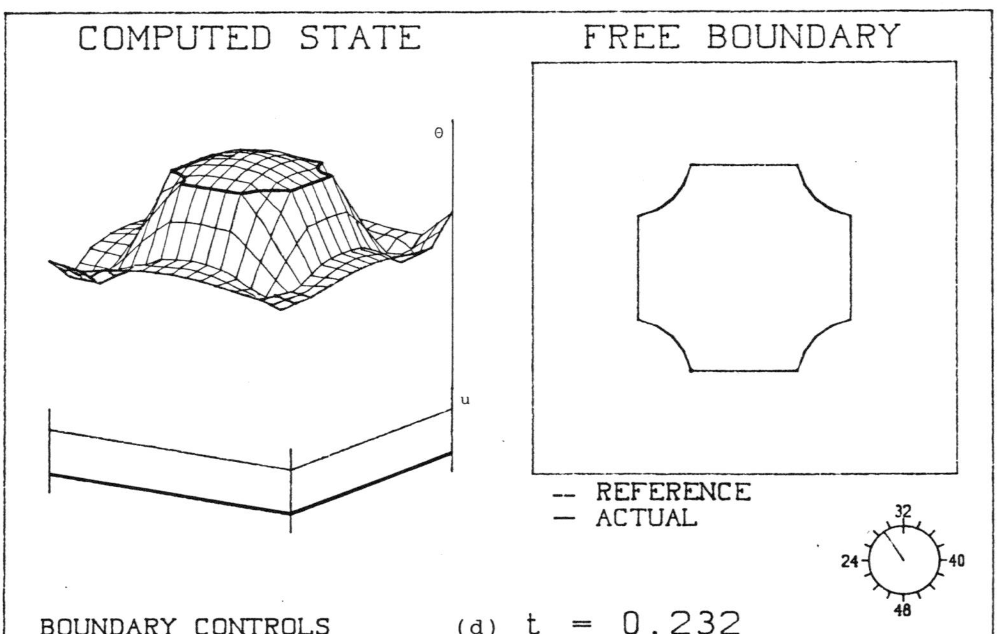

FIGURE 4, A-B : Experiment (E2)

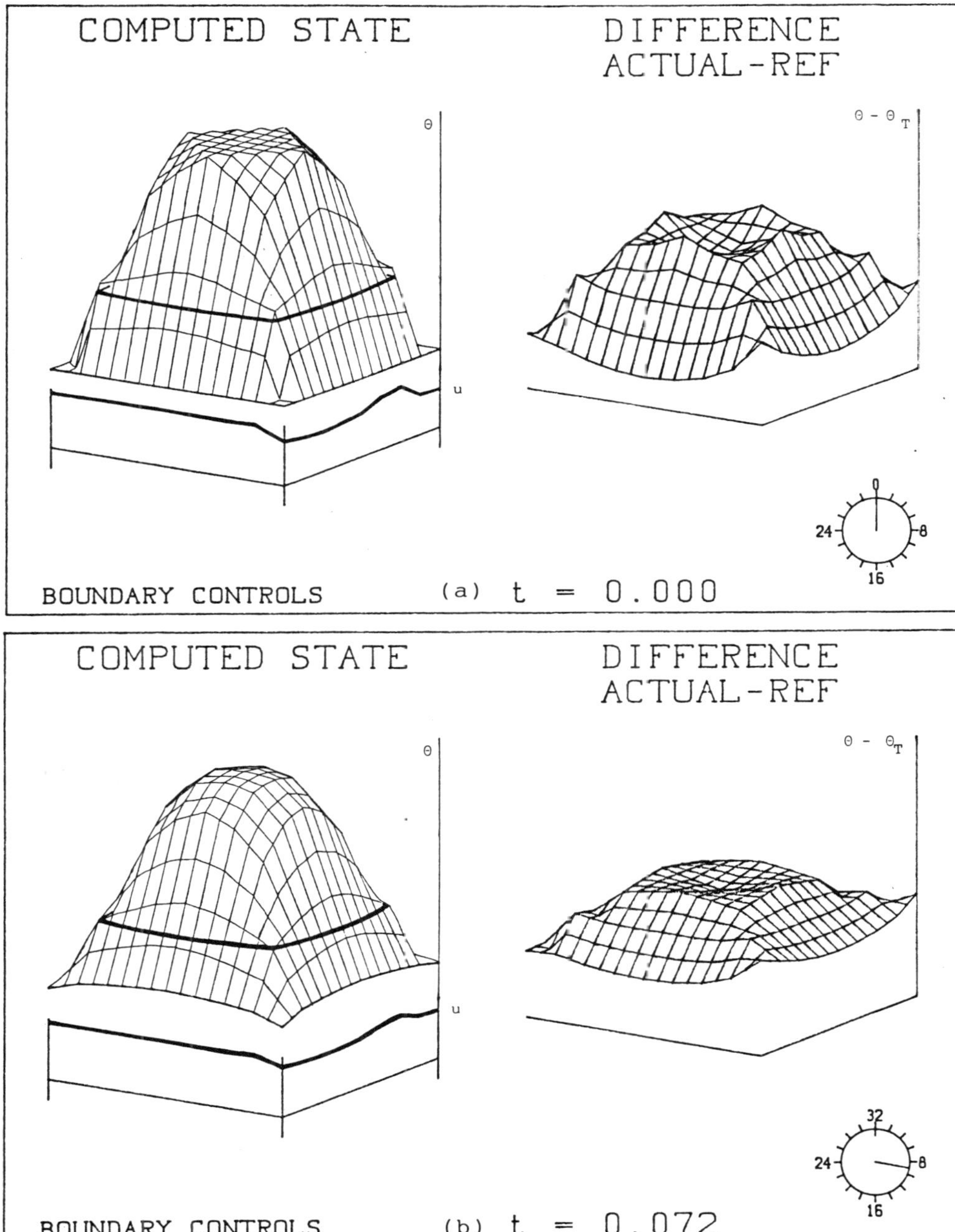

FIGURE 4, C-D : Experiment (E2) - continuation

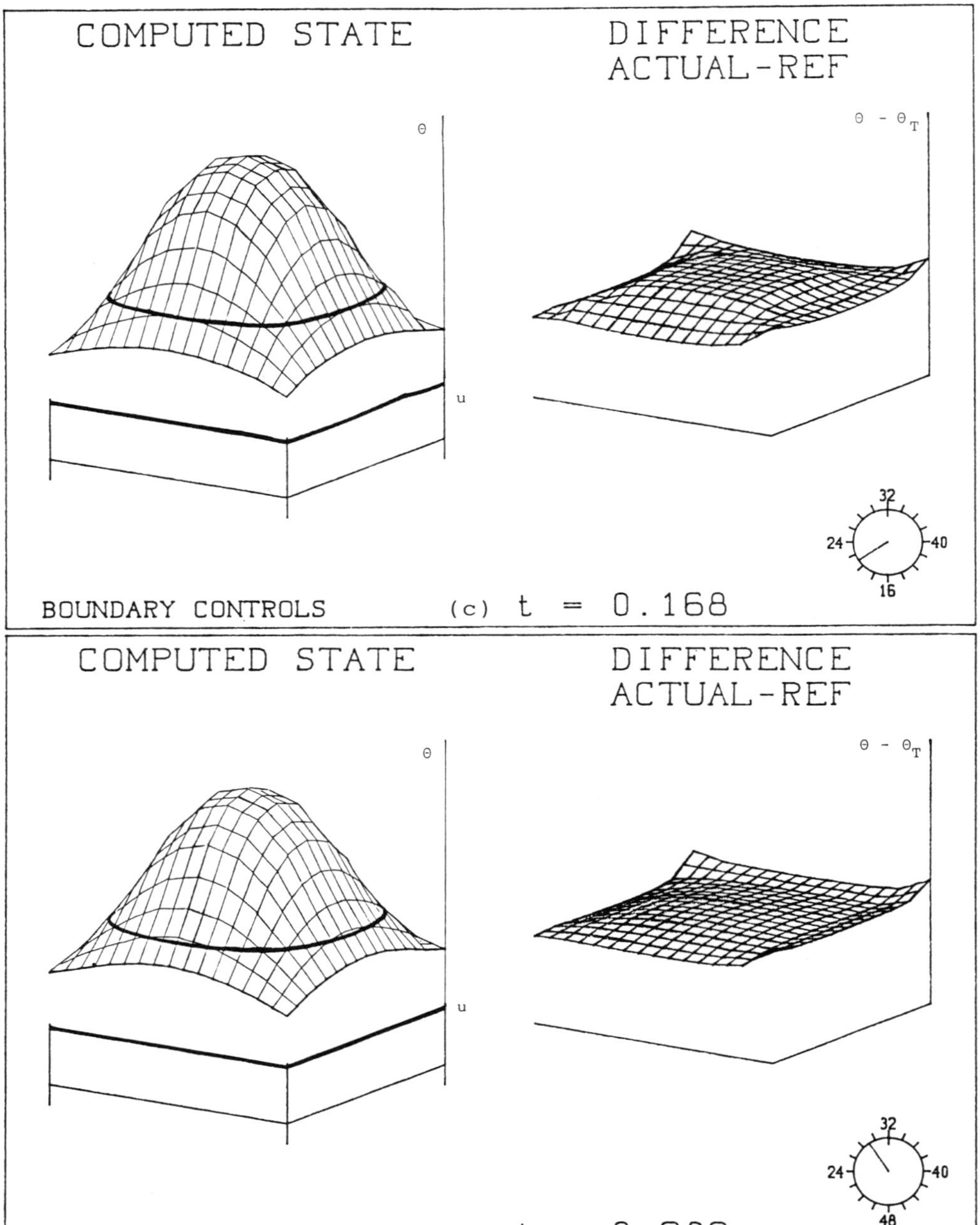

FIGURE 5, A-D : Experiment (E2)

FREE BOUNDARY - MOVEMENT

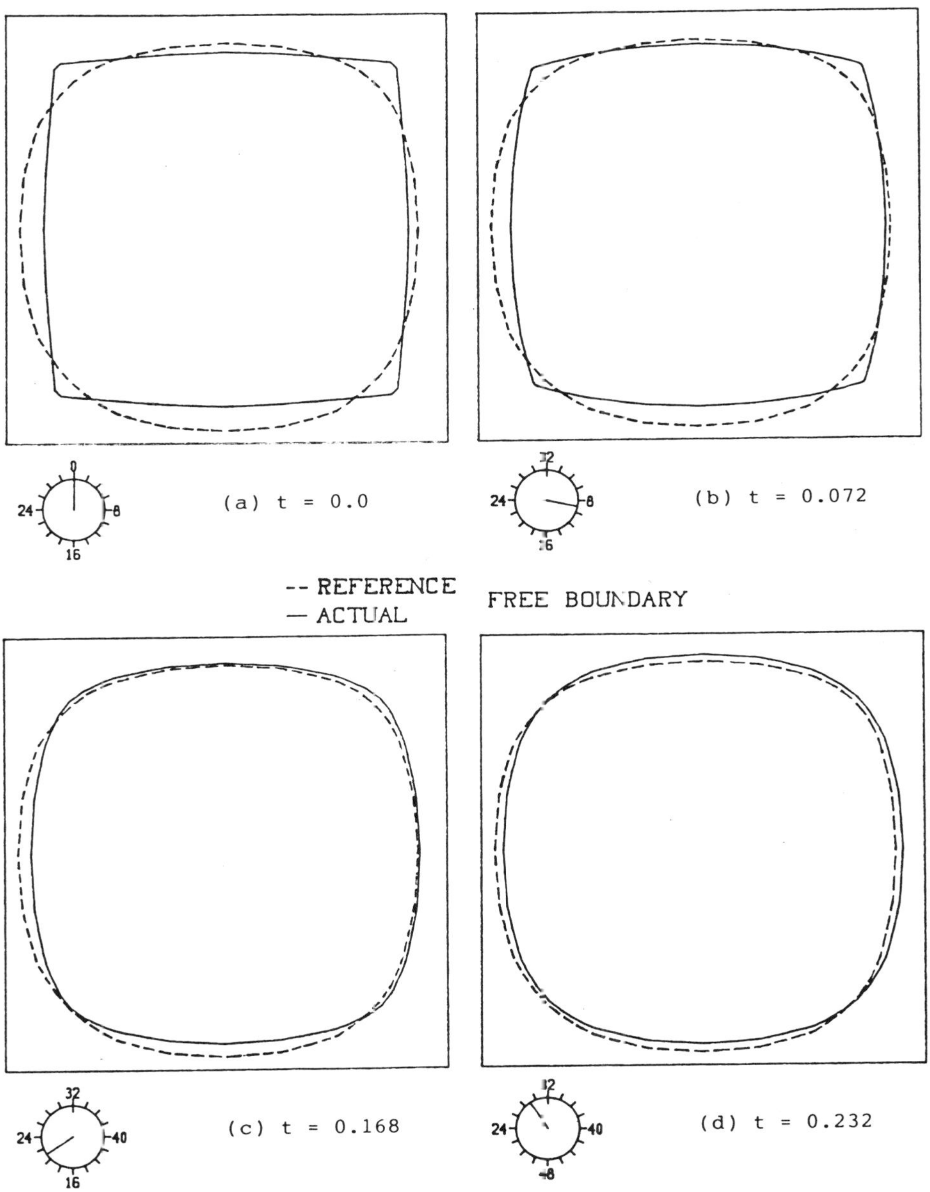

with α_o , α_1 - some positive constants. The objective of the control is to stabilize the complete distribution of the field function Θ at a given time-independent reference pattern Θ_T .

The assumed data were: $\rho(\Theta) = 10$ if $\Theta < 0$ and $\rho(\Theta) = 5$ if $\Theta > 0$, $L = 0.5$ and $p = 1$; the regularization parameters were taken as $\mu = 0$ and $\varepsilon = 0.01$, the discretization remained the same as in the foregoing experiment.

This time, the reference Θ_T was assumed nonsymmetric in (x_1, x_2) . The initial space distribution of Θ and the relevant difference distribution $\Theta - \Theta_T$ are depicted in Fig. 4a (on the left and right, respectively). The corresponding inital form of the computed free boundary and the reference interface are shown in Fig. 5a . The following Figures 4,b-d show the distributions of Θ and $\Theta - \Theta_T$ at time instants $t = 0.072$, $t = 0.168$ and $t = 0.232$, respectively. The relevant evolution of the free boundary (again compared with the reference) is given by Figures 5,b-d . Let us also in this case notice the stabilization effect. Equally the distribution of Θ and the free boundary stabilize about the references.

Because of the nonsymmetry of Θ_T-distribution, the control variable u is nonsymmetric, as well. Nevertheless, the distribution of u over Γ , initially quite strongly nonsymmetric turns out to show some symmetrizing trend, approaching a value constant throughout (observe the lower parts of the left pictures in Figures 4,a-d).

Experiment (E3) is related with an observation of the characteristic function $\chi(u)$, as in (E1), but this time compared with some space- and time-dependent reference χ_g , defined by $\chi_g(x,t) = 1$ for $(x,t) \in Q_g$ ($\subsetneq Q$) and $\chi_g(x,t) = 0$ for $(x,t) \in Q \setminus Q_g$, where $Q_g = \{(x,t) \in Q \mid \Theta_g(x,t) > 0\}$, Θ_g is a given reference distribution.

This type of observation refers, at least implicitly, to an attempt of providing the free boundary evolution along a given trajectory; the corresponding control problem consists in assuring

FIGURE 6, A-B : Experiment (E3)

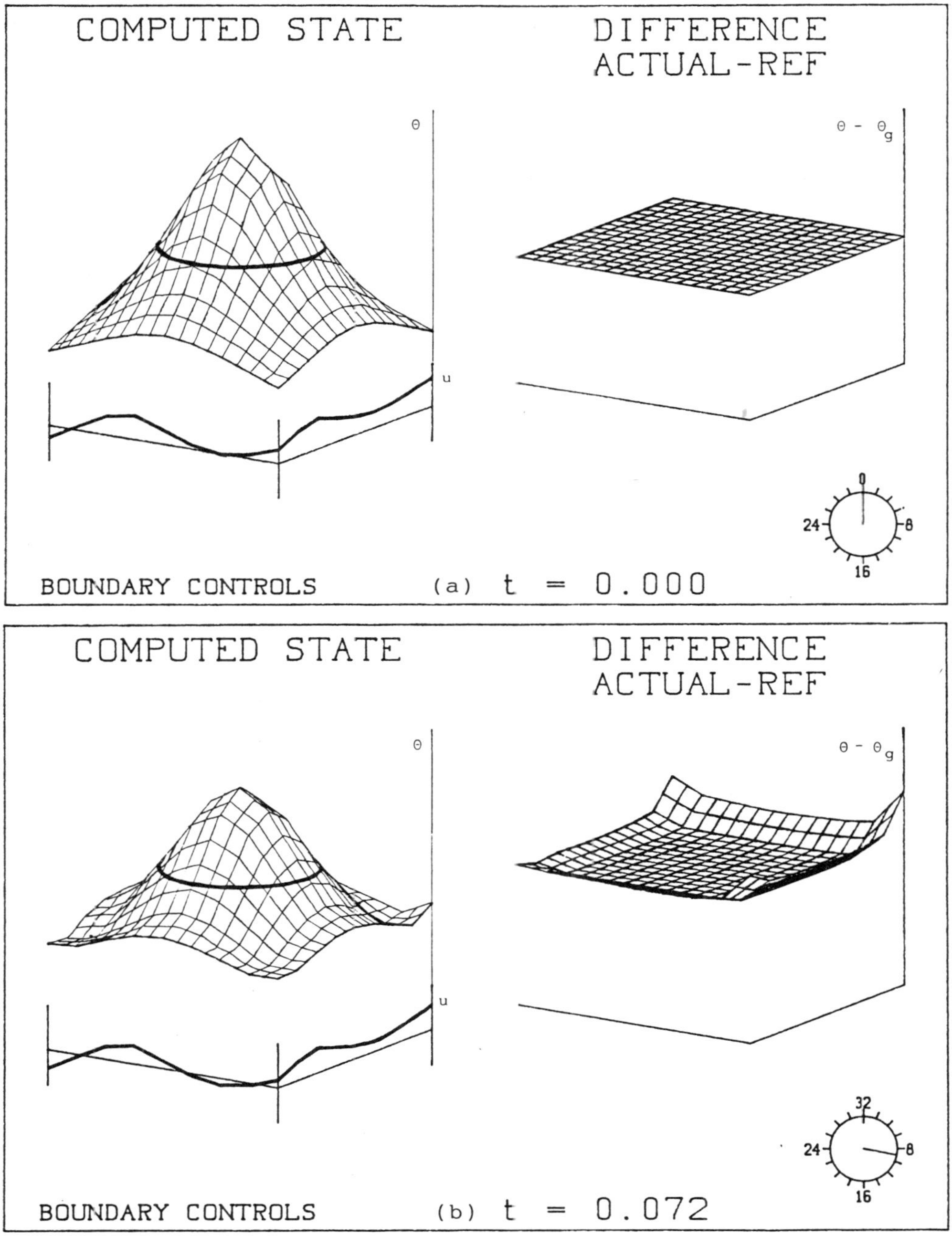

FIGURE 6, C-D : Experiment (E3) - continuation

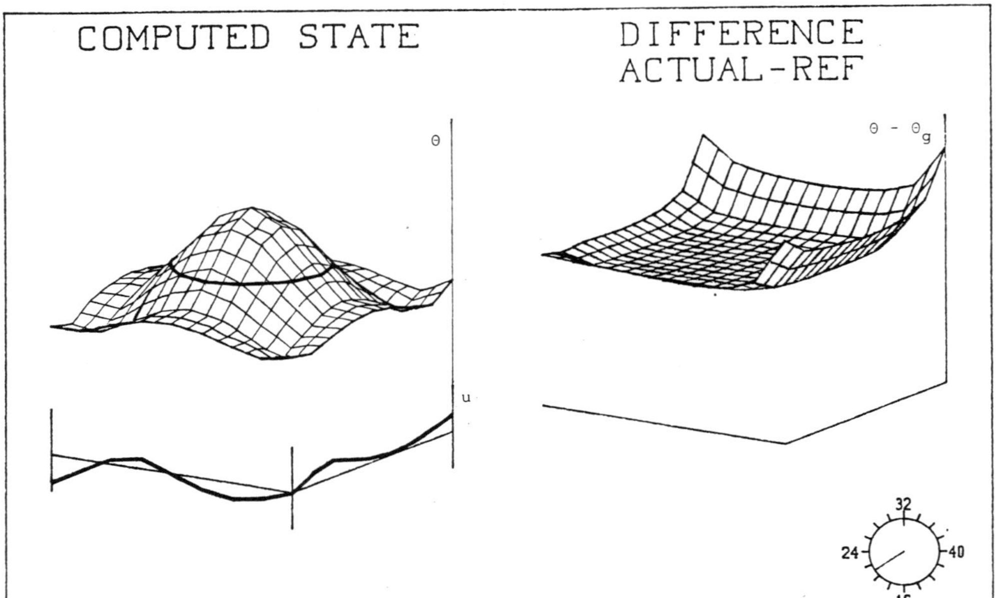

(c) t = 0.168

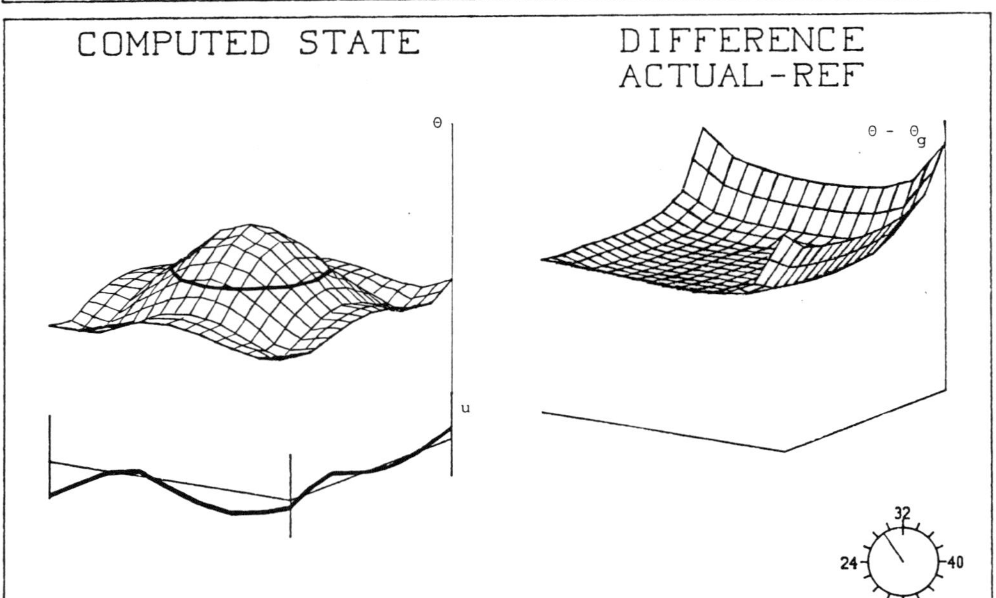

(d) t = 0.232

FIGURE 7, A-D : Experiment (E3)

FREE BOUNDARY - MOVEMENT

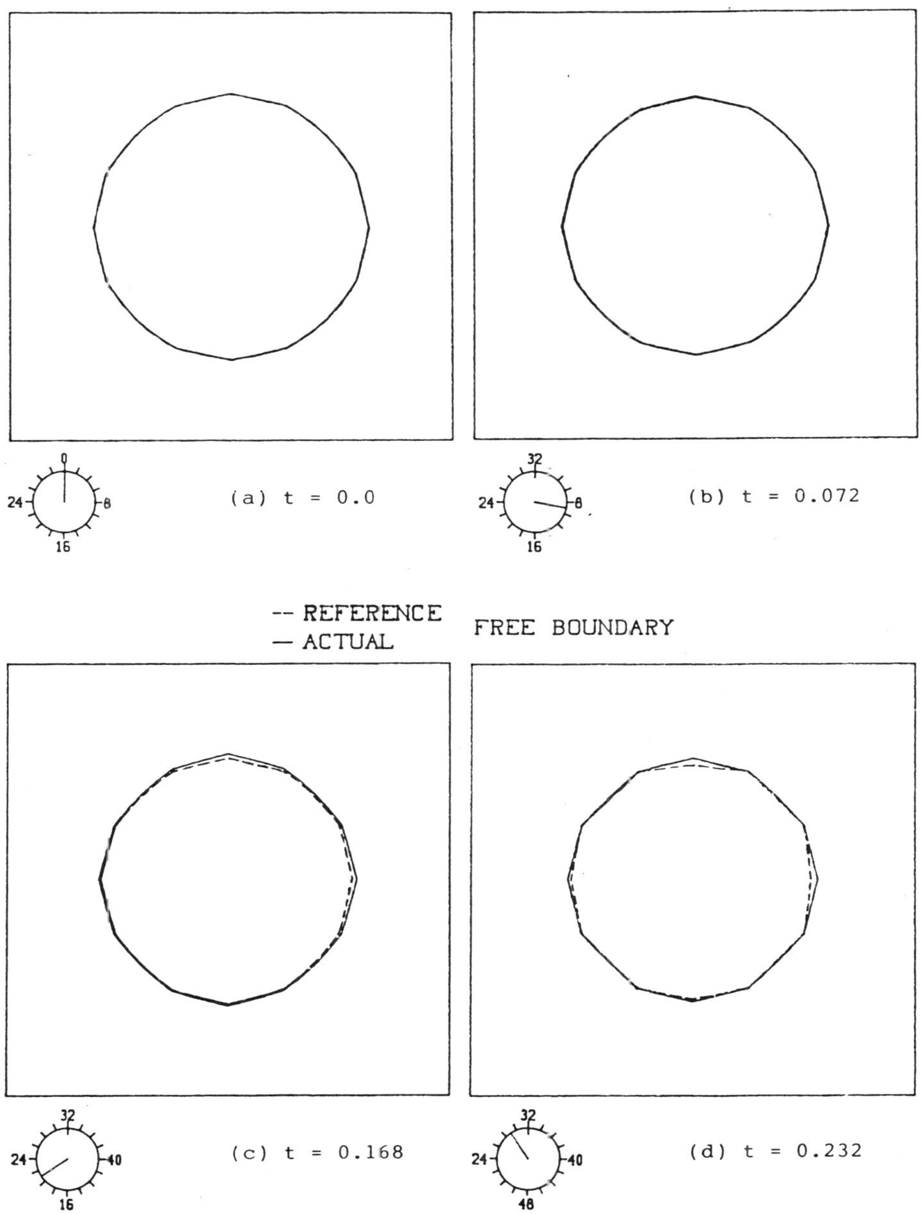

$$\inf_{u \in \mathcal{U}^1} \{ I(u) = \frac{1}{2} \|\chi(u) - \chi_g\|^2_{L^2(Q)} + \alpha_o \|u(0)\|^2_{L^2(\Gamma)} + \alpha_1 \|u'\|^2_{L^2(\Sigma)} \} .$$

The problem was solved with the following data: $\rho(\Theta) = 10$ if $\Theta < 0$ and $\rho(\Theta) = 5$ if $\Theta > 0$, $L = 5$, $p = 1$; as well as $\mu = 0$, $\varepsilon = 0.01$ and the same discretization as previously.

In this experiment we have assumed that the initial conditions, i.e., the distribution of Θ and the free boundary at $t = 0$ are quite close to the reference at $t = 0$ (the difference of the actual and reference distributions is nearly zero), see Fig. 6a and Fig. 7a . The purpose of the control is to preserve the proximity of the computed and reference free boundaries throughout the whole time interval. The relevant illustrations are given by Figures 7, b-d ; see also Figures 6,b-d which show the corresponding distributions of Θ and $\Theta - \Theta_g$.

The time-dependent reference free boundary was remaining well reproduced allover the time interval. This behaviour has been produced by means of the controls u nonsymmetrically distributed over Γ , as visible from the lower left parts of Figure 6,a-d .

To summarize the results of all performed experiments (not only those above discussed), let us remark the following:

(i) In general, the controls u from $\mathcal{U}^1$, more regular in time, turn out to be preferable to the controls from $\mathcal{U}^o$, as far as the convergence of the optimization procedure, and consequently efficiency of the control action are concerned.

(ii) The lack of convexity in the discussed control problems causes a possible nonuniqueness of the optimal controls, therefore the resulting minimum is heavily dependent on an assumed starting point of the iterative process of computations; in this connexion let us also mention the decisive role of the weighting factors in the cost functionals, since too high priority of the control components might give rise to underbalancing the state term.

(iii) Since the whole control action is concentrated on the fixed boundary Γ of only one of the phases, to achieve a desired evolution also within the other phase some local inaccuracy of the

state reproduction in a vicinity of Γ must be accepted.
(iv) Due to relatively high dimensionality of the discrete control problem (1056 - in the discussed examples), the choice of a possibly simple minimization algorithm is preferable; according to our experience, a steepest descent algorithm is to be recommended as long as the initial state is not too far from the reference and some qualitative information on the control function is available so as to permit a reasonable selection of the starting control in the iterative process of optimization.
(v) In the case of a time-dependent reference, at an actual initial state far from the desired one, the L^2-observation as employed in our experiments, seems insufficient for providing an accurate tracking of the reference state.

REFERENCES

1. A. Bermudez and C. Saguez, Optimal control of variational inequalities. In: Recent Advances in Free Boundary Problems, M. Niezgódka, I. Pawlow, Eds., Control & Cybernetics, 14 (1985), 9-30.

2. C.M. Elliott and J.R. Ockendon, Weak and Variational Methods for Moving Boundary Problems. Pitman, Boston (1982).

3. K.-H. Hoffmann and M. Niezgódka, Control of parabolic systems involving free boundaries. In: Free Boundary Problems - Theory and Applications, A. Fasano, M. Primicerio, Eds., Pitman, Boston (1983), 431-462.

4. A.M. Meirmanov, The Stefan Problem. Nauka, Novosibirsk (1986). (in Russian)

5. P. Neittaanmäki and D. Tiba, A descent method for the boundary control of a two-phase Stefan problem. Report No. 2, Lappenranta Univ. Techn. (1983).

6. P. Neittaanmäki and D. Tiba, A finite element approximation of the boundary control of two-phase Stefan problems. Report No. 4, Lappenranta Univ. Techn. (1983).

7. I. Pawlow, A variational inequality approach to generalized two-phase Stefan problem in several space variables. Annali Matem. Pura ed Applicata, 131 (1982), 333-373.

8. I. Pawlow, Variational inequality formulation and optimal control of nonlinear evolution systems governed by free boundary problems. In: Applied Nonlinear Functional Analysis, K.-H. Hoffmann, R. Gorenflo, Eds., Verlag P. Lang, Frankfurt/Main (1983), 213-250.

9. I. Pawlow, Approximation of variational inequality arising from a class of degenerate multi-phase Stefan problems. Submitted to Numerische Mathematik.

10. I. Pawlow, Analysis and Control of Evolution Multi-Phase Problems with Free Boundaries. Habilitation Thesis, Warszawa (1986).

11. L. Rubinstein, The Stefan problem: Comments on its present state. J. Inst. Math. Applics, 24 (1979), 259-277.

12. C. Saguez, Contrôle optimal de systèmes à frontière libre. Thése, Univ. Techn., Compiegne (1980).

13. D. Tiba, Boundary control for a Stefan problem. In: Optimal Control for Partial Differential Equations, K.-H. Hoffmann, W. Krabs, Eds., Birkhäuser-Verlag, Basel (1984), 229-242.

Irena Pawlow
Systems Research Institute,
Polish Academy of Sciences
Newelska 6, 01-447 Warsaw
Poland

International Series of
Numerical Mathematics, Vol. 78

JUSTIFICATION OF NECESSARY OPTIMALITY CONDITIONS FOR CERTAIN INTEGRAL FUNCTIONALS

Thomas I. Seidman

Abstract. We consider the justification of formally obtained first order optimality conditions to be satisfied by the minimizer of an integral functional. The functionals with which we are concerned need not be convex and are not differentiable. The principal hypothesis (H_1) is merely that the integrand be "locally smooth where finite."

1. INTRODUCTION

We consider minimization of an integral functional of the form:

$$J := \int_\Omega F(s,u(s),x(s))\,\mu(ds). \tag{1.1}$$

Here the primary variable $u(\cdot)$ is viewed as determining $x(\cdot) = G[u(\cdot)]$ where, for example, the map G might be defined through a differential equation in which u appears as a control. In addition, we might have (a finite number of) constraints

$$\xi_k(u) = c_k \quad \underline{\text{or}} \quad \leq c_k \qquad (k = 1,\dots,K). \tag{1.2}$$

Thus, the admissible set $\mathcal{U}_{ad}$ is

$$\mathcal{U}_{ad} := \{u(\cdot) \text{ measurable on } \Omega\text{: each } \xi_k(u) \text{ is defined and satisfies (1.2); } G(u) \text{ is defined; } F(\cdot,u,G(u)) \text{ is in } L^1(\Omega) \text{ so } J \text{ is finite}\}. \tag{1.3}$$

We assume that we are given $[\bar{u},\bar{x}]$ with $\bar{u} \in \mathcal{U}_{ad}$ and $\bar{x} = G(\bar{u})$ for which J attains its minimum.

Our object here is to justify the "usual" first order necessary conditions for optimality under quite weak conditions on the integrand F, without concern for any independent considerations involved in attempting to demonstrate existence of such a minimizer. In particular, we impose no hypothesis regarding convexity[1)] in ω for $F(s,\omega,\xi)$. We also impose directly neither growth conditions nor coercivity conditions for the integrand F or the functional J.

<u>What is the condition which we seek to justify</u>? Formally, the derivative of $J(u,G(u))$ with respect to a perturbation at $\bar{u}$ in a direction η is given by

$$\left.\frac{d}{d\varepsilon}\right|_{\varepsilon=0} \int_\Omega F(\cdot,\bar{u}+\varepsilon\eta,G(\bar{u}+\varepsilon\eta))$$

$$= \int_\Omega [\bar{F}_\omega\cdot\eta + \bar{F}_\xi\cdot(\underset{\sim}{\Gamma}\eta)] = \langle \bar{F}_\omega + \underset{\sim}{\Gamma}^*\bar{F}_\xi,\eta\rangle$$

where $\underset{\sim}{\Gamma} := G'(\bar{u})$ (The Fréchet derivative of G at $\bar{u}$) and $\bar{F}_\omega$, $\bar{F}_\xi$ are the (pointwise) partial derivatives:

$$\text{(1.4)} \qquad \bar{F}_\omega(s) := \left.\frac{\partial}{\partial\omega}F(s,\omega,\xi)\right|_{\omega=\bar{u}(s),\,\xi=\bar{x}(s)},$$

$$\bar{F}_\xi(s) := \left.\frac{\partial}{\partial\xi}F(s,\omega,\xi)\right|_{\omega=\bar{u}(s),\,\xi=\bar{x}(s)}.$$

Then, as in elementary calculus, since $[\bar{u},G(\bar{u})]$ minimizes J we have

$$\text{(1.5)} \qquad 0 - \langle \bar{F}_\omega + \underset{\sim}{\Gamma}^*\bar{F}_\zeta,\eta\rangle + \Sigma_k\lambda_k\langle \xi_k'(\bar{u}),\eta\rangle$$

for each η. Where the $\{\lambda_j\}$ are Lagrange multipliers. Setting

$$\text{(1.6)} \qquad z_k := \xi_k'(\bar{u}), \qquad Z := \text{span}\{z_1,\ldots,z_K\},$$

the condition (1.5) gives:

$$\text{(1.7)} \qquad \bar{F}_\omega + \underset{\sim}{\Gamma}^*\bar{F}_\xi =: z \quad \underline{\text{is in}} \quad Z.$$

It is this which we call the (first order) "necessity condition

---

1) We take this opportunity to note an existence theorem for a minimizer which is independent of convexity assumptions — although its hypotheses are, in their own way, much stronger than those employed here: we are here concerned, for example, to eschew (Gâteaux) differentiability of J.

<u>THEOREM</u> (Barbu-Seidman [1]). <u>Let</u> $\mathfrak{X}$ <u>be a reflexive Banach space and let</u> $\mathcal{K}$ <u>be a subset of</u> $\mathfrak{X}$ <u>defined by a finite set of linear constraints</u> ($\mathcal{K} := \{u \in \mathfrak{X}$: (1.3) <u>with</u> $\xi_k \in \mathfrak{X}^*\}$). <u>Let</u> $J\colon \mathfrak{X} \to \bar{\mathbb{R}} := \mathbb{R}\cup\{+\infty\}$ <u>be lower semicontinuous and Gâteaux differentiable on</u> dom(J). <u>Assume a decomposition</u> $J' = G + R$ <u>with</u> $G(\cdot)$ <u>"inverse compact"</u> (<u>i.e.</u>, $\{u_n\}$ <u>bounded in</u> $\mathfrak{X}$ <u>and</u> $\{G(u_n)\}$ <u>convergent in</u> $\mathfrak{X}^*$ <u>implies</u> $\mathfrak{X}$<u>-convergence for a subsequence of</u> $\{u_n\}$) <u>and</u> R <u>continuous and compact</u>. <u>Assume</u> $\mathcal{K}$ <u>is nonempty and</u> J <u>is bounded below and coercive on</u> $\mathcal{K}$. <u>Then there exists a minimizer</u> $\bar{u} \in \mathcal{K}$: <u>more precisely, any minimizing sequence</u> $\{u_n\}$ <u>in</u> $\mathcal{K}$ <u>has a subsequence converging in</u> $\mathfrak{X}$ <u>to such a minimizer</u>. □

This has subsequently been generalized [2] to admit certain nonlinear (differentiable) ξ_k in defining $\mathcal{K}$.

for optimality."

The difficulty which we wish to address in this paper is that, even apart from the constraints (1.2) $\bar{u}+\varepsilon\eta$ need not be admissible: $J(\bar{u}+\varepsilon\eta, G(\bar{u}+\varepsilon\eta))$ need not be finite, much less differentiable with respect to ε as above. We will focus our attention on the difficulties associated with dependence of $F(s,\omega,\xi)$ on ω and so will freely impose hypotheses regarding the dependence on ξ and regarding G' and ξ_j'. It is reasonable to assume that we know

(1.8) $\quad \bar{F}(\cdot) \;:=\; F(\cdot,\bar{u}(\cdot),\bar{x}(\cdot))$ $\quad$ _is in_ $L^1(\Omega)$

for the minimizer $[\bar{u},\bar{x}]$ and, while we do not directly impose coercivity conditions, also to assume

If $[\hat{u},\hat{x}]$ are such that $\hat{x}=G(\hat{u})$ and $F(\cdot,\hat{u},\hat{x})$ is in $L^1(\Omega)$, then

(H_0-1) For any v in $L^\infty(\Omega)$ one has $G(\hat{u}+v)$ and $\xi_k(\hat{u}+v)$ well-defined, indeed,

$$v \mapsto [G(\hat{u}+v)-G(\hat{u})],\xi_k(\hat{u}+v)$$

are (continuously) Fréchet differentiable from $L^\infty(\Omega)$ to $L^\infty(\Omega)$, $\mathbb{R}$, respectively;

(H_0-2) The constraint functionals are "locally independent" in that $\dim Z = K$ with

$$Z = Z(\hat{u}) := \operatorname{span}\{\xi_k'(\hat{u}) : k=1,\dots,K\};$$

(H_0-3) The functional

$$y \mapsto J(\hat{u},\hat{x}+y)$$

is continuous and, indeed, differentiable from $L^\infty(\Omega)$ with

$$\frac{d}{dy}J(\hat{u},\hat{x}+y) \;=\; F_\xi(\cdot,\hat{u},\hat{x})$$

in some specifiable space $\mathcal{Q}$ of functions on Ω embeddable in $L^1(\Omega\to\mathbb{R}^n)$;

(H_0-4) The derivatives $\xi_k'(\hat{u})$ (_a priori_ in the dual of $L^\infty(\Omega)$) are actually in $L^1(\Omega)$ and the derivative $G'(\hat{u})$ (_a priori_ a bounded linear map from $L^\infty(\Omega)$ to $L^\infty(\Omega)$) has an adjoint which extends, by continuity, as an operator $\mathcal{Q}\to L^1(\Omega)$ so $[G'(\hat{u})]^*F_\xi(\cdot,\hat{u},\hat{x})$ is in $L^1(\Omega)$.

Note that with (H_0-4) (or hypotheses giving Z and $\tilde{\Gamma}^*\bar{F}_\xi$ in spaces of functions even smoother than $L^1(\Omega)$), the condition

(1.7) will also provide a regularity theorem for the minimizer $\bar{u}$ whenever one might have solvability of $F_\omega(s,\omega,\bar{x}(s)) = b(s)$ for ω with some smoothness in s.

Having imposed (H_0) en passant, we focus our attention on the ω-dependence of F. The essential hypothesis is that F is "locally smooth where finite":

(H_1) For a.e. $s \in \Omega$, if $F(s,\hat{\omega},\hat{\xi})$ is finite then there is some neighborhood of $[\hat{\omega},\hat{\xi}]$ on which $F(s,\cdot\cdot)$ is finite, continuous, and continuously differentiable.

Our object is to justify (1.7) on the basis of this rather weak hypothesis (H_1). This expands on an argument in [3].

2. FORMULATION AND LEMMAS

As we are primarily concerned with exposition of the basic argument, we do not seek the most general setting for the result. We assume $u(\cdot)$ is to be a (measurable) $\mathbb{R}^m$-valued function on Ω and $x(\cdot) = G(u)$ is to be $\mathbb{R}^n$-valued on Ω where $[\Omega,\mathcal{S},\mu]$ is a finite measure space[2)]. That $u(\cdot)$, $x(\cdot)$ are taken as defined on the same space Ω leads to no loss of generality; see the "trick" noted in discussing Example 3.2, below. The integrand F appearing in (1.1) is then a function from $\Omega \times \mathbb{R}^m \times \mathbb{R}^n$ to $\bar{\mathbb{R}} := \mathbb{R} \cup \{+\infty\}$; we assume throughout that $F(\cdot,u(\cdot),x(\cdot))$ will always be measurable when $u(\cdot)$, $x(\cdot)$ are measurable, etc. Note that the partial derivative F_ω will then be $\mathbb{R}^m$-valued and F_ξ will be $\mathbb{R}^n$-valued; the references to $L^\infty(\Omega)$, $L^2(\Omega)$ in (H_0) must be taken, even, without explicit indication, as referring to spaces of vector-valued functions.

Suppose, then, we are given such an F, satisfying (H_0) and

[2)] In the paper [3], for example, the state $x = G(u)$ took values in a manifold $\mathcal{M}$ [there, $\mathbb{R}^3 \times SO(3)$] and, in addition to the explicit constraints [there, specification of $x(T)$ where $\Omega = (0,T)$; specification of $x(0)$ was the initial condition for an ODE on $\mathcal{M}$ defining G], it was required that $x(\cdot)$ was in a particular homotopy class of continuous functions joining $x(0)$ to $x(T)$. The modifications needed to replace the state space $X = \mathbb{R}^n$ by a manifold $\mathcal{M}$ (without boundary) or by an infinite-dimensional state space X or an infinite-dimensional manifold $\mathcal{M}$ are easy enough and may be left to the reader; compare [3]. Similarly, the easy modifications to treat σ-finite Ω — e.g., an unbounded region in $\mathbb{R}^d$ with Lebesgue measure — are also left to the reader.

(H_1), and a specified function $\bar{u} \in \mathcal{U}_{ad}$ with $\bar{x} = G(\bar{u})$. Later we will take $[\bar{u},\bar{x}]$ to minimize J but already, based only on (1.8) and (H_1), we can make a simple but important observation.

LEMMA 2.1. *Let F satisfy (H_1) and assume $[\bar{u},\bar{x}]$ gives (1.8): integrability of $\bar{F}(\cdot) := F(\cdot,\bar{u}(\cdot),\bar{x}(\cdot))$. For $M > 0$ let Ω_M be the set of $s \in \Omega$ such that*

(2.1) *For each $[\omega,\xi] \in \mathbb{R}^{m+n}$ with $|\omega-\bar{u}(s)|, |\xi-\bar{x}(s)| \le 1/M$, one has $|F(s,\omega,\xi)|, |F_\omega(s,\omega,\xi)|, |F_\xi(s,\omega,\xi)| \le M$.*

Then $\Omega_\infty := \cup_M \Omega_M$ is almost all of Ω; $\mu(\Omega \setminus \Omega_M) \to 0$.

Proof. By (1.8), $\bar{F}(s)$ is finite for almost every $s \in \Omega$. For almost every such s (H_1) asserts (2.1) for large enough M. I.e., almost every s is in some Ω_M. Denoting the characteristic function of Ω_M by χ_M, we have $\chi_M \to 1$ a.e. so the Monotone Convergence Theorem gives $\mu(\Omega\setminus\Omega_M) = \mu(\Omega) - \int \chi_M \to 0$. □

We will write $\mathcal{U}_M = L^\infty(\Omega_M)$ for the subspace of $\mathcal{U} := L^\infty(\Omega \to \mathbb{R}^m)$ consisting of functions η vanishing (a.e.) on $\Omega\setminus\Omega_M$, i.e., multiplication by χ_M maps $\mathcal{U}$ to $\mathcal{U}_M$. The significance of the sets Ω_M and the key to our approach lies in the following technical lemma. For this lemma we continue to take Ω as above but, without regard for (1.6) and (2.1), we assume only that:

(2.2-i) $\Omega_M \uparrow \Omega$ (*i.e.*, $\Omega_{\bar{M}} \subset \Omega_M$ *for* $\bar{M} \le M$ *and* $\mu(\Omega\setminus\Omega_M) \to 0$),

(2.2-ii) Z *is a finite-dimensional space of functions on* Ω (*dim*$Z =: K$) *such that each* $Z_M := \{\chi_M z\colon z \in Z\}$ ($\chi_M :=$ *characteristic function of* Ω_M) *is in* $L^1(\Omega_M)$.

We assume, with no loss of generality, that Z_M is K-dimensional for each M; this is necessarily true for large enough M since (2.2-i) gives $\chi_M z \to z$ for every $z \in L^1(\Omega)$ by the Monotone Convergence Theorem. As before, we write $\mathcal{U}_M$ for $\{\eta \in L^\infty(\Omega)\colon \eta = 0 \text{ on } \Omega\setminus\Omega_M\}$.

LEMMA 2.2. *Assume (2.2) and suppose f is any function on Ω such that*

(2.3-i) *f is integrable on each Ω_M,*

(2.3-ii) $\int_{\Omega_M} f\eta = 0$ *for each* $\eta \in \mathcal{U}_M \cap Z^\perp$

where $Z^{\perp} := \{\eta \in L^{\infty}(\Omega): \int_{\Omega} \eta z = 0$ *for* $z \in Z\}$. *Then* f *is actually an element of* Z.

Proof. On each Ω_M we have $f_M := \chi_M f$ in L^1 by (2.3-i) and can also consider Z_M as a K-dimensional (hence, closed) subspace of $L^1(\Omega_M)$ — which may be identified with the set of L^1 functions on Ω vanishing on $\Omega \setminus \Omega_M$. Since the dual of $L^1(\Omega_M)$ is just $\mathcal{U}_M := L^{\infty}(\Omega_M)$, the Hahn-Banach Theorem would give an $\eta_M \in \mathcal{U}_M$ orthogonal to Z_M such that $\int f_M \eta_M = 0$ if we were to have $f_M \notin Z_M$. Since η_M vanishes on $\Omega \setminus \Omega_M$ the orthogonality to Z_M means orthogonality to Z; thus, η_M is in $\mathcal{U}_M \cap Z^{\perp}$. Taking $\eta = \eta_M$ in (2.3-ii) would then give a contradiction. Thus, $f_M \in Z_M$ for each M.

Fixing $\bar{M}$, we thus have $f_{\bar{M}} = \chi_{\bar{M}} \bar{z}$ for some $\bar{z} \in Z$. Since $\dim Z_M = K$ for each M, multiplication by $\chi_{\bar{M}}$ is an injection: $Z_M \to Z_{\bar{M}}$ for each $M > \bar{M}$. Thus, noting that $\chi_{\bar{M}} f_M = f_{\bar{M}} = \chi_{\bar{M}}(\chi_M \bar{z})$, we see that $f_M = \chi_M \bar{z}$ for all $M \geq \bar{M}$ using this fixed element $\bar{z} \in Z$. The definition of χ_M means, with (2.2-i), that as $M \to \infty$ one has $f_M := \chi_M f \to f$ pointwise a.e. on Ω and $\chi_M \bar{z} \to \bar{z}$ pointwise a.e. on Ω whence $f = \bar{z}$ a.e. on Ω. I.e., f "is" the element $\bar{z} \in Z$. □

We now fix $\bar{u} \in \mathcal{U}_{ad}$ and set $\bar{x} = G(\bar{u})$ under the hypotheses (H_0), (H_1), (1.8). Using Lemma 2.1, we may define the subsets $\{\Omega_M\}$ by (2.1); we can also define $Z = \text{span}\{z_k := \xi_k'(\bar{u})\}$ as in (1.6).

LEMMA 2.3. *Assuming* (H_0), (H_1), *let* $\bar{u} \in \mathcal{U}_{ad}$ *be given with* $\bar{x} := G(\bar{u})$; *take* Z, $\{\Omega_M\}$ *as given by* (1.6), (2.1) *for this* $[\bar{u},\bar{x}]$; *suppose* M *is fixed* (*large enough*) *so* $Z_M := \{\chi_M z \colon z \in Z\}$ *is* K-*dimensional* ($K := \dim Z$ *as in* $(H_0\text{-}2)$). *Then for any* $\bar{\eta}$ *in* $\mathcal{U}_M \cap Z^{\perp}$ *one can find* $u(\varepsilon)$ (*for small* ε: $|\varepsilon| < \bar{\varepsilon}$) *such that*

(2.4) $[u(\varepsilon) - \bar{u}]$ *is in* $\mathcal{U}_M$, $u(\varepsilon)$ *is in* $\mathcal{U}_{ad}$,

(2.5) $\varepsilon \mapsto [u(\varepsilon) - \bar{u}]$ *is in* C^1 *to* $\mathcal{U}_M$ *with* $u(0) = \bar{u}$ *and* $u'(0) = \bar{\eta}$.

Proof. Since $\bar{u}$ is fixed we may ignore the inactive contraints (any strict inequalities in (1.2) at $\bar{u}$); assume Z has already been so reduced and (1.2) consists only of equalities. Since $\dim Z_M = K$ we have $\{\tilde{z}_k := \chi_M z_k\}$ a basis for Z_M so the Hessian matrix $\underline{\tilde{H}}$ (with entries $\{\langle \tilde{z}_j, \tilde{z}_k \rangle = \langle z_j, \tilde{z}_k \rangle : j,k = 1,\dots,K\}$ is nonsingular. By density, we can approximate $\tilde{z}_k$ by $\hat{z}_k \in \mathcal{U}_M$ closely enough that the $K \times K$ matrix $\underline{\hat{H}}$ with entries $\{\langle z_j, \hat{z}_k \rangle\}$ is also nonsingular.

We take $u(\varepsilon)$ to have the form:

$$u(\varepsilon) = \bar{u} + \varepsilon\bar{\eta} + \underline{\alpha}\underline{\hat{z}} \qquad (=: u(\varepsilon,\underline{\alpha})) \tag{2.6}$$

where $\underline{\alpha} \in \mathbb{R}^K$ (so $\underline{\alpha}\underline{\hat{z}}$ means $\sum_k \alpha_k \hat{z}_k$) is to be chosen suitably: $\underline{\alpha} = \underline{\alpha}(\varepsilon)$. Thus, automatically one has $[u(\varepsilon) - \bar{u}]$ in $\mathcal{U}_M$. We apply the Implicit Function Theorem to

$$f: \mathbb{R}^{K+1} \to \mathbb{R}^K : [\underline{\alpha},\varepsilon] \mapsto [\xi_k(u(\varepsilon,\underline{\alpha})) - c_k : k = 1,\dots,K].$$

Clearly f is C^1 in $[\underline{\alpha},\varepsilon]$ by $(H_0\text{-}1)$. At $[\underline{0},0]$ we have $f = [\xi_k(\bar{u}) - c_k] = \underline{0}$ as $\bar{u} \in \mathcal{U}_{ad}$ by assumption; we also have there

$$\partial f/\partial\underline{\alpha} = \{\langle \partial\xi_j/\partial u, \partial u/\partial\alpha_k \rangle\} = \{\langle z_j, \hat{z}_k \rangle\} = \underline{\hat{H}},$$

which is invertible. Thus, there is a C^1 $\mathbb{R}^K$-valued function $\underline{\alpha}(\varepsilon)$ with $\underline{\alpha}(0) = \underline{0}$ such that $f(\varepsilon,\underline{\alpha}(\varepsilon))$ vanishes identically for small ε — which just means that (1.2) holds for $u(\varepsilon)$. By $(H_0\text{-}1)$ we have $x(\varepsilon) := G(u(\varepsilon))$ a C^1 function of ε staying near $\bar{x}$ (in the sense of $L^\infty(\Omega)$) for small ε.

To see that J is finite for $[u(\varepsilon), x(\varepsilon)]$, completing the argument that $u(\varepsilon) \in \mathcal{U}_{ad}$, we analyze separately the situation on Ω_M and on $\Omega \setminus \Omega_M$: consider

$$J_1(\varepsilon) := \int_{\Omega_M} F(s,u(\varepsilon,s),x(\varepsilon,s))\,\mu(ds), \tag{2.7}$$

$$J_2(\varepsilon) := \int_{\Omega\setminus\Omega_M} F(s,\bar{u}(s),\bar{x}(s)+y(\varepsilon,s))\,\mu(ds)$$

where $y = y(\varepsilon,s) := \{0 \text{ \underline{on} } \Omega_M; [x(\varepsilon,s) - \bar{x}] \text{ \underline{else}}\}$. Since $y(\varepsilon)$ is in $L^\infty(\Omega)$ by $(H_0\text{-}1)$, we see that $J_2(\varepsilon)$ is well-behaved by $(H_0\text{-}3)$. By continuity in $\mathcal{U}_M$, we have $u(\varepsilon,s) - \bar{u}(s)|$, $|x(\varepsilon,s) - \bar{x}(s)| \le 1/M$ for small enough ε so (2.1) bounds $|F(s,u(\varepsilon,s),x(\varepsilon,s)) - \bar{F}(s)|$ by M for $s \in \Omega_M$. Since $\bar{F}$ is integrable on Ω_M by (1.8), this makes $J_1(\varepsilon)$ also well-behaved. Thus, $J(u(\varepsilon),x(\varepsilon)) = J_1(\varepsilon) + J_2(\varepsilon)$ is finite for such small ε and $u(\varepsilon) \in \mathcal{U}_{ad}$. We have (2.4).

Finally, to complete the argument for (2.5) we need only show that $u'(0) = \bar{\eta}$. Differentiating the identity $f(\varepsilon,\underline{\alpha}(\varepsilon)) = 0$, one has $f_\varepsilon(0) + \underline{\hat{H}}\,\underline{\alpha}'(0) = 0$ at $\varepsilon = 0$ so $\underline{\alpha}'(0) = -\underline{\hat{H}}^{-1} f_\varepsilon(0)$. We have $f_\varepsilon = [\langle \partial\xi_k/\partial u, \partial u/\partial\varepsilon\rangle = \langle \partial\xi_k/\partial u, \bar{\eta}\rangle]$ by (2.6) so $f_\varepsilon(0) = [\langle z_k, \bar{\eta}\rangle]$. Since $\bar{\eta} \in Z^\perp$ by assumption, this gives $f_\varepsilon(0) = \underline{0}$ whence $\underline{\alpha}'(0) = \underline{0}$. We then have $u' = \bar{\eta} + \underline{\alpha}'\hat{z}$ from (2.6) giving $u'(0) = \bar{\eta}$ as desired. □

<u>COROLLARY 2.4</u>. <u>Assume the hypotheses of Lemma</u> 2.3 <u>for</u> $[\bar{u},\bar{x}]$ <u>and</u> $\bar{\eta}$; <u>let</u> $u(\varepsilon)$ <u>be as in</u> (2.4), (2.5) <u>with</u> $x(\varepsilon) := G(u(\varepsilon))$. <u>Then</u> $\varepsilon \mapsto J(u(\varepsilon),x(\varepsilon))$ <u>is</u> C^1 <u>for small</u> ε <u>with</u>

$$\frac{d}{d\varepsilon}J(u(\varepsilon),x(\varepsilon))\Big|_{\varepsilon=0} = \int_{\Omega_M} \bar{F}_\omega\bar{\eta} + \int_\Omega \bar{F}(\underset{\sim}{\Gamma}\bar{\eta}) = \langle \bar{F}_\omega + \underset{\sim}{\Gamma}^*\bar{F}_\xi, \bar{\eta}\rangle. \tag{2.8}$$

<u>Proof</u>. We note, to start, that the right hand side of (2.8) makes sense since $\bar{F}_\omega$ is actually bounded (by M, in view of (2.1)) on Ω_M where $\bar{\eta}$ can be non-zero while $\underset{\sim}{\Gamma}^*\bar{F}_\xi$ is in $L^1(\Omega)$ by $(H_0\text{-}3,4)$. It is adequate to show differentiability at $\varepsilon = 0$ with the derivative as in (2.8); essentially the same argument shows C^1 regularity for small ε.

Return to the analysis above of (2.7). Since $(H_0\text{-}1)$ gives C^1 dependence (in the sense of L^∞) for $x(\varepsilon)$ and so for $y(\varepsilon)$, we have $x' = (G'|_{u=u(\varepsilon)})u'$ whence $x'(0) = \underset{\sim}{\Gamma}\bar{\eta}$ by (2.5) and then $y'(0)$ is the restriction of this to $\Omega\setminus\Omega_M$. Thus, by $(H_0\text{-}3)$,

$$J_2'(0) = \langle \frac{d}{dy}J(\bar{u},\bar{x}+y), y'(0)\rangle = \langle \bar{F}_\xi, y'(0)\rangle = \int_{\Omega\setminus\Omega_M} \bar{F}_\xi(\underset{\sim}{\Gamma}\bar{\eta}). \tag{2.9}$$

On Ω_M we have, for small enough ε,

$$\frac{1}{\varepsilon}[J_1(\varepsilon) - J_1(0)] = \int_{\Omega_M} [F(s,u(\varepsilon),x(\varepsilon)) - F(s,\bar{u},\bar{x})]/\varepsilon\;\mu(ds)$$

with $|u(\varepsilon)-\bar{u}|, |x(\varepsilon)-\bar{x}| \le 1/M$ so (H_1) gives continuous differentiability whence, by the Mean Value Theorem, the integrand is (pointwise in s) $F_\omega u' + F_\xi x'$, evaluated at $[s,u(\tilde{\varepsilon},s),x(\tilde{\varepsilon},s)]$ with $\tilde{\varepsilon} = \tilde{\varepsilon}(s)$ between 0 and ε. We note that $u'(\tilde{\varepsilon},s) = \bar{\eta}(s) + \underset{\sim}{\alpha}'(\tilde{\varepsilon})\hat{\underset{\sim}{z}}(s) \to \bar{\eta}(s)$ as $\varepsilon \to 0$ forces $\tilde{\varepsilon} \to 0$ and, correspondingly, $x'(\tilde{\varepsilon}) = G'(u(\tilde{\varepsilon}))u'(\tilde{\varepsilon}) \to \underset{\sim}{\Gamma}\bar{\eta}$ in $L^\infty(\Omega)$ as $\varepsilon \to 0$ by $(H_0\text{-}1)$. Thus we have convergence (pointwise in $s \in \Omega_M$) of the integrand of the difference quotient $[J_1(\varepsilon) - J_1(0)]/\varepsilon$ to $[\bar{F}_\omega\bar{\eta} + \bar{F}_\xi(\underset{\sim}{\Gamma}\bar{\eta})]$ as $\varepsilon \to 0$. By (2.1), we can then apply the Dominated Convergence Theorem to get

$$J_1'(0) = \int_{\Omega_M} [\bar{F}_\omega\bar{\eta} + \bar{F}_\xi(\underset{\sim}{\Gamma}\bar{\eta})]. \tag{2.10}$$

Since $J(u(\varepsilon),x(\varepsilon)) = J_1(\varepsilon) + J_2(\varepsilon)$, we obtain the first equality of (2.8). By $(H_0\text{-}4)$ we can take the adjoint: $\langle\bar{F}_\xi,\underset{\sim}{\Gamma}\bar{\eta}\rangle = \langle\underset{\sim}{\Gamma}^*\bar{F}_\xi,\bar{\eta}\rangle$ to complete the proof of (2.8). □

3. THEOREM AND AN EXAMPLE

With the lemmas of the previous section in hand, it is now easy to justify the assertion that the "first order optimality condition" (1.7) is, indeed, necessary at a minimizer $[\bar{u},\bar{x}]$. Indeed, with the definition:

(3.1) $[\bar{u},\bar{x}]$ is a <u>local minimizer</u> of J if $\bar{u} \in \mathcal{U}_{ad}$ with $\bar{x} = G(\bar{u})$ and, for some $\delta > 0$, one has $J(u,G(u)) \geq J(\bar{u},\bar{x})$ for every $u \in \mathcal{U}_{ad}$ with $\|u-\bar{u}\|_\infty \leq \delta$

we will obtain (1.7) for any such local minimizer.

<u>THEOREM 3.1. Assume (H_0), (H_1) and let $[\bar{u},\bar{x}]$ be a local minimizer of</u>

$$J = \int_\Omega F(s,u(s),G(u)(s))\, \mu(ds) \tag{3.2}$$

<u>in the sense of (3.1). Then</u>

$$[\bar{F}_\omega + \underset{\sim}{\Gamma}^*\bar{F}_\xi] \text{ is an element of } Z := \operatorname{span}\{\xi_k'(\bar{u})\} \tag{3.3}$$

<u>where $\bar{F}_\omega, \bar{F}_\xi$ are the partials F_ω, F_ξ evaluated at $[\bar{u},\bar{x}]$ and</u> $\underset{\sim}{\Gamma} := G'(\bar{u})$.

<u>Proof</u>. Let $\{\Omega_M\}$ be given by (2.1) and let $\bar{\eta}$ be any element of $\mathcal{U}_M \cap Z^\perp$. By Lemma 2.3 there exists $u(\varepsilon)$ satisfying (2.4), (2.5) so $\|u(\varepsilon) - \bar{u}\|_\infty \leq \delta$ for ε small enough whence

$\hat{J}(\varepsilon) := J(u(\varepsilon),G(u(\varepsilon))) \geq J(\bar{u},\bar{x}) = \hat{J}(0)$. By Corollary 2.4 we have $\hat{J}$ differentiable — necessarily $\hat{J}'(0) = 0$ since $\varepsilon = 0$ gives a (local) minimum of $\hat{J}$ — with $\hat{J}'(0) = \langle \bar{F}_\omega + \underset{\sim}{\Gamma}^*\bar{F}_\xi, \bar{\eta}\rangle$. Thus,

$$(3.3) \qquad \int_{\Omega_M} [\bar{F}_\omega + \underset{\sim}{\Gamma}^*\bar{F}_\xi]\bar{\eta}\;\mu(ds) = 0 \qquad \underline{\text{for each}}\ \bar{\eta} \in \mathcal{U}_M \cap Z^\perp.$$

Note that our hypotheses give integrability of $[\bar{F}_\omega + \underset{\sim}{\Gamma}^*\bar{F}_\xi]$ when restricted to (any) Ω_M: we have $|\bar{F}_\omega| \leq M$ and $\underset{\sim}{\Gamma}^*\bar{F}_\xi \in L^1(\Omega)$. Thus, (2.3) is verified and Lemma 2.2 gives the desired conclusion (3.3). □

Example 3.2. We consider boundary control for the heat equation. Thus, with $\mathcal{R}$ a bounded region in $\mathbb{R}^d$ and $T > 0$ specified, consider

$$(3.4) \qquad \begin{array}{llll} \dot{v} = \Delta v & \text{in } Q := (0,T)\times\mathcal{R}, & v(0) = v_0 & \text{on } \mathcal{R}, \\ v = \phi & \text{on } \Sigma := (0,T)\times\partial\mathcal{R} & & \end{array}$$

where ϕ is the control. We impose the condition

$$(3.5) \qquad \|v(T,\cdot) - v_T(\cdot)\|_{L^2(\mathcal{R})} \leq \delta$$

and seek to obtain (3.5) with a strictly positive control ϕ; suppose such a control exists, say in $L^2(\Sigma)$. In this case we view the minimization to be a device for selection of a specific control: we minimize the usual quadratic criterion $\|\phi\|^2$ ($L^2(\Sigma)$-norm) with a penalty term to ensure positivity so

$$(3.6) \qquad J := \int_\Sigma [\phi^2 + \lambda/\phi_+]$$

where λ is a positive constant (and $\phi_+ = \max\{\phi,0\}$ so the integrand would be infinite where $\phi \leq 0$). Since, in this example, J is coercive and convex in ϕ, standard methods give existence of a minimizer in $L^2(\Sigma)$. Indeed, one also has, here, other known methods for justifying the optimality conditions but this nevertheless provides a useful expository example for application of Theorem 3.1.

In this case we have ϕ defined on Σ and v defined on Q (although its trace to $\mathcal{R}$ at $t = T$ is also relevant) rather than having both defined on a common set Ω. A simple "trick" takes care of this: Take Ω to be $\Sigma \cup Q$ (disjoint union of copies with the appropriate Lebesgue measure on each) and set

$u := \{\phi \text{ on } \Sigma;\ 0 \text{ on } Q\}$, $x := \{0 \text{ on } \Sigma;\ v \text{ on } Q\}$, $F = \{\phi^2 + \lambda/\phi_+ \text{ on } \Sigma;\ 0 \text{ on } Q\}$. Having pointed this formalism out, we note that, since v does not occur in the functional, we will take $\Omega = \Sigma$ and pass over direct consideration of the domain of v.

The map G is here the affine map: $\phi \mapsto v_* + \underset{\sim}{\Gamma}\phi$ where v_* satisfies (3.4) with $\phi = 0$ and $\underset{\sim}{\Gamma}$ gives the solution of (3.4) with $v_0 = 0$; then $G'(\phi) = \underset{\sim}{\Gamma}$, independent of ϕ. We note that $\underset{\sim}{\Gamma}^*: f \mapsto w_\nu$ (normal on Σ) where

$$\text{(3.7)} \qquad \dot{w} + \Delta w = f \quad \text{on } Q; \qquad w(T) = 0 \quad \text{on } \Omega; \qquad w = 0 \quad \text{on } \Sigma.$$

We have, here, $K = 1$ and

$$\text{(3.8)} \qquad \xi(\phi) := \frac{1}{2}\|(v_* + \underset{\sim}{\Gamma}\phi)\big|_T - v_T\|^2 \qquad (L^2(\Omega)\text{-norm})$$

so $Z := \operatorname{span}\{\zeta\}$ where $\zeta := \xi'(\phi)$ is z_ν with

$$\text{(3.9)} \qquad \dot{z} + \Delta z = 0 \quad \text{on } Q; \qquad z(T) = v_T - (v_* + \underset{\sim}{\Gamma}\phi)\big|_T \quad \text{on } \Omega;$$
$$z = 0 \quad \text{on } \Sigma.$$

Assuming $v_T \in L^2(\Omega)$, we note that finiteness of (3.6) gives $\phi \in L^2(\Sigma)$ whence $v := v_* + \underset{\sim}{\Gamma}\phi \in C([0,T] \to L^2(\Omega))$ (so the constraint makes sense easily) and (e.g., using semigroup methods) the $H^{3/2}(\Omega)$-norm of $z(t)$ is bounded by $C(T-t)^{-3/4}$ so ζ is certainly in $L^1(\Sigma)$. The maximum principle ensures that $\underset{\sim}{\Gamma}$: $L^\infty(\Sigma) \to L^\infty(\Omega)$ but, since the functional is independent of v (so $F_\xi \equiv 0$), this is irrelevant. We have (H_0). The form of (3.6) obviously gives (H_1) and we have $F_\omega = 2\phi - \lambda/\phi^2$.

Theorem 3.1 now applies to give either $2\phi - \lambda/\phi^2 = 0$ (i.e., $\phi = \text{const.} = (\lambda/2)^{1/3}$) if this would give v satisfying (3.5) so the constraint is inactive or, when the constraint is active,

$$\text{(3.10)} \qquad 2\phi - \lambda/\phi^2 = c\zeta$$

with the constant c determined by (3.10) and (3.5), noting that $\zeta = z_\nu$ depends on ϕ as in (3.9). As noted following the statement of (H_0), this gives a regularity result for the optimal ϕ: assuming $\partial\mathcal{R}$ is smooth, one has regularity of ζ (except at $t = T-$) and so, solving (3.10) for ϕ, regularity of ϕ. In particular, this regularity ensures that ϕ must stay strictly positive — as desired — for $0 \le t < T$ since one would otherwise get, from (3.10), an impossible singularity in ζ.

REFERENCES

1. V. Barbu and T.I. Seidman, Existence for minimization in Banach space with some applications. To appear in J. Math. Anal. and Appl.

2. D. Motreanu, Existence for minimization with nonconvex constraints. J. Math. Anal. and Appl. 117 (1986) 128-137.

3. T.I. Seidman and P. Wolfe, Equilibrium states of an elastic conducting rod in a magnetic field. (Submitted)

Thomas I. Seidman
Department of Mathematics
University of Maryland Baltimore County
Catonsville, Maryland 21228
U.S.A.

BITNET:seidman@umbc

Acknowledgments. This paper developed out of the earlier joint work[3] with P. Wolfe. The research presented here was partially supported under grant # AFOSR-82-0271. Thanks are also due to the organizers both for the opportunity to present this and for a most stimulating conference.

International Series of
Numerical Mathematics, Vol. 78

SEMIDISCRETE FINITE ELEMENT APPROXIMATION OF PARABOLIC BOUNDARY CONTROL PROBLEMS - CONVERGENCE OF SWITCHING POINTS

F. Tröltzsch

Abstract

For several classes of convex parabolic control problems the structure of the optimal control can be characterized by a certain type of switching points (even in the non-bang-bang case). In this paper the convergence of switching points is investigated, when the parabolic equation for the state is treated by a semidiscrete finite element scheme.

1. Introduction

In this paper we shall discuss some aspects of approximation of parabolic boundary controls. As a model problem we consider the minimization of

$$F(y(T)-q) + \frac{r}{2} \|u\|^2_{L_2(0,T)} \tag{1.1}$$

subject to the parabolic initial-boundary value problem for the state $y(t,x)$

$$\begin{aligned} y_t(t,x) &= \Delta y(t,x) && \text{on } (0,T]\times D \\ y(0,x) &= 0 && \text{on } D \\ \frac{\partial y}{\partial n}(t,x) + by(t,x) &= g(x)u(t) && \text{on } (0,T]\times \Gamma \end{aligned} \tag{1.2}$$

and to the constraints

(1.3) $|u(t)| \leq 1$ on $[0,T]$

on the control $u(t)$. In this setting we are given a bounded domain $D \subset \mathbb{R}^N$ with C^∞-boundary Γ, such that D is locally at one side of Γ, a continuously Fréchet-differentiable real functional $F: L_2(D) \longrightarrow \mathbb{R}$, real numbers $T \geq 0$, $r \geq 0$, $b > 0$, and real functions $q \in L_2(D)$, $g \in L_2(\Gamma)$. By $\partial/\partial n$ the outward normal derivative at Γ is denoted.

An important particular case for F in (1.1) is $F(w) = \| w \|^2$. We should note that the choice of the Laplace operator Δ is only for convenience, the theory works for other uniformly elliptic self-adjoint operators with C^∞-coefficients as well. Moreover, the theory extends directly to the more general boundary condition $\partial y/\partial n + b\, y = \sum_{i=1}^{k} g_i\, u_i(t)$ in the system (1.2).

It can be shown along the lines of the paper [5] by GLASHOFF and WECK that the optimal control of (1.1-3) is bang-bang for $r = 0$, provided that some natural assumptions on the eigenfunctions of Δ are satisfied. This behaviour can be exploited for computational methods. For instance, KNOWLES [8] investigated the finite element approximation of an analogous time-optimal control problem taking advantage of bang-bang properties. We refer also to GLASHOFF and SACHS [4], HACKBUSCH and WILL [6], KIRSCH [7], or to the considerations by ŁASIECKA [9] and MACKENROTH [10].

But even in the coercive case $r > 0$ the structure of the optimal control can be characterized by means of a certain type of switching points, which has been defined appearently first by EPPLER and TRÖLTZSCH [2]. On the numerical application of a corresponding switching point technique in a one-dimensional domain is reported in the author's paper [15].
Here we shall consider the question of convergence of switching points, when (1.2) is treated by a semi-discrete finite element scheme.

2. Semigroup approach to (1.2)

We denote by H the space $L_2(D)$ with norm $\|\cdot\|$ and introduce $A: D(A) \subset H \longrightarrow H$ by

$$D(A) = \{v \in H^2(D) \mid \frac{\partial v}{\partial n} + bv|_{\Gamma} = 0\}, \quad Av = -\Delta v \quad \text{for } v \in D(A).$$

A is self-adjoint and positive, and $-A$ generates an analytic semigroup $\{S(t)\} = \{\exp(-At)\}$, $t \geq 0$, of linear continuous operators in H. It is known

$$\|A^{\alpha} S(t)v\| \leq c\, t^{-\alpha}\|v\| \quad (0 \leq \alpha \leq 1,\ t > 0), \tag{2.1}$$

where c depends on α (cf. PAZY [14]).
We define the state y corresponding to the control u as the mild solution of (1.2) by the Cauchy type formula

$$y(t) = (Lu)(t) = \int_0^t AS(t-s)Ng\, u(s)ds, \tag{2.2}$$

where $N: L_2(\Gamma) \longrightarrow H^{3/2}(D)$ assigns to $g \in L_2(\Gamma)$ the solution w of the elliptic boundary value problem $\Delta w = 0$, $\partial w/\partial n + bw = g$.

The expression (2.2) was discussed extensively in the literature, we refer for instance to FATTORINI [3], WASHBURN [16], or to ŁASIECKA [10]. Proceeding similarly as KNOWLES [8] we can show that L is a linear and continuous operator from $L_p(0,T)$ into $C([0,T],H^{\alpha}(D))$, provided that $0 \leq \alpha < 3/2$ and $p > 4/(3-2\alpha)$.
In particular, $L_{\infty}(0,T)$ is transformed into $C([0,T],H^{3/2-\varepsilon}(D))$ $(\varepsilon > 0)$.
In the following we keep the pair $\alpha = 1$, $p > 4$ fixed. Then by

$$u \longmapsto Ru = (Lu)(T) = y(T)$$

a linear continuous operator $R: L_p(0,T) \longrightarrow H$ is defined (actually we have $R: L_p \longrightarrow H^1$, hence R is compact, as the embedding of H^1 into H is compact).
In this way we can express the optimal control problem (1.1-3) in the short form of a convex programming problem in $L_p(0,T)$,

$$(P_r) \qquad \Phi(u) = F(Ru-q) + r/2\,\|u\|^2 = \min, \quad u \in U_{ad},$$

where $U_{ad} = \{u \in L_p(0,T) \mid |u(t)| \leq 1 \text{ a.e. on } [0,T].\}$

3. The structure of the optimal control

From the weak compactness of U_{ad} and the weak lower semicontinuity of Φ we infer the existence of an optimal control of (P_r), which we shall denote by $u_r(t)$ (in particular $u_o(t)$ for $r = 0$). For $r > 0$ this optimal control is unique by strong convexity, for $r = 0$ we shall suppose bang-bang properties of $u_o(t)$ implying in turn the uniqueness of $u_o(t)$.
In the optimality conditions for $u_r(t)$ the function

$$f_r(t) = -(R^* \nabla F(Ru_r - q))(t)$$

will play the main role (R^* is the adjoint operator of R, $\nabla F \in H$ the Fréchet-derivative of F).

For u_r the following necessary and sufficient optimality conditions are known:

Lemma 1: u_r is optimal if and only if
in the case $r = 0$

(i) $\qquad u_o(t) = \operatorname{sign} f_o(t)$

and in the case $r > 0$

(ii) $$u_r(t) = \begin{cases} r^{-1} f_r(t), & |r^{-1} f_r(t)| < 1 \\ \operatorname{sign}(r^{-1} f_r(t)), & |r^{-1} f_r(t)| \geq 1 \end{cases}$$

$t \in [0,T]$ (cf. [1], [2], or [12]).

Note that the statement (ii) can be formulated shorter by

$$u_r(t) = \min\{1, \max\{-1, r^{-1} f_r(t)\}\}.$$

Definition: A point τ is said to be a switching point of $u_r(t)$ ($r \geq 0$), if $0 < \tau < T$, $|f_r(\tau)| = r$ and (exactly) one of the two functions $f_r(t) \pm r$ changes its sign in τ.

For $r = 0$ this definition covers "bang-bang" points, where the control switches from 1 to -1 or reversed. In the coercive case $r > 0$ the switching points separate the intervals where $|u_r(t)| < 1$ from those where $|u_r(t)| = 1$.

The function $f_r(t)$, which is responsible for the switching behaviour of $u_r(t)$ is defined via the adjoint operator R^*. One can show that $R^*: H \longrightarrow L_q(0,T)$ $(1/p+1/q = 1)$ is given by

$$(3.1) \qquad (R^* v)(t) = (g\,,\,S(T-t)v)_\Gamma = (g\,,\,z(t))_\Gamma$$

on $[0,T)$, where $(\cdot\,,\cdot)_\Gamma$ is the inner product of $L_2(\Gamma)$ and $z(t)$ from $C^1([0,T),D(A)) \cap C([0,T],H)$ is the solution of the <u>adjoint Cauchy problem</u>

$$(3.2) \qquad z'(t) - A\,z(t) = 0\,, \quad z(T) = v \quad (t \in [0,T)).$$

The analyticity of the semigroup $\{S(t)\}$ and $S(T-t)v \in D(A)$ for $t < T$ imply that $z(t)$ can be continued holomorphically to a function from the complex half-plane $\{\, t \in \mathbb{C} \mid Re(t) < T\}$ to $H^1(D)$. Therefore, $(R^*v)(t) = (g,z(t))_\Gamma$ extends to an analytic function on this half-plane, as the mapping $z \longmapsto tr\, z$ (trace of z at Γ) is continuous from $H^1(D)$ to $L_2(\Gamma)$.

It was already mentioned that we need bang-bang properties of $u_0(t)$ in the case $r = 0$. To this aim, we formulate at next sufficient conditions:
Let $\{c_n\}$ and $\{v_n\}$ be the non-trivial solutions (eigenvalues and eigenfunctions of $-\Delta$) of the elliptic problem

$$-\Delta v_n = c_n v_n \quad \text{on } D\,, \quad \partial v_n/\partial n + b\,v_n = 0 \quad \text{on } \Gamma$$

and define

$$K(g) = \{\, n \in \mathbb{N} \mid (g\,,\,v_n)_\Gamma \neq 0\,\}\,.$$

Then it can be shown along the lines of [5] that the two conditions

(3.3) $\nabla F(Ru_o - q) \neq 0$ (in the sense of H)

(3.4) $c_i \neq c_j$ for $i \neq j$, $i,j \in K(g)$

imply together $u_o(t)$ to be a bang-bang control.
Now we are able to investigate the structure of $u_r(t)$.

Lemma 2: Suppose that (3.3-4) hold in the case $r = 0$. Then $u_r(t)$ has at most countably many switching points, which can accumulate only at $t = T$. The control $u_r(t)$ is continuous on $[0,T)$ for $r > 0$ and piecewise constant ± 1 for $r = 0$.

Proof: The statement for $r = 0$ follows from [5]. Now assume $r > 0$. $f_r(t)$ is analytic on $\{t \in \mathbb{C} \mid \mathrm{Re}(t) \leq T-\Delta\}$ for all fixed $\Delta > 0$. Therefore either $f_r(t)$ is identically constant on $[0,T)$ (then $u_r(t)$ has no switching points) or the equations $f_r(t) = \pm r$ have at most finitely many solutions on $[0,T-\Delta]$. This observation yields the statement of the lemma. □

4. Approximation and convergence

In preparation for a finite element discretization of (1.2) we regard in this section a general approximation scheme for (P_r). Aiming to investigate the dependence of $u_r(t)$ on perturbations of R, q, and r we suppose that appropriate sequences $\{q_n\} \subset H$, $r_n \geq 0$, and linear continuous operators $R_n: L_p(0,T) \longrightarrow H$ are given ($n \in \mathbb{N}$), which satisfy

(4.1) $r_n \longrightarrow r \quad (r \geq 0), \qquad q_n \longrightarrow q$ in H

(4.2) $\|R - R_n\|_{L_\infty \to H} \longrightarrow 0$

(4.3) $\|R^* - R_n^*\|_{H \to C^1[0,T-\Delta]} \longrightarrow 0 \qquad (\Delta > 0)$

for $n \longrightarrow \infty$. We note that R_n^*, R^* are supposed to transform H even into $C^1[0,T-\Delta]$ for arbitrary $\Delta > 0$. This will be satisfied in the applications.

Now we investigate the approximate control problem

$$(P^n) \qquad \Phi_n(u) = F(R_n u - q_n) + r_n/2 \; \|u\|^2 = \min, \qquad u \in U_{ad}.$$

We do not approximate U_{ad}, because we shall later combine switching point techniques with a semidiscrete finite element scheme. For a more general consideration, including perturbations of U_{ad}, we refer to the detailed discussions in MALANOWSKI [12], who applies his results to obtain convergence estimates for the approximation of convex control problems, in particular to parabolic ones. We cannot use his results for our purposes directly, as we will not suppose strong convexity of F and Φ.
Moreover, we refer to the general considerations by MOROZOV [13].

The optimal control of (P^n) will be denoted by u^n. Recall that the solution of the unperturbed problem (P_r) is u_r.

Lemma 3: Suppose that u_r is unique. Then $u^n \rightharpoonup u_r$, $n \to \infty$.

Proof: U_{ad} is weakly compact, hence $u^{n_k} \rightharpoonup \bar{u}$ for a certain sub-sequence of $\{u^n\}$ and a certain $\bar{u} \in U_{ad}$. To simplify our notation let us introduce $m = m(k) = n_k$. By definition of u^m

$$(4.4) \qquad \Phi_m(u^m) \le \Phi_m(u_r).$$

The differentiability of F yields

$$\begin{aligned} |\Phi(u^m) - \Phi_m(u^m)| &\le |F(Ru^m - q) - F(R_m u^m - q_m)| + |r_m - r| \, \|u^m\|^2 \\ &\le c\{\|R - R_m\| \|u^m\|_{L_\infty} + |q - q_m\|\} + |r_m - r| \|u^m\|^2, \end{aligned}$$

hence $\Phi(u^m) - \Phi_m(u^m) \to 0$, $k \to \infty$, by (4.1-2) and $|u^m(t)| \le 1$.
Analogously we find $\Phi(u_r) - \Phi_m(u_r) \to 0$, $k \to \infty$.
As Φ is weakly lower semicontinuous

$$\underline{\lim}_{k\to\infty} \Phi_m(u^m) = \underline{\lim}_{k\to\infty} \Phi(u^m) + \lim_{k\to\infty}(\Phi(u^m) - \Phi_m(u^m)) \ge \Phi(\bar{u})$$

$$\Phi(\bar{u}) \leq \underline{\lim}_{k\to\infty} \Phi_m(u^m) \leq \lim_{k\to\infty} \Phi_m(u_r) = \Phi(u_r),$$

and the uniqueness of u_r implies $\bar{u} = u_r$. This holds for all weakly converging sub-sequences of $\{u^n\}$, and a known argument implies $u^n \rightharpoonup u_r$, $n \to \infty$. □

For the next statement we define

$$f^n(t) = -(R_n^* \nabla F(R_n u^n - q_n))(t).$$

Lemma 4: If u_r is unique, then $f^n(t) \to f_r(t)$ on $[0,T-\Delta]$ in the sense of $C^1[0,T-\Delta]$ for arbitrary but fixed $\Delta > 0$.

Proof: Lemma 3, (4.2), and the compactness of R yield

$$R_n u^n = Ru^n + (R_n - R)\, u^n \to Ru_r$$

in H. Consequently, $v_n = \nabla F(R_n u^n - q_n) \to v = \nabla F(Ru_r - q)$ in H, thus

$$(R_n^* v_n)(t) = (R^* v_n)(t) + ((R^* - R_n^*)v_n)(t) \to (R^* v)(t)$$

in the sense of $C^1[0,T-\Delta]$. The convergence of the first term follows from the representation (3.1) for R^* and the smoothing property of S(T-t), the convergence of the second one is ensured by (4.3). □

Corollary: For $r > 0$ the sequence $\{u^n(t)\}$ converges uniformly to $u_r(t)$ on each subinterval $[0,T-\Delta]$, $\Delta > 0$. If (3.3-4) is satisfied, then for $r = 0$ $\{u^n(t)\}$ converges pointwise on $[0,T)$ to $u_o(t)$ with exception of the switching points of $u_o(t)$.

Proof: If $r > 0$, then u_r is unique by strong convexity. Hence

$$u^n(t) = \min\{1, \max\{-1, r_n^{-1} f^n(t)\}\} \to u_r(t)$$

uniformly on $[0,T-\Delta]$ by lemma 4 and the representation for $u_r(t)$. For $r = 0$ we know from (3.3-4) that u_o is bang-bang, hence unique. The statement follows from lemma 1, lemma 4, and

$$\operatorname{sign} r_n^{-1} f^n(t) \to \operatorname{sign} f_o(t)\ ,\ n \to \infty\ ,\ \text{if } f_o(t) \neq 0. \ \square$$

Note: For $r>0$ we can estimate the convergence rate for $u^n \to u_r$ in appropriate Sobolev spaces by means of the results of MALANOWSKI [12]. In this paper, however, we focus our attention to the convergence of switching points.

We conclude this section with the investigation of the switching behaviour of $u^n(t)$.
For $n \to \infty$ we expect the convergence of switching points of u^n to those of u_r. However, illustrating the meaning of lemma 1 geometrically, we realize that we need an additional slope condition:

$$(4.5) \qquad \text{If } t \in [0,T) \text{ and } |f_r(t)| = r \text{ , then } \frac{d}{dt} f_r(t) \neq 0 \text{ .}$$

We regard at first the simplest case $r_n \to r>0$. Note that, by lemma 2, $u_r(t)$ has only finitely many switching points, say $k(\Delta)$, on each sub-interval $[0,T-\Delta]$ $(\Delta>0)$.

Theorem 1: Assume that $r>0$ and (4.5) holds true. Let $u_r(t)$ have the switching points $0<t_1<\ldots<t_k<T-\Delta$ on $[0,T-\Delta]$ $(0<\Delta<T,\ k = k(\Delta))$ and take $\delta \in (0,t_1)$.
Then, for all sufficiently large n, $u^n(t)$ has on $[\delta,T-\Delta]$ 1) the switching points $\delta<t_1^n<\ldots<t_k^n<T-\Delta$, and $\lim_{n\to\infty} t_i^n = t_i$ $(i = 1,\ldots,k)$.

Proof: u_r is unique by strong convexity of Φ. Using lemma 4 we obtain $f^n(t) \to f_r(t)$ in $C^1[0,T-\Delta]$ and $r_n \to r>0$ is known. Therefore the slope condition (4.5) ensures that the k-vector of zeroes of $f^n(t) \pm r_n = 0$ converges to the vector of corresponding zeroes of $f_r(t) \pm r = 0$.
This is equivalent with our statement. □

Now we consider the case $r_n>0$ for all $n \in \mathbb{N}$, but $r = 0$. To this aim, we arrange the switching points of $u^n(t)$ in another manner:

---

1) We restrict our attention to $[\delta,T]$ in order to avoid the discussion of possible switching points converging to zero, if $|f_r(0)| = r$.

For $r_n > 0$ we regard pairs of switching points $t_i^n < s_i^n$ such that $|u^n(t_i^n)| = |u^n(s_i^n)| = 1$ and $|u^n(t)| < 1$ on (t_i^n, s_i^n).

Theorem 2: Suppose that $r = 0$, $r_n > 0$ for all $n \in \mathbb{N}$, and that the conditions (3.3-4), (4.5) are satisfied. Let $u_o(t)$ have the switching points $0 < t_1 < \ldots < t_k < T-\Delta$ on $[0, T-\Delta]$ and take $0 < \delta < t_1$. Then, for all sufficiently large n, $u^n(t)$ has the switching points $\delta < t_1^n < s_1^n < \ldots < t_k^n < s_k^n < T-\Delta$ and

$$\lim_{n \to \infty} t_i^n = \lim_{n \to \infty} s_i^n = t_i \qquad (i = 1, \ldots, k).$$

Proof: From (3.3-4) we have that $u_o(t)$ is bang-bang, hence unique. Now lemma 4 applies to show $f^n(t) \to f_o(t)$ in $C^1[0, T-\Delta]$. The switching points of u_o are the zeroes of $f_o(t)$, the switchings of $u^n(t)$ are located at the zeroes of $f^n(t) \pm r_n$. Now, invoking the slope condition, the statement of the lemma is easy to verify. □

Completely analogous we can discuss the case $r_n \equiv 0$ for all n. Then we find under the assumptions of theorem 2 that $u^n(t)$ has the switching points $\delta < t_1^n < \ldots < t_k^n < T-\Delta$ and $\lim_{n \to \infty} t_i^n = t_i$ (note that $u^n(t)$ must be a bang-bang control for sufficiently large n, as $f^n(t) \to f_o(t)$ in $C^1[0, T-\Delta]$).

Remark: It follows from the results of this section that the bang-bang principle can be used as a substitute for strong convexity assumptions, if convergence of optimal controls is to be achieved.

5. Application to finite element approximation

Let $h > 0$ be a discretization parameter and V_h be a family of finite-dimensional subspaces of $H^1(D)$ such that

$$(5.1) \qquad \inf_{w \in V_h} \{ \|v - w\| + h \|v - w\|_1 \} \leq c\, h^s \|v\|_s \quad , v \in H^s(D)$$

for $1 \leq s \leq 2$ (by $\|\cdot\|_k$ we denote the norm of $H^k(D)$) and the inverse estimate

(5.2) $\qquad \|w\|_1 \leq c\, h^{-1} \|w\|, \qquad w \in V_h$

are satisfied. The semidiscrete approximation $y_h(t):[0,T] \to V_h$ of $y(t)$ is obtained as the solution to the finite element scheme

$$\frac{d}{dt}(y_h(t),w) + (\nabla y_h(t),\nabla w) + b(y_h(t),w)_\Gamma = (g,w)_\Gamma u(t) \tag{5.3}$$
$$(y_h(0),w) = 0$$

for all $w \in V_h$ ($(\cdot,\cdot)$ is the inner product of $L_2(D)$).
Now we introduce an approximation of the control operator R of section 2 by $R_h: L_p(0,T) \to V_h \subset H$,

$$R_h u = y_h(T)$$

and define the approximate control problem (P^h) by

$(P^h) \qquad F(R_h u-q) + \frac{r}{2}\|u\|^2 = \min, \qquad u \in U_{ad}.$

In order to investigate the convergence of the solution of (P^h), the approximate control, we must estimate the norms $\|R-R_h\|_{L_\infty \to H}$ and $\|R^*-R_h^*\|_{H \to C^1[0,T-\Delta]}$. Both estimations can be obtained from recent results of ŁASIECKA [10].
At first we consider $\|R - R_h\|$: We define the error $e(t):[0,T] \to H$

$$e(t) = y(t) - y_h(t).$$

Then we have (cf. [10], theorem 3.1, $p = \infty$)

$$\max_{t \in [0,T]} \|e(t)\| \leq c\, h^{3/2} \ln h \|u\|_{L_\infty}.$$

Consequently,

$$\|R - R_h\|_{L_\infty(0,T) \to H} \leq c\, h^{3/2} \ln h. \tag{5.4}$$

For the estimation of $\|R^*-R_h^*\|$ some additional considerations are necessary. We introduce $A_h: V_h \to V_h$ by

$$(A_h v_h, w_h) = (A v_h, w_h) \quad \text{for all } v_h, w_h \in V_h.$$

A_h generates an analytic semigroup $\{S_h(t)\} = \{\exp(-A_h t)\}$ of linear continuous operators in V_h. We can show with some effort that

(5.5) $\quad (R_h^* v)(t) = (g, S_h(T-t)Q_h v)_\Gamma$ on $[0,T)$, $\quad v \in H$,

where Q_h is the projector of H onto V_h.

Lemma 5: It holds

(5.6) $\quad \|R^* - R_h^*\|_{H \to C^1[0,T-\Delta]} \leq c\, h/\Delta^2$,

where c is independent of h, Δ, and v $(0<\Delta<\min(1,T))$.

Proof: The arguing makes heavy use of two basic estimates formulated by ŁASIECKA in [10]:

(5.7) $\quad \|AS(t) - A_h S_h(t)Q_h\|_{H \to H} \leq c\, h^2/t^2, \quad t>0,$

(5.8) $\quad \|S_h(t)Q_h - Q_h S(t)\|_{H \to H} \leq c\, h^2/t \quad , \quad t>0$

(cf. [10], theorem 4.1 and corollary 4.1).
We put $z(t) = S(T-t)v$, $z_h(t) = S_h(T-t)Q_h v$ and find for $t<T$

$$\|\tfrac{d}{dt}(z(t) - z_h(t))\|_1 = \|AS(T-t)v - A_h S_h(T-t)Q_h v\|_1$$

$$\leq \|AS(T-t)v - Q_h AS(T-t)v\|_1 + \|Q_h AS(T-t)v - A_h S_h(T-t)Q_h v\|_1$$

$$\leq c\, h\, \|AS(T-t)v\|_2 + c\, h^{-1}\|Q_h AS(T-t)v - A_h S_h(T-t)Q_h v\|$$

(using (5.1) and (5.2))

$$\leq c\, h\, \|A^2 S(T-t)v\| + c\, h^{-1}\|AS(T-t)v - A_h S_h(T-t)Q_h v\|$$

(by $\|v\|_s \leq c\, \|A^{s/2}v\|$, [14], and $\|Q_h\| \leq 1$), and (2.1), (5.7) yield

$$\leq c\, h\, (T-t)^{-2}\, \|v\| \leq c\, h\, \Delta^{-2}\, \|v\|.$$

Similarly $\|z(t) - z_h(t)\|_1 \leq c\, h\, \Delta^{-1}\|v\|$ is obtained. The mapping $z \longmapsto \operatorname{tr} z$ is continuous from $H^1(D)$ into $L_2(\Gamma)$. This implies in turn

$$\left|\frac{d}{dt}((R^*-R_h^*)v)(t)\right| + \left|((R^*-R_h^*)v)(t)\right| = \left|\frac{d}{dt}(g\,,\,z(t)-z_h(t))_\Gamma\right| + \left|(g\,,\,z(t)-z_h(t))_\Gamma\right|$$

$$\leq c\,\|g\|_{L_2(\Gamma)}\,(h/\Delta^2 + h/\Delta)\,\|v\| \leq c\,h/\Delta^2\,\|v\|$$

for $\Delta<1$, being equivalent with the statement of the lemma. □

Now we can apply the results of section 4 to obtain the convergence of switching points: We take a sequence $h_n \to 0$, $n \to \infty$, denote the solution of (P^{h_n}) by u^n, and set in section 4 $R_n = R_{h_n}$, $q_n = q$, $r_n = r$. Then the assumptions (4.1-3) are fulfilled. Therefore the theorems 1 and 2 and the other statements of section 4 are true for the convergence of the optimal controls u^n for the finite element approximation of problem (P_r) to the exact optimal control u_r of (P_r).

References

[1] Alt, W. and U. Mackenroth: On the numerical solution of state-constrained coercive parabolic optimal control problems. In: Optimal control of partial differential equations (K.H. Hoffmann, W. Krabs eds.). ISNM 68, Birkhäuser-Verlag Basel, Boston, Stuttgart 1984.

[2] Eppler, K. and F. Tröltzsch: On switching points of optimal controls for coercive parabolic boundary control problems. Optimization 17 (1986), 93-102.

[3] Fattorini, H.O.: Boundary control systems. SIAM J. Contr. Opt. 6 (1986), 349-385.

[4] Glashoff, K. and E. Sachs: On theoretical and numerical aspects of the bang-bang principle. Num. Math. 29 (1977), 93-114.

[5] Glashoff, K. and N. Weck: Boundary control of parabolic differential equations in arbitrary dimensions: Supremum norm problems. SIAM J. Contr. Opt. 14 (1976), 662-681.

[6] Hackbusch, W. and Th. Will: A numerical method for a parabolic bang-bang problem. In: Optimal control of partial differential equations (cf. Ref. 1).

[7] Kirsch, A.: Some remarks concerning the computation of bang-bang controls. In: Optimal control of partial differential equations (cf. Ref. 1).

[8] Knowles, G.: Finite element approximation of parabolic time optimal control problems. SIAM J. Contr. Opt. 20 (1982), 414-427.

[9] Łasiecka, I.: Ritz-Galerkin approximation of the time-optimal boundary control problem for parabolic systems with Dirichlet boundary conditions. SIAM J. Contr. Opt. 22 (1984), 477-500.

[10] Łasiecka, I.: Galerkin approximations of abstract parabolic boundary value problems with "rough" boundary data - L_p-theory. To appear in Mathematics of Computation.

[11] Mackenroth, U.: Some remarks on the numerical solution of bang-bang type optimal control problems. Num. Funct. Anal. Opt. 5 (1982-83), 457-484.

[12] Malanowski, K.: Convergence of approximations vs. regularity of solutions for convex, control-constrained optimal control problems. Appl. Math. Opt. 8 (1981), 69-95.

[13] Morozov, V.A.: Methods for solving incorrectly posed problems. Springer-Verlag, Berlin, New York, Heidelberg, Tokyo 1984.

[14] Pazy, A.: Semigroups of linear operators and applications to partial differential equations. Springer-Verlag New York, Berlin, Heidelberg, Tokyo 1983.

[15] Tröltzsch, F.: On a numerical method for coercive parabolic boundary control problems. Appears in Z. Angew. Math. Mech.

[16] Washburn, D.: A bound on the boundary input map for parabolic equations with application to time optimal control. SIAM J. Contr. Opt. 17 (1979), 652-671.

Fredi Tröltzsch
Technische Universität
Karl-Marx-Stadt
Sektion Mathematik
DDR-9010 Karl-Marx-Stadt
PSF 964

List of participants

Prof. Dr. H. W. ALT
Institut für Angewandte Mathematik
Universität Bonn
Wegelerstr. 6
5300 Bonn

Prof. Dr. Th. S. ANGELL
Dept. of Mathematical Sciences
University of Delaware
Newark, Delaware 19716
USA

Dr. M. BROKATE
Institut für Mathematik
Universität Augsburg
Memminger Str. 6
8900 Augsburg

Prof. Dr. R. BULIRSCH
Mathematisches Institut der
Universität München
Arcisstr. 21
8000 München 2

Prof. Dr. A. G. BUTKOVSKIY
Institut Problem Upravlenija
A. N. SSSR
ul Profsoyuynaja 65
117 342 Moskau
UdSSR

Prof. Dr. Lothar COLLATZ
Eulenkrugstr. 84
2000 Hamburg 67

Dr. F. COLONIUS
Fachbereich 3 - Mathematik
Universität Bremen
Postfach 330 440
2800 Bremen 33

Prof. Dr. H. ENGL
Institut für Mathematik
Kepler-Universität Linz
A-4040 Linz
Österreich

Prof. Dr. H. O. FATTORINI
Dept. of Mathematics
University of California
Los Angeles, California 90024
USA

Dr. Zhicheng GUAN
Institut für Mathematik
Universität Augsburg
Memminger Str. 6
8900 Augsburg

Prof. Dr. K.-H. HOFFMANN
Institut für Mathematik
Universität Augsburg
Memminger Str. 6
8900 Augsburg

Dr. Qiyuan JIANG
Institut für Mathematik
Universität Augsburg
Memminger Str. 6
8900 Augsburg

Prof. Dr. N. KENMOCHI
Faculty of Education, Dept. Math.
Chiba University
Chiba-Shi 260, Yayi-Cho
Japan

Prof. Dr. Andreas KIRSCH
Institut für Numerische und
Angewandte Mathematik
Georg-August-Universität
Lotzestr. 16 – 18
3400 Göttingen

Dr. Peter KNABNER
Institut für Mathematik
Universität Augsburg
Memminger Str. 6
8900 Augsburg

Prof. Dr. W. KRABS
Fachbereich Mathematik
Technische Hochschule
Schloßgartenstr. 7
6100 Darmstadt

Prof. Dr. F. LEMPIO
Mathematisches Institut
Universität Bayreuth
Postfach 10 12 51
8580 Bayreuth

Dr. U. MACKENROTH
Mathematisches Institut
Universität Bayreuth
Postfach 10 12 51
8580 Bayreuth

Prof. Dr. K. MALANOWSKI
Systems Research Institute
Polish Academy of Sciences
Newelska 6
01-447 Warsaw
Poland

Prof. Dr. P. NEITTAANMÄKI
Lappeenranta University of Technology
Department of Physics and Mathematics
Box 20
53851 Lappeenranta
Finland

Dr. Irena PAWLOW
Systems Research Institute
Polish Academy of Sciences
Newelska 6
01-447 Warsaw
Poland

Prof. Dr. E. SACHS
Fachbereich IV - Mathematik
Universität Trier
Postfach 38 25
5500 Trier

Prof. Dr. G. SCHMIDT
Department of Mathematics
and Statistics
McGill University
Montreal, Quebec
Canada

Prof. Dr. Th. I. SEIDMAN
Dept. of Math. & Computer Sci.
University of Maryland
Baltimore County
Catonsville, MD 21228
USA

Prof. Dr. J. STOER
Institut für Angewandte
Mathematik und Statistik
Am Hubland
8700 Würzburg

Dr. F. TRÖLTZSCH
Technische Hochschule
Sektion Mathematik
Postfach 964
DDR-9010 Karl-Marx-Stadt

Prof. Dr. J. ZABCZYK
Institute of Mathematics
Polish Academy of Sciences
Sniadeckich 8
00-950 Warsaw
Polen

Edited by
I. Gohberg

This series of monographs is devoted to the publication of current research in operator theory, with particular emphasis on applications to classical analysis and the theory of integral equations, as well as to numerical analysis, mathematical physics and mathematical methods in electrical engineering.

Operator Theory: Advances and Applications

Volumes 1–18 are also available

Volume 19
I. Gohberg/H. Bart/M. A. Kaashoek
Operator Theory and Systems
ISBN 3-7643-1783-3

Volume 20
D. Amir
Isometric Characterization of Inner Product Spaces
ISBN 3-7643-1774-4

New in the Series

Volume 21
I. Gohberg/M. A. Kaashoek (Eds.)
Constructive Methods of Wiener-Hopf Factorization
1986. 424 pages, Hardcover
ISBN 3-7643-1826-0

Volume 22
V. A. Marchenko
Sturm-Liouville Operators and Applications
1986. 378 pages. Hardcover
ISBN 3-7643-1794-9

Volume 23
W. Greenberg
Boundary Value Problems in Abstract Kinetic Theory
1986. 532 pages, Hardcover
ISBN 3-7643-1765-5

In Preparation

Volume 24
Gr. Arsene et al. (Ed.)
Operators in Indefinite Metric Spaces, Scattering Theory and other Topics
10th International Conference on Operator Theory, Bucharest (Romania), August 26 – September 5, 1985
1987. approx. 372 pages, Hardcover
ISBN 3-7643-1843-0